READING SAUSSURE

READING SAUSSURE

A critical commentary on
the *Cours de linguistique générale*

ROY HARRIS

Professor of General Linguistics
in the University of Oxford

Open ✳ Court

La Salle, Illinois

OPEN COURT and the above logo are registered in the U.S. Patent and Trademark Office.

Published by arrangement with Gerald Duckworth & Co. Ltd., London.

Printed and bound in Great Britain.

Library of Congress Cataloging-in-Publication Data

Harris, Roy, 1931–
    Reading Saussure.

    Bibliography: p.
    Includes index.
    1. Saussure, Ferdinand de, 1857-1913.   Cours de linguistique générale.   2. Linguistics.   I. Title.
P121.S369H37   1987   410   87-11101
    ISBN 0-8126-9049-4
    ISBN 0-8126-9050-8 (pbk.)

Contents

Preface   vii

Part One: The Syntagmatics of the *Cours*

Introduction   3
I. General Principles   55
II. Synchronic Linguistics   103
III. Diachronic Linguistics   139
IV. Geographical Linguistics   171
V. Questions of Retrospective Linguistics; Conclusion   181

Part Two: Saussurean Linguistics

I. Strategy and Programme   195
II. Saussure's Theory of Communication   204
III. Individuals, Collectivities and Values   219

Bibliography   238
Index   243

Preface

... quoi que je n'aie pas de plus cher vœu que de ne pas avoir à m'occuper de la langue en général.
   Cela finira malgré moi par un livre ...

... although I have no dearer wish than not to have to concern myself with language in general.
   It will come to a book in the end, in spite of my reluctance ...

– F. de Saussure, letter to A. Meillet, 4.1.94.

History was to prove Saussure right. It produced, *malgré lui* and twenty-two years later, a book: the *Cours de linguistique générale.* Evidently, Saussure had not tried hard enough to prevent that reluctant consummation. His ultimate trump cards (premature decease; fragmentary notes; failure to leave a manuscript) were blandly overtrumped by his pupils and colleagues. It took them barely more than a couple of years to bring out the book that Saussure had managed to avoid writing for the previous twenty.

What Bally and Sechehaye published in 1916 can certainly be read. But *Reading Saussure* might perhaps be regarded as a controversial title for a study of a book which Saussure never wrote. In one sense, we can no more read the Saussure who was the founder of Saussurean linguistics than we can read the Socrates who was the founder of Socratic philosophy. Our access to Saussure's ideas through reading the *Cours de linguistique générale* is indeed comparable to our access to the ideas of Socrates through reading the Platonic dialogues. Inevitably, all we can read on the page is a second-hand account of what a particular thinker is represented as having said, or as likely to have meant. Saussure and Socrates are classic examples of our cultural reliance on written reports, and even on reports which take the form of imaginative reconstructions. Such reports are, for obvious reasons, wide open to the charge of 'misrepresentation'; but, ironically, the more influential the thinker the less relevant the charge of misrepresentation becomes.

It is a measure of their importance that the possibility of misrepresentation hardly matters in either Saussure's case or that of Socrates. Just as 'Socratic' ideas reached a far wider public through Plato's written reconstruction of them (however misguided) than could ever have been the case otherwise, so more people assimilated 'Saussurean' ideas by reading the *Cours* than ever attended Saussure's lectures or asked him questions about points of linguistic theory. (It may come as something of a shock today to realize that none of Saussure's three courses at Geneva was attended by more than a handful of students.) As readers, we have no option but to read the Saussure who is presented as the author of the *Cours*, unless we renounce all possibility of investigating the source of some of the most basic notions current in contemporary discussions of language. It is not that nothing readable at all survives from the hand of Saussure: but this does not differentiate the Socratic from the Saussurean problem. For there is no doubt that the formative influence was exercised not by Saussure in person but by the text which his editors published after his death.

A quarter of a century after the appearance of the *Cours*, one of its editors wrote:

> Even if Ferdinand de Saussure's *Cours de linguistique générale* were eventually to become entirely outdated, it would be destined to remain alive in the memory of linguistic science because of its powerful and productive influence at a certain point in the evolution of that science. (Sechehaye 1940:1)

A quarter of a century had given the editors ample time to realize that as far as most people were concerned 'reading Saussure' was to all intents and purposes reading their version of Saussure's teachings.

The question then is – and has been for many years – how to make sense of reading this Saussure who is the presumptive author of the *Cours*; not whether what we read is a correct or an incorrect account of 'what the real Saussure really meant'. For whatever that may have been is arguably irrecoverable anyway. As mere 'readers', we shall never know what Saussure actually 'said'. (But whether that puts us in a position of disadvantage or, on the contrary, of advantage as compared to his original hearers is debatable: for none of them heard it all.) At the very worst, the Saussure of the *Cours* is a literary – and literal – fabrication of his editors. So might Socrates, conceivably, be a fabrication of Plato's. But as far as modern linguistics is concerned, it would have been necessary, as Voltaire said of God, to invent him had he not existed. In the modern academic world a book demands an author. We cannot blame the editors of the *Cours* for supplying one. They – rightly – sensed that this mode of presentation would be infinitely more authoritative than any publication of the original students' notes.

Less wise than Plato, however, Saussure's editors – on their own initiative – raised the question of authenticity in the reader's mind. Will anyone, they publicly wondered, 'be able to distinguish between Saussure and our interpretation of Saussure?' ([11]) It is undoubtedly the silliest query executors of Saussure's linguistic testament could possibly have raised; particularly if the executors had already rejected the idea of quoting their source material *verbatim*, and were therefore offering the reader no alternative basis for forming a judgment. Plato was not given to silliness of this order (in part, doubtless, because it never fell to his intellectual lot to endure the nineteenth century).

More unfortunately still, a later generation of Saussureans belatedly took this question of authenticity seriously, and proposed to deal with it by comparing the published text of the *Cours* with the surviving manuscript notes. Textual Pelion was thus piled upon textual Ossa (to the dismay of linguistic historiographers and the delight of university examiners). To say this is not to deny the interest of knowing what Saussure's pupils made of his lectures. It is simply to acknowledge the irony of the fact that this approach to Saussurean linguistics validates at Saussure's expense the methods of philology versus the methods of semiology. That may be one way of 'reading Saussure'. But the present study proposes, on the contrary, a semiological reading of Saussure, as against a philological reading, wherever the two conflict.

For some scholars, it would seem, it is only a 'philological' approach to the text which has any value at all. At least one eminent commentator on Saussure has been charged outright with lacking the requisite *formation philologique* to undertake a competent exegesis of the *Cours* (Frei 1950). Evidently 'philological' standards are so high that very few would-be commentators can hope to escape whipping. The shortcomings of the present commentary in that respect will doubtless be judged to be severe, if not positively provocative. Why is the reader not constantly referred to what survives of Saussure's manuscript notes and to his students' notebooks in order to elucidate obscure or contentious points? One reply might be that those who are looking for that kind of philological apparatus already have it available in Engler's monumental critical edition: but that is not the relevant reason. The rejection of a 'philological' approach to the *Cours* in the present commentary is based on conviction that such an approach would be quite misleading. For anyone who is interested in the *Cours* as linguistic theory, the 'philological' questions that can be both asked and answered concerning the text are simply the wrong questions. Quite apart from the fact that it was the Saussure of the *Cours* and not the Saussure of the Geneva lectures who was responsible for the 'Copernican' revolution in linguistic thought, and quite apart from the fallacy that there is just one 'authentic' version of Saussure lurking somewhere behind the textual facade, waiting to be discovered, there are two considerations which combine to call in question whether a 'philological' study of the *Cours* can tell us anything of critical value. One is simply that it begs the question to suppose that the alleged 'sources' confirm or modify certain possible interpretations of the *Cours*: for the 'sources' stand in just as much need of interpretation as the *Cours* itself. The other consideration is that all the crucial theoretical problems are raised in the *Cours* in any case: the 'sources' do not add to that inventory. It is certainly interesting to have confirmation that Bally and Sechehaye did not in that crude sense 'miss anything out'; but it would be obviously rash to conclude that anything not in the 'sources' Bally and Sechehaye simply invented. In short, apart from failing to reveal omissions, the 'sources' leave us no wiser on any substantive critical issue. To suppose that subjecting them to a sufficiently rigorous 'philological' analysis would throw light on any point of theory is either to confuse theory with biography or else to demand of philology more than philology is capable of giving.

No attempt either is made in the following chapters to enter into the labyrinthine and unending controversy concerning 'influences' on Saussure, important as these issues may be for historians. Are the key concepts of the *Cours* to be viewed as deriving specifically from the work of Humboldt, or Paul, or Gabelentz, or Durkheim, or Whitney ...? Or were they, as Bloomfield brusquely claimed in his review of the book (Bloomfield 1923), just ideas which had been 'in the air' for a long time? There is a sense in which detailed answers to such questions could make a difference to one's reading of Saussure. But there is also a sense in which they need not matter a jot. Saussure, as it happens, provides an awkward test case for the claims of 'influential' historiography, inasmuch as the Saussurean influence on his successors was manifestly unrelated to the extent of their curiosity about the influence of Saussure's predecessors on Saussure. To acknowledge this is not to belittle the researches of historiographers. Nor is it to espouse an idealistic 'context-neutral' approach to reading the *Cours*. For it is always worth considering what is to be gained by comparing the ideas of one thinker with those of another working within the same (or some other) intellectual tradition. Saussure's case is no exception. It is, indeed, virtually impossible for intelligent readers not to place what they read within the context of some kind of 'history of ideas', however minimal. To that extent, the concept of historical contextualization is already implicit in the concept of reading. But the contextualization thus implied is of a quite different order from the historiographer's. The comparisons occasionally drawn between Saussurean ideas and those of other thinkers in the course of the present commentary are to be understood with this important distinction in mind. They are not intended as contributions to the history of linguistics.

It is therefore the reader's Saussure, the hypothetically reconstructable author of the *Cours*, who is the focus of attention and interpretation in the chapters that follow. This Saussure is neither complete fact nor complete fiction, neither an authority on the 'real' Saussure nor an authorial persona. Elusive as he may be, it is this author who drafted the Magna Carta of modern linguistics. He is also the author whom Bühler, Hjelmslev, Merleau-Ponty, Lévi-Strauss, Piaget and Derrida – to mention but a few – read: and their various readings of Saussure became part of the mainstream of twentieth-century thought.

Perhaps it will be objected that to proceed in this manner is to interpose 'between the image of Saussure and the man Saussure simply the ideological projection and the epistemological imperfections of two generations of linguists' (Calvet 1975: 54). The answer to this objection is that we have no alternative nowadays but to read Saussure through the academic spectacles provided by the subsequent history of Saussurean linguistics. The case is at least less desperate than that of Socrates, whom we read through the distorting lens of two thousand years of Western philosophy.

May it, alternatively, be objected that such an approach to reading Saussure simply conflates author and editors? This is not so. For a reader is still free to distinguish between the two roles whenever there is occasion to do so. The author is the presumptive source of ideas, terminology, arguments and examples: the editors are responsible for their arrangement and the construction of an articulated text. That distinction, contentious though it must inevitably be, is what makes possible the projection of different readings of Saussure, of which his editors have given us just theirs – albeit a consciously 'open' version. Only those readers who cling to the vain hope of uncovering some unique and 'authentic' version of Saussure will be unduly worried by the prospect. His editors clearly were not. Saussure, they tell us, was one of those thinkers for whom thinking is a constant process of intellectual renewal ([9]). They 'edited' Saussure in just that spirit; and that is one merit of their version which cannot be denied, however much later critics may carp. Sechehaye subsequently said of Saussure's lectures that Saussure thought aloud in front of his students, in order to make them think for themselves (Sechehaye 1940:2). Similarly, to read Saussure is to be invited to re-think Saussure, and it is precisely for this reason that Saussure on linguistic theory is far more worth reading today than many of his more 'advanced' successors.

Saussure had already become compulsory reading for linguists within five years of the publication of the *Cours*, which was widely reviewed (de Mauro 1972:366). What linguists read into Saussure is a different question. It was to become almost a commonplace of Saussurean exegesis to point out that even those who were originally most sympathetic and most directly influenced by Saussure (Meillet, for instance; de Mauro 1972:368) did not always seem to understand some of his basic ideas. That this should have been so, if it was so, is doubtless an indication of the difficulty which a generation brought up to accept the assumptions of nineteenth-century comparative and historical linguistics experienced in coming to terms with Saussurean structuralism. More eloquent still, perhaps, is what Jespersen says in 1922 in his much acclaimed book *Language, its Nature, Development and Origin*.

He lists the first edition of the *Cours* in his bibliography, but nevertheless begins by announcing: 'The distinctive feature of the science of language as conceived nowadays is its historical character' (Jespersen 1922:7). In the four chapters Jespersen gives to the 'History of Linguistic Science', Saussure is mentioned just once, and then simply in an alphabetical list of scholars who 'have dealt with the more general problems of linguistic change or linguistic theory' (Jespersen 1922:98). By 1925, however, Jespersen felt obliged to devote a substantial part of the opening chapter of his new book, *Mankind, Nation and Individual from a Linguistic Point of View*, to a criticism of Saussure's distinction between *langue* and *parole* (here misleadingly – but influentially – rendering those terms into English as 'language' and 'speech'). Why that distinction had been passed over in silence three years previously in *Language, its Nature, Development and Origin* Jespersen does not explain. It was not that in 1922 he had not yet read the *Cours*: for he had published a review of it in 1917.

Part of the answer is that Saussure the scholar had already established himself in the minds of his contemporaries in a quite different but less distinguished – and less threatening – role. As Calvet points out (Calvet 1975:16), the entry under *Saussure* in the 1923 edition of the *Larousse Universel* refers to his work of 'capital importance' on the primitive system of Indo-European vowels, but makes no mention at all of the *Cours de linguistique générale*. These attested cases of historical myopia go to reinforce the thesis that Saussure falls into that Shakespearian category of those who, retrospectively, 'have greatness thrust upon them'. This leads in turn to an academic reading of Saussure in which the author of the *Cours* was really a happy, orthodox historical comparativist, who suffered intermittently from an unfortunate neurosis about terminological distinctions. Or, to borrow Calvet's metaphor, Saussure appears as an intellectual Columbus who by accident discovered America while exploring in search of the Indies.

Another eloquent piece of evidence about academic readings of Saussure comes from Leonard Bloomfield's book *Language*, published a decade after Jespersen's. Here too Saussure is given a single passing mention (Bloomfield 1935:19) in an introductory chapter on the history of linguistics. At first sight, it might seem that, like Jespersen in 1922, Bloomfield had somehow failed to register the fact that the *Cours* was a major landmark in the development of the subject. This is not the case, however. Bloomfield too had published a previous review of the *Cours* (Bloomfield 1923). This review makes interesting reading. In it, Bloomfield begins by acknowledging Saussure's standing as the scholar who first faced the problems involved in constructing a comprehensive theory of language. Bloomfield says of Saussure, 'in lecturing on "general linguistics" he stood very nearly alone, for, strange as it may seem, the nineteenth century, which studied intensively the history of one family of languages, took little or no interest in general aspects of human speech.' Here, in effect, Bloomfield acknowledges Saussure as the founder of modern general linguistics, even though Bloomfield's earlier book *An Introduction to the Study of Language* had come out in 1914, thus preceding the original publication of the *Cours* by two years. Saussure, says Bloomfield, 'has here first mapped out the world in which historical Indo-European grammar (the great achievement of the past century) is merely a single province: he has given us the theoretical basis for a science of human speech.' But by the time he wrote *Language*, Bloomfield had changed his first estimate of Saussure's *Cours* and its significance.

The reason for the disparity between Bloomfield's eulogy of Saussure in 1923 and his virtual dismissal of Saussure ten years later is not difficult to explain. The Bloomfield of the 1923 review is Bloomfield in his pre-behaviourist period; and in his pre-behaviourist period Bloomfield was a follower of the psychologist Wundt. So the 1923 review gives us a reading of the *Cours* as viewed by an American Wundtian who was also a Germanic philologist of the traditional stamp (and a student of Amerindian languages as well). But ten years later Bloomfield had rejected Wundt in favour of Watson. His reading of Saussure had altered accordingly. Saussure was now read not as the adventurous founder of modern linguistics, but as a perpetuator of the endemic psychologism of late-nineteenth-century approaches to language. That later Bloomfieldian reading was to dictate the relationship between American and European versions of structuralism for the next quarter of a century.

A complementary but interestingly different Anglo-Saxon reading of Saussure is manifest in the objections to the *Cours* raised by Ogden and Richards (1923), Gardiner (1932) and Firth (1950). Nevertheless, although different individual positions might be taken whether in Europe or America, few theorists were prepared to deny that the distinctions drawn by Saussure provided the basis on which a modern science of language might be established. In this respect, Saussure eventually appeared to be less innovative and less controversial than had formerly been supposed. Thus whereas Firth in 1950 (Firth 1950:179) could still classify professional linguists into four groups ('Saussureans, anti-Saussureans, post-Saussureans, or non-Saussureans'), by 1957, the centenary year of Saussure's birth, a fellow professional linguist could make the bland pronouncement: 'We are all Saussureans now' (Spence 1957:15).

As the case-history of Bloomfield demonstrates, the question of 'reading Saussure' merges inextricably with that of reading readings of Saussure. For when Bloomfield wrote *Language* nothing of the readable Saussure had changed since 1916 (with the exception of trivial emendations to the 1922 edition). Furthermore, it would be a mistake to infer from the way in which Bloomfield's *Language* deliberately ignores Saussure that Saussurean ideas left no trace in American academic linguistics of the interwar period. Bloomfield himself admitted to

Jakobson that reading the *Cours* was one of the events which had most influenced him (de Mauro 1972:371). Editing a collection of papers spanning the period 1925-1956, Joos (1957:18) wrote: 'At least half of these authors had read the *Cours*. The others got it second-hand: in an atmosphere so saturated with those ideas, it has been impossible to escape that. The difference is hard to detect, and it is generally unsafe to accuse a contemporary linguist of not having read the *Cours* ...' In other words, by the late 1950s the experience of reading Saussure seemed to have been so thoroughly absorbed as to make a distinction between Saussureans and non-Saussureans meaningless.

However, as if to give the lie to the dictum that 'we are all Saussureans now', there appeared in the very same year of 1957 the first manifesto of a new school of transatlantic linguistics which apparently owed little if anything to Saussure, however directly or indirectly assimilated. This was A.N. Chomsky's *Syntactic Structures*. The new theory proposed to treat a language as 'a set (finite or infinite) of sentences, each finite in length and constructed out of a finite set of elements' (Chomsky 1957:13) – a definition which might well have made the author of the *Cours* turn in his authorial grave. The essential novelty of transformational-generative grammar, as proposed in *Syntactic Structures*, was the eminently unSaussurean notion of considering languages as mathematical systems, on a par with the formal systems of mathematical logic. In retrospect, that approach may well now appear to have been naive or misguided; but in 1957 – to some at least – it looked full of promise. So rapidly did the new school win adherents that it doubtless seemed to many by the late 1950s that the advent of transformational grammar meant that Saussurean ideas had at last exhausted their usefulness, and a radically different era of linguistic theorizing had dawned.

From its inception, transformational-generative linguistics was based on a distinctly second-hand – if not third-hand – idea. Already in the nineteenth century, Boole had mathematicized logic. Subsequently Frege re-mathematicized it, by generalizing function-theory instead of algebra. The formal linguistics of the twentieth century was destined to follow – surprise, surprise – an exactly parallel course. Saussure's thinking about language owed nothing to this 'mathematical' tradition whatsoever, and was in spirit opposed rather than congenial to any unification of logical and linguistic formalism.

All the more remarkable is the fact that in less than ten years from the publication of *Syntactic Structures* a significantly altered and much more Saussurean theory of language was being proclaimed under the same 'transformational-generative' banner. This new version of transformational-generative linguistics drew a fundamental distinction between linguistic 'competence' and linguistic 'performance': furthermore the distinction was acknowledged as echoing Saussure's classic dichotomy between *langue* and *parole* (Chomsky 1964:62, Chomsky

1965:4), and the 'generative grammar internalized by someone who has acquired a language' identified as the Saussurean *langue* (Chomsky 1964:52). It can hardly be dismissed as mere coincidence that the first English translation of the *Cours* was published in the U.S.A. in 1959, and that in the 1957 manifesto of transformationalism Saussure's name had not even appeared in a footnote. In other words, it took less than a decade (a mere hiccough in the history of linguistics) before we were 'all Saussureans again'. Needless to say, the recently discovered author of the *Cours* had to be castigated for failure to teach transformationalism *avant la lettre* (Chomsky 1964:59-60, Chomsky 1965:4); but, nevertheless, a reading of Saussure had evidently left its mark on the formulation of a doctrine which was to become as important in the linguistics of the 60s and 70s as Saussurean structuralism itself had been in the linguistics of the 20s and 30s.

* * *

'Well-known but little understood,' said Firth epigrammatically of the *Cours* (Firth 1950:179). It is not the purpose of the present study to document or evaluate the various readings of Saussure which have influenced, either positively or negatively, the course of twentieth-century linguistics to date. That, in any case, would be a task far beyond the scope of a single book. The project to hand is a much more modest one, and in one respect has quite the opposite aim: to seek out what in the *Cours* remains 'unread'.

It would be presumptuous to present this as the discovery of an 'alternative Saussure'. However, reading the 'unread' Saussure will involve, in the interpretation of various aspects of the work, an implied contrast between how the twentieth century in fact chose to read the *Cours* and how it might have been read. In many cases this may appear to be merely a difference of emphasis, or a difference in what is taken for granted and left unsaid. But such differences may have a cumulative value which in the end refocuses the whole. The spirit of such an enterprise is eminently Saussurean, for obvious reasons. Central to Saussure's thinking is the idea that every semiological fact is constituted by an imaginative juxtaposition of other unrealized possibilities. To explore such possibilities at points where it is of interest to do so is not so much to offer a reassessment of the *Cours* as part of the history of linguistics, but rather to reaffirm its potential for our understanding of language in the present.

Most of what remains 'unread' in Saussure is not in any way obscure or difficult to read. On the contrary, no exegetic excavation is required to dig it out: it already lies conspicuously on the surface of the text. But it lies there rather like some hidden object in a puzzle picture, which remains 'invisible' until we look at the picture in a certain way. Once the object is 'seen', it becomes clear that it was visible all the time. Its invisibility was simply due to the fact that our visual attention was concentrated on other things. So it is with our 'reading attention' in the *Cours*.

Reading the 'unread' Saussure will include bringing into visibility the hidden premisses about language and linguistics – and there are not a few of these – which, although never explicitly acknowledged in the text as 'principles' or 'postulates', nevertheless play such a role in the work. To examine this theoretical infrastructure would itself justify writing a commentary on the *Cours*, even in the absence of any other motive.

Last but not least, reading the 'unread' Saussure will involve reading the book as a book, as distinct from reading it as a collection of theses about language, or as the palimpsest of a set of lectures. The present commentary is not intended to be an apologia for the book or for its editors. No one, however, who has taken the trouble to read the text with the attention that a commentary requires can fail to be struck by the fact that it commands the reader's respect on a level for which it is rarely given credit. The *Cours* is not merely an important scientific document. It is also a work of literature in the same sense as Plato's dialogues: an example of the art of imaginative exposition at its best.

The form of treatment adopted in the present study has been in part determined by this last consideration. Any literary work deserves to be read in the way it was intended to be read; that is to say as a consecutive text which unfolds 'syntagmatically', to use the appropriate Saussurean term. Hence the chapter-by-chapter analysis presented here in Part One. A commentary which did not respect this syntagmatic development would be particularly inappropriate in the case of the *Cours*; for its expository method relies heavily on a technique of presenting successive reformulations of major points, examined in gradually increasing detail and from slightly different angles. (Some of the 'internal contradictions' in the work which critics have detected can be traced to the use of this technique.) In any case, as Calvet pertinently remarks, 'to undertake, in the wake of the immense bibliography devoted to the *Cours de linguistique générale*, yet another account of the theses there put forward would today be an enterprise of no interest whatsoever' (Calvet 1975:13).

Calvet adds: 'Any reader can refer to the text itself ...' which is true enough but hardly sufficient. Most readers making a serious study of the *Cours* will also need to refer to notes of the kind to be expected from a good critical edition. The present commentary assumes that the reader will have access to the standard modern edition of the text (de Mauro 1972), and no attempt is made here to repeat the detailed factual information which that edition supplies. The page references to the *Cours* (given throughout in square brackets) are to the 1922 version of the text, the pagination of which is retained in de Mauro 1972. A chapter-by-chapter commentary of the kind here presented in Part One, however, inevitably has to leave on one side certain more general issues of interpretation which arise in connexion with the work as a whole. Such issues have been reserved for consideration in Part Two.

Recent commentary on Saussure seems to be obsessed with steering a middle course between the Scylla of adulation and the Charybdis of contempt. Commentators do not wish to be seen either as defending Saussure *contre vents et marées* (Engler 1974: 120): or as guilty of *la chicane de ceux qui ne veulent pas comprendre* (Martinet 1974: 225). Steering such a course may be a feat of admirable academic navigation. It has not been attempted here.

Hardly anyone nowadays tackles the *Cours* without having in advance some notion of what ideas it contains and why they are said to be important – in short, without having at least an elementary background in linguistics and knowing where Saussure stands in the history of the subject. That too is taken for granted throughout the following chapters, since it would have been naive to assume otherwise. The task of a commentator is neither to duplicate that of an editor nor to usurp that of a historiographer, but to construct and justify a reading of the text which makes sense. The richer the text, the more readings it will support. Any commentator who recognizes this has already dismissed the notion of the 'definitive' commentary as a will o' the wisp, and will be satisfied to have contributed in even a minor way to that continued renewal of thought which is the permanent legacy of every great text.

PART ONE

The Syntagmatics of the *Cours*

I believe it to be one of the most penetrating books I have ever read, but it is also one of the most obscure.

A.H. Gardiner

INTRODUCTION

CHAPTER I

A Brief Survey of the History of Linguistics

Saussure begins by offering the reader a five-act historical scenario. Act I comprises 'Grammar'. Grammar is characterized as a prescriptive discipline which aims solely at providing rules which distinguish between correct and incorrect forms. It is concerned with the study of language, but a study which is 'unscientific'. Act II is 'Philology'. Philology is said to aim primarily at establishing, interpreting and commenting on written texts. Act II makes an advance over Act I, in that it is, at least within certain limits, 'scientific'; but inasmuch as it is concerned mainly with written texts, fails to be a *linguistic* science. Act III is 'Comparative Philology' or 'Comparative Grammar'. This is both linguistic and also a science, but a very limited one, principally concerned with determining relationships between languages of the Indo-European family. Act IV in the scenario is 'linguistics proper' ([18]). This emerged from the nineteenth-century historical study of the Romance and Germanic languages. In its development the Neogrammarian school played a key role. Whereas the comparativists had failed to place the results of their investigations in the right historical perspective, the Neogrammarians succeeded; and whereas the comparativists misguidedly treated a language as if it were a natural organism, the Neogrammarians correctly saw it as a product of the collective mind of a community ([19]). In spite of this, however, the Neogrammarians left unresolved the fundamental problems of general linguistics. Finally, Act V concerns the foundation of a 'true' science of language: and it is on this fifth act that the *Cours* claims to raise the curtain.

It is worth noting at the outset the recurrent use of the terms *science* and *scientifique* throughout this first chapter (thirteen times in all). The reader is never told exactly what the requirements for a 'science' in Saussure's sense actually are. Certain inferences can nevertheless be drawn which tie in with later claims in the *Cours*. A principal requirement is evidently that a science must have identified its 'true object'. What this in turn means is not at all clear, but it is assumed from the start that linguistics has *son véritable et unique objet* ([13]). Furthermore, it was because the comparativists failed to identify this object that comparative philology did not succeed in becoming a *véritable science linguistique* ([16]). More remarkable still is the statement that Romance studies inaugurated by Diez brought linguistics nearer to this *véritable objet* ([18]). Evidently, then, a science (*la linguistique*) can exist which has not yet discovered its 'true object', but is somehow engaged in a historical process of working progressively towards it. How anyone knows when the 'true object' has at last been discovered Saussure does not explain. The 'true object' thus appears as a kind of intellectual holy grail which initiates will recognize when they see it, and whose eventual discovery makes sense of previous unsuccessful quests in search of it. Nothing could more clearly illustrate than these opening pages the late-nineteenth-century romanticism of science with which the *Cours* is deeply imbued.

As is typical of the period, the scientific romanticism of the *Cours* is an evolutionary romanticism. Each of the historical phases identified by Saussure marks a certain progress towards the ultimate scientific goal. Later is better and earlier is worse. At the opposite end of the historical scale from the 'true' science of language we find its implied antithesis: 'grammar' as developed originally by the Greeks and subsequently by the French. Although very diverse types of activity connected with language are approved in this chapter as 'scientific' – Wolf is credited with founding a 'scientific' philology, Bopp with creating an autonomous 'science' of comparativism – and although these scientific efforts are criticized on various counts, it is only the work of the grammarians which is condemned in this perspective as *dépourvue de toute vue scientifique et désintéressée sur la langue elle-même* ([13]).

This condemnation is of interest in several ways. The attitude towards traditional grammarians is not consistently hostile throughout the *Cours*. The concepts developed in traditional grammar are later said to provide the basis on which linguistics has to work ([153]). Traditional grammarians are even praised for having adopted a strictly synchronic approach to their subject ([118]). The twin sins of traditional grammar for Saussure are apparently that it is 'based on logic' and is prescriptive ([13]). The first of these two charges might certainly be levelled at Port Royal, but it is difficult to see in what sense the work of a Dionysius Thrax or a Priscian is based on logic. As for the second, Saussure conveniently overlooks the extent to which prescriptivism is also inherent in certain kinds of philological work (for instance, in editing texts) and remains latent in much nineteenth-century historical linguistics (lexicography in particular). Yet these endeavours, unlike traditional grammar, are given the Saussurean 'scientific' seal of approval.

Saussure never explains why a prescriptive linguistic discipline cannot be 'scientific' in his sense. What seems to lie behind his initial condemnation of grammar is its tacit identification as a kind of anti-science of language. It purports to teach linguistic truths for which there is no basis. More specifically, its prescriptivism is perhaps implicitly equated with propagating an erroneous linguistic theory. For anyone who holds, as Saussure does, not only that the linguistic sign is arbitrary but that this is a foundational principle of the 'true' science of language, it may be tempting to present the prescriptive grammarian as a Cratyline figure, committed to denying this principle and proclaiming that certain linguistic forms are 'naturally' right and others 'naturally' wrong. If so, then it would make sense from the viewpoint of evolutionary scientific romanticism to see the first step towards the 'true' science of language as being the abandonment of this deeply 'false' view.

Straight away, then, in this opening chapter – and even in its title – we meet the first of the hidden theoretical premisses of the *Cours*. Usually these premisses are 'hidden' by being disguised either as undisputed historical facts or as matters of commonsense observation. This initial premiss is no exception. It is the premiss that linguistics is a subject with an identifiable history. Since Saussure's day, that premiss has not merely remained hidden but has become even more effectively concealed, buried ever deeper under layers of accumulated scholarship. Histories of linguistics unknown to Saussure have become standard works, and 'the history of linguistics' has been promoted to the status of a university subject, with specialized journals devoted to it. All this serves to obscure from the present-day reader the significance of the fact that Saussure declines to acknowledge that we are here dealing with a theoretical decision to treat linguistics in a certain way, and that neither history nor historians have any authority to impose that decision upon anyone. By just not admitting this, Saussure avoids the necessity of undertaking any theoretical defence of the decision. He can therefore simply omit the most difficult part of a prolegomena to any general inquiry into language. The Saussurean programme for linguistics is able to start *in medias res* by presenting a spurious certificate of authentication from the academic past.

The full piquancy of adopting this 'historical' approach to linguistics cannot be savoured except retrospectively. For it has to be compared with Saussure's attitude towards adopting a 'historical' approach to linguistic phenomena; and this does not emerge until later in the *Cours*. For the moment, the reader has to be content with noting the fact that the first question Saussure deals with is not 'What is language?' but 'What is linguistics?'. The tension between these two questions will be a persistent *leitmotiv* throughout the book. At times the former question appears to be dominant and at times the latter. But in the end neither is subordinated to the other: that, at least, is one way of reading the *Cours*.

Did academic linguists of Saussure's generation think of their subject with sufficient detachment to see how dubious its historical status was? Doubtless many did not, and would therefore have been all the less likely to treat Saussure's initial premiss as contentious. That in no way alters the role this premiss plays in the overall rationale of the *Cours*. In some respects it is rather surprising that the theoretical manoeuvre of the opening chapter has not been more clearly recognized as such; for it treats the history which it alleges to exist in such a conspicuously cavalier way as to attract adverse comment from later scholars who took the subject more seriously. Aarsleff's observation (1982:395 n.15) that 'Saussure's understanding of the history of linguistics is often not well informed' is a mild understatement. Saussure's 'history of linguistics' is grotesque. The significant point is that it does not matter for Saussure's purposes. What matters theoretically is that the subject has had *some* such history. Saussure nevertheless takes the opportunity of slanting his selected history in a way which will suit the pattern of exposition which immediately follows. Chapters I and II of the Introduction are essentially complementary, and serve to direct the reader's attention along certain lines.

Once the 'orientational' function of these two chapters is grasped, some of the details which might otherwise be puzzling can be explained. For example, it explains the omission of any reference to philosophical discussion of linguistic topics in Graeco-Roman antiquity, or to the modistic grammarians of the Middle Ages. It also explains why c.1870 is chosen as the date which marks the beginning of 'inquiry into the conditions governing the life of languages'; why Schleicher is selected as a target for criticism; and why the Neogrammarians emerge in such a favourable light, in spite of the fact that, as de Mauro points out, the Neogrammarians had been hostile to the *Mémoire sur le système primitif des voyelles dans les langues européennes* of 1879 (de Mauro 1972:413, n.37). The expository aim of this potted 'history' is to make clear what, in Saussurean terms, a 'science of language' *was not and could not be*. It is a chapter which deals with possible misconceptions of the subject, a kind of 'warning to the reader' about what not to expect from this particular 'course in general linguistics'.

To appreciate the possibility of this reading, it may be helpful to compare the opening pages of the *Cours* in the first instance to the opening pages of another general book on linguistics published forty years earlier (almost at the same time as the precocious *Mémoire sur le système primitif des voyelles*): Abel Hovelacque's *La linguistique*.

Hovelacque's book begins, in a vein remarkably similar to the *Cours*, by drawing a distinction between *linguistique* and *philologie*, pointing out that even scholars confuse the two, and taking the great French lexicographer Littré to task for the definitions of these terms given in the latter's monumentally authoritative *Dictionnaire*. Furthermore, the way in which Hovelacque defines philology (as distinct from linguistics) corresponds in certain respects exactly to the account given in the opening paragraphs of the *Cours*. On this point, clearly, nothing had changed much throughout the second half of the nineteenth century. The *Cours* merely accepted an intradisciplinary commonplace of the times (namely, that linguistics was not philology), even if it involved a distinction still obscure to the generality of academics. (The incomprehension of fellow academics remains today: 'But it's all to do with languages, isn't it?' End of discussion.) Hovelacque's opening chapter also contains the quasi-obligatory academic genuflexions to Sir William Jones, à propos of Sanskrit, and to Bopp for his inauguration of comparative philology. But there the similarity ends.

The way Hovelacque's opening chapter then proceeds is not at all along Saussurean lines. In Hovelacque we find no criticism of Bopp and the comparativist school. Worse still, we find that the authority cited on the crucial distinction between linguistics and philology is none other than the misguided Schleicher. For Hovelacque, Schleicher is 'the man of method' (*l'homme de la méthode* (Hovelacque 1877:6)): whereas others, including Wertheimer's successor at Geneva, thought him a complete mediocrity and pretentious to boot (de Mauro 1972: 412 n.32). Furthermore, Hovelacque praises Schleicher for precisely the reasons that Saussure attacks him. These are: Schleicher's view of languages as organisms, the concomitant assimilation of linguistics to botany, and the ranking of linguistics among the 'natural' (as opposed to the 'historical') sciences. Seen from this angle, the first chapter of the *Cours* reads almost like a deliberate rebuttal of Hovelacque's introduction to the subject.

Support for such an interpretation would be provided by the lukewarm remarks in this chapter ([16]) about Max Müller, Oxford's German-born first Professor of Comparative Philology, and chief propagandist for the subject in Victorian England. Already in the early 1860s Müller had loudly proclaimed the advent, at long last, of a 'science of language'. This new science, moreover, was in Müller's view one of the natural sciences, on a par with geology and botany (Müller 1864: 1):

... the language which we speak, and the languages that are and that have been spoken in every part of our globe since the first dawn of human life and human thought, supply materials capable of scientific treatment. We can collect them, we can classify them, we can reduce them to their constituent elements, and deduce from them some of the laws that determine their origin, govern their growth, necessitate their decay; we can treat them in fact, in exactly the same spirit in which the geologist treats his stones and petrifactions, – nay, in some respects, in the same spirit in which the astronomer treats the stars of heaven, or the botanist the flowers of the field.

It is difficult not to see in this passage a reflection of Schleicher's famous parallel likening the difference between linguistics and philology, on the one hand, to the difference between botany and horticulture on the other (Schleicher 1860: Intr.). This parallel Hovelacque cites with approval as explaining better than any other what linguistics aims to do.

A second comparison may be even more helpful. This is between the *Cours* and a general book on language published some twenty years later: Leonard Bloomfield's *Language*. The comparison is telling in this instance too, because Bloomfield's book – unlike Hovelacque's, but like the *Cours* – established a landmark in the subject.

We find in Chapter I of *Language* another variation on the strategy of using an introductory discussion of the 'history' of language studies in order to explain to the reader what linguistics is not (or should not be). Bloomfield's attack is directed in the first instance against the tradition of school 'grammar' and the accompanying 'preconceptions which are forced upon us by our popular-scholastic doctrine' (Bloomfield 1935:4), and more generally against any approach to linguistic analysis based on philosophical or psychological premisses. Thus he criticizes the ancient Greeks for taking it for granted 'that the structure of their language embodied the universal forms of human thought' (Bloomfield 1935:4) and for stating their grammatical observations 'in philosophical form'; while on the other hand praising the Sanskrit and Hindu grammarians for demonstrating that it is possible to present 'a complete and accurate description of a language, based not upon theory but upon observation' (Bloomfield 1935:11). He is particularly severe on the European medieval scholastic philosophers, whom the *Cours* never mentions. They, in his view, contributed much less than the ancients and mistakenly 'saw in classical Latin the logically normal form of human speech' (Bloomfield 1935:6). Nor has he anything but condemnation for the post-Renaissance attempts to write 'general grammars'; for these embody the same error of seeking to force language into the mould of logic. 'Philosophers, to this day, sometimes look for truths about the universe in what are really nothing but formal features of one or another language' (Bloomfield 1935:6). The Port Royal grammar of 1660 in particular, which received qualified praise from Saussure ([118]), Bloomfield singles out for criticism on this score. What eventually rescued the European tradition of language studies from this dismal plight, according to Bloomfield, was the discovery of Sanskrit. 'Hindu grammar taught Europeans how to analyze speech-forms' (Bloomfield 1935:12). The European comparativist school took it from there; and henceforward Bloomfield speaks only of 'progress', until he comes to the Neogrammarians. His exemplar-target here is Hermann Paul, whose 'standard work' (*Principien der Sprachgeschichte*, 1880) suffers from two 'great weaknesses'. One of these weaknesses is 'neglect of descriptive language study' and concentration on questions of linguistic change, a fault Paul shared with his contemporaries. 'The historical language students of the nineteenth century suffered under these limitations, but they seem not to have grasped the nature of the difficulty' (Bloomfield 1935:17). The other 'great weakness' of which Paul is guilty is 'his insistence upon "psychological" interpretations'. As a behaviourist, Bloomfield was utterly opposed to discussing language in terms of mental processes. 'The only evidence for these mental processes is the linguistic process; they add nothing to the discussion but only obscure it. In Paul's book and largely to the present day, linguistics betrays its descent from the philosophical speculations of the ancient Greeks' (Bloomfield 1935:17). Bloomfield's *Language*, like the *Cours*, lists many names on its roll-call of honours in nineteenth-century linguistics. One of the names mentioned is that of Saussure: but he is only one among several others (Böhtlingk, Müller and Finck) credited with having seen 'the natural relation between descriptive and historical studies' (Bloomfield 1935:18-19).

Thus comparison between the opening chapter of the *Cours* and of Bloomfield's book is particularly revealing. It alerts any intelligent reader of the *Cours* to the fact that what to look for is the balance of praise and blame; and, more important still, the reasons given for both praise and blame. Whether the judgments formulated are 'historically accurate' is a quite secondary – and almost irrelevant – matter. For example, while it is perfectly true, as Aarsleff points out (Aarsleff 1982: 395 n.15), that the *Cours* gives the Neogrammarians credit for a view which Bréal had expressed long before (i.e. that a language is the product of a 'collective mind'), the point to note in context is that, historically accurate or not, this attribution is part of the Saussurean case against the comparativists. It could hardly be so for Bloomfield, since behaviourism is no less suspicious of collective minds than of individual minds; perhaps even more suspicious. (In fact, Bloomfield has nothing but praise for the comparativists: they at least were not guilty of 'psychologism'.)

The reader who grasps that the 'history' of linguistics with which the *Cours* opens can be read simply as an account of 'what linguistics is not' will also see that the misconceptions attacked fall into two groups. The first group are the three 'popular' misconceptions: that linguistics is prescriptive (= 'grammar'), that linguistics is concerned with textual study (= 'philology'), and that linguistics is to be equated with the investigation of relationships between languages (= 'comparative philology'). The second group are the 'academic' misconceptions: that linguistics studies languages a-historically, and that linguistics studies languages as organisms. The second group is by far the more interesting, the two 'academic' misconceptions being presumably chosen for their complementarity. In other words, for many of Saussure's contemporaries it must have seemed that the choice for linguistics as an academic discipline lay, precisely, between treating languages as living organisms – and hence studying what Müller (in the passage cited above) called their 'origin', 'growth' and 'decay' – as opposed to treating languages as abstract systems with no 'life'. The latter alternative is particularly significant inasmuch as Saussurean synchronic linguistics itself is sometimes represented as taking an a-historical approach to languages. The point of criticizing comparativism for its a-historicity is thus an important one. It hinges on what has been called the 'radical historicity' of Saussure's view of languages (de Mauro 1972:448 n.146, Culler 1976:35). The comparativists come under attack from a Saussurean vantage-point because they simply disregard history altogether: their approach is a-historical because it is non-historical. Saussurean synchronic linguistics, on the other hand, is a-historical in a quite different way; namely, that it rejects a conflation of data pertaining to different historical states. But it is at the same time 'radically historical' in that it proposes an analysis based solely on data which are historically coherent in the sense of belonging to a single system. Such a system does indeed have a 'life', as far as Saussure is concerned; and in at least two quite different respects. First, it may last for hundreds or even thousands of years. Second, while it lasts it functions as an active generator of the consistency of speech (*parole*). Perhaps the essence of Saussure's 'radical historicity' might be crystallized in two aphorisms which the Saussure of the *Cours*, despite his apparent love of paradox, never formulated: 'There are no dead languages' and 'Languages live by resisting change'.

CHAPTER II

Data and Aims of Linguistics:
Connexions with Related Sciences

Having first been told what linguistics is *not*, a reader of the *Cours* now presumably expects to be told what it *is*. If so, the expectation will be frustrated. A point which commentators have missed here is that the exposition adopted in the *Cours* exemplifies admirably – and presumably not coincidentally – the Saussurean concept of 'value' (*valeur*). Just as the identity of a Saussurean linguistic sign is determined by its place in a system of related but contrasting signs, so the identity of Saussurean linguistics is determined by its place in an academic system of related but contrasting disciplines (anthropology, sociology, psychology, etc.). Here we glimpse the possibility of a full Saussurean semiology of the forms of intellectual inquiry in society. What is significant is the avoidance in the *Cours* of any naively 'positive' definition of the kind commonly encountered in dictionaries and introductory textbooks, where the term *linguistics* itself is presented as the established name of a certain branch of study ('the study of language and languages', for example). Such a definition would have been incongruous to say the least, in view of Saussure's forthright and absolute condemnation of nomenclaturism ([97]f.). It is to the credit of the editors that they recognized the expository problem, and managed to deal with it in a way faithful to the principles of Saussurean structuralism. They saw that the implications of a Saussurean approach to languages forbade any simplistic definition of linguistics in terms of its subject matter. They also saw that, from a Saussurean viewpoint, the way linguistics is to be defined and the way languages are to be defined will be head and tail of the same coin.

To pursue the notion of a semiology of intellectual inquiry a little further, it may also strike the alert reader that the distinction drawn between the data (*matière*) of linguistics and its object (*objet*) is parallel to the distinction Saussure later draws for languages between substance and form. Linguistics accepts as raw material, the *Cours* tells us, 'all manifestations of human language', including written texts ([20]). But the form linguistics takes, the organization it imposes upon this raw material, is determined by the aims (*tâche*) of the discipline. Exactly the same data could in principle be treated in many different ways (of which philology, anthropology and other disciplines offer concrete examples). The aims of linguistics are thus of crucial importance; and at the same time raise an obvious question. How are *they* determined? For presumably a discipline's internal aims do not drop unbidden out of a clear blue academic sky. The answer is that Saussure's 'radical historicity' can be read as applying not merely to languages but also – and *in the first instance* – to linguistics itself.

That this answer is plausible can be immediately confirmed by considering the account now given ([20]) of what the specific disciplinary aims of linguistics are. They are just three in number. The first ('to describe all known languages and record their history') sounds like a fairly straightforward – albeit interminable – task of cataloguing and classifying linguistic data; in short, an enterprise of the kind already very familiar to the linguists of the nineteenth century. The second, however, ('to determine the forces operating permanently and universally in all languages, and to formulate general laws which account for all particular linguistic phenomena historically attested') is of an entirely different stamp. By no stretch of the academic imagination could this second aim be accomplished by processes of cataloguing and classification. But it is the third aim which gives the game away: 'to delimit and define linguistics itself.' Was not that the very question we started with? Indeed, it was. And the moment we realize this we also realize that what have been offered as the three aims of Saussurean linguistics are simply the result of applying to the study of linguistic phenomena a general paradigm from the philosophy of science. (For any science S, it falls to that science to describe the phenomena within its domain. Second, it falls to that science to explain the same phenomena as particular instances of the general laws of S. Third, the way S accomplishes these twin objectives defines S as a science.) The 'radical historicity' of Saussurean linguistics can be construed as residing precisely in the application of this paradigm as a paradigm dictated by the cultural context of the historical Saussure's day and age.

Thus the claim, on this reading, will be that the development of linguistics (in the early years of the twentieth century) has reached a turning point at which only two historical paths into the future are possible. Either it must establish itself as a unified science, or else it is doomed to fragmentation and will be absorbed piecemeal into other disciplines which deal in their own terms with various aspects of human linguistic activity. The question therefore is: how can linguistics meet the conditions required of a modern science? Saussure's proposed solution, all commentators agree, is to identify *la langue* as the object of linguistic study. This is presented initially in the *Cours* as a solution dictated by fundamental difficulties, which are seen as arising out of the very nature of linguistic phenomena.

CHAPTER III

The Object of Study

The first difficulty a theorist has to face ([23]) is that whereas other sciences study objects 'given in advance', in linguistics, on the contrary, 'it is the viewpoint adopted which creates the object'. The single example provided to illustrate this point, however, is in some respects an unhappy one. The reader is invited to consider the word *nu* in spoken French and to realize that there are various ways of considering it: (i) as a sound, (ii) as the expression of an idea, (iii) as corresponding to Latin *nūdum*, etc. The different viewpoints thus briefly identified make it appear, unfortunately, as if all that is being claimed here is that words may be studied in different ways and with different interests in mind by the phonetician, by the lexicographer, by the etymologist, and so on. And since no linguist of the late nineteenth century would ever have contested this, what was intended to illustrate a fundamental problem for linguistics collapses into a banality which fails completely to perform its intended function. On the contrary, linguistics seems in this respect to be in the same boat as many other disciplines. Medical science, for example, both allows and requires consideration of the human body from various points of view, depending on the interests of different specialists. But it would be odd to cite this as a reason for claiming that the human body constitutes a number of different objects, or for denying that the human body is 'given in advance' of the efforts of medical science to understand how it works.

Saussure's point can hardly be the academic banality which the laconically glossed example of *nu* makes it seem. For this the editors must take responsibility. In claiming that where language is concerned the point of view precedes the object, Saussure is saying something much more basic: that the phonetician, the lexicographer, the etymologist and their fellow specialists having *nothing to make statements about at all* unless what we hear as a certain sound and write as *nu* is first seen as having a certain linguistic status, namely as being the utterance of a particular French word. As Barthes (1964: 1.1.4) puts it: 'any speech, as soon as it is grasped as a process of communication, is *already* part of the language'. To which we might add that *until* it is thus grasped, it does not exist at all as a linguistic phenomenon. In this respect there is no parallel with the human body and medical science: that is to say, there is no question of physicians having first to 'see' a human body as a human body, or its parts as parts of a human body. Whereas, *mutatis mutandis*, that is precisely what is required in the linguistic case. If *nu* were not a word but a sneeze or grunt, the linguist would not be interested in it, even though it might sound no different: and if *nu* were not a French word but English or Japanese then both lexicographer and etymologist would be looking at quite a different linguistic unit. In short, there just is no linguistically relevant item *nu* which exists independently of the processes of linguistic identification. It is in this sense that the linguistic viewpoint creates the linguistic object. That is not, admittedly, the only possible way of taking Saussure's point: but it makes far more sense of the *Cours* than any other.

The second general difficulty ([23-6]) is that at no level of linguistic observation are simple autonomous units to be found. On the contrary, at all levels of linguistic observation the observer finds dualities. Furthermore, these dualities involve combinations of apparently quite disparate kinds. For example, the 'consonant *n*' is a duality involving on the one hand articulatory movements and on the other hand auditory impressions; the 'word *nu*' is a duality involving on the one hand an audible sound and on the other hand an inaudible meaning; and so on. There is never just a single dimension or a single criterion involved in identifying such units. How, in view of this diversity, will any uniform method of analysis be possible in linguistics at all? A discipline forced to choose between a variety of methodologically diverse approaches, which examine different aspects of the phenomena selected for study but are never brought together in any meaningful synthesis, will have no claim to be an independent science.

The foregoing difficulties will be resolved, and can only be resolved – the *Cours* tells us – if linguistics takes *la langue* as its object of study. Again, it is to be noted how the exposition adopted by the editors presents, in a typically Saussurean manner, the related conceptual framework into which the notion of *la langue* is required to fit, before making any attempt to enlighten the reader as to just what *la langue* is. In fact, the reader is never told exactly what *la langue* is at any point in the *Cours*: there is no definitive or final formulation. All we find are successive reformulations which bring out different contrasts between *la langue* and everything which *la langue* is not. The procedure is an object-lesson in Saussurean methodology, and in this sense the *Cours* itself is the great masterpiece of Saussurean linguistics.

Typically, the first statement made about *la langue* is negative: *la langue* is not to be equated with *le langage* ([25]). And the first paragraph of this much-quoted passage proceeds to concentrate not on *la langue* at all but on language in general, explaining why the very heterogeneity of language makes it impossible for us to place it in any one category of human phenomena. *La langue*, on the contrary, it claims, is 'both a self-contained whole and a principle of classification'. But how or why that might be the reader is not yet told. Instead the discussion veers off into dealing in advance with a possible objection to taking this as the *appropriate* principle of classification for purposes of linguistics. Again, the expository procedure adopted here is quite remarkable. Before any explanation is given of what was meant by claiming that *la langue* provides a 'principle of classification' for linguistics we find an account of why an alternative principle of classification will *not* do.

The objection brought up for consideration at this point is that the language faculty is one of humanity's basic natural endowments; whereas particular languages are simply sets of acquired social conventions established on the basis of this natural endowment. Should not linguistics, therefore, give priority to the natural endowment, rather than to the socially superimposed conventions (*la langue*)? The way this objection is dealt with in the *Cours* is revealing. First of all, argues Saussure, although it is true that all (normal) human beings can speak, it is not at all clear that the human vocal apparatus is naturally designed for speaking in the way human legs are designed for walking. Saussure rejects Whitney's view that humanity might just as easily have opted for a different medium (than speech) for linguistic expression; but nevertheless accepts the American linguist's insistence that the vocal nature of linguistic signs is a matter of secondary importance. In other words, what is natural to the human species is not spoken language, but rather the ability to construct and use systems of signs, whether spoken or not. Brief reference is made at this point to Broca's investigation of the localization of language in the brain. What Broca discovered, the *Cours* claims, is that the brain's control of speech is bound up inseparably with its control of other forms of communication, including writing; and consequently there is no separate physiological basis for treating speech as a distinct natural endowment. Finally, in any case, even if speech were a separate natural (i.e. physiological) endowment, it could not be exercised unless society provided a public instrument (*la langue*) for its exercise. The particular form this instrument takes will vary from one society to another: and here the distinction between *langage* and *langue* ties in with the Saussurean doctrine of the arbitrariness of the linguistic sign, to be developed later in the *Cours*.

But the question inevitably now arises as to whether the rational strategy for the scientific investigation of language ought not to take as its starting point this natural faculty of using signs, which Saussure recognizes as the *faculté linguistique par excellence* ([27]). The answer to this brings us to the next 'hidden premiss' of the *Cours*: more precisely, to two 'hidden premisses', which underlie Saussure's apparently unquestioning acceptance of the doctrine of the 'primacy of speech'. The first and more general of these premisses is that implicational relationships may hold between sign systems: that is to say, that one system may be semiologically dependent upon another. The second premiss is that what constitute from a lay point of view spoken and written forms of 'the same language' are examples of this relationship, the spoken system being semiologically presupposed by the written. Why Saussure needs these premisses becomes apparent not so much from the arguments he advances, but from the arguments he does not advance. What these missing arguments are must now be examined.

First, it should be noted that it is by no means clear that Saussure accepts the doctrine of the 'primacy of speech'; at least, not in the crude form in which it was usually presented in the nineteenth century. It would certainly be rash to infer too much simply from the fact that when the *Cours* refers to French, English, Greek, etc. as *langues* the reference is to the spoken language, even though in some cases the linguist may have access to the spoken form only indirectly through written records. What the *Cours* states quite unambiguously is that *écriture* and *langue* constitute two separate systems of signs, and that the former exists only to represent the latter ([45]). The conclusion from this is that writing is of interest to the linguist only insofar as it is amenable to treatment as a representation of *langue*: its other properties are strictly irrelevant. (Later theorists were to insist on this even more emphatically than Saussure. Bloomfield, for instance, stated bluntly: 'Writing is not language' (Bloomfield 1935:21).) So in practice Saussure proceeds *as if* accepting the 'primacy of speech' doctrine, but nevertheless stops short of offering any theoretical justification for it.

Given that the *Cours* is a work of linguistic theory, this reticence is striking. Was the assumption that the arguments were so obvious as not to be worth stating? This scarcely seems plausible, given the evident concern elsewhere in the *Cours* to reject popular misconceptions about the status of writing. In general, the *Cours* shows no evidence of reluctance to state the obvious, provided that the point is of sufficient importance. A more likely explanation of Saussure's reticence is that it corresponds to an unresolved problem of semiological theory, for which Saussure has no option but to assume a solution.

That this is the most probable reason for Saussure's silence emerges if we consider the usual arguments which linguists have offered in favour of the doctrine of the primacy of speech. These arguments have been summarized by Lyons (1972: 62-3) under four heads. (i) *Phylogenetic priority*. In all communities, the emergence of writing, if and when it occurs, is subsequent to the establishment of a spoken language. (ii) *Ontogenetic priority*. The normal child learns a spoken language first, and only later, if at all, a written language. (iii) *Functional priority*. A spoken language normally has a wider range of communicative functions than a written language. (iv) *Structural priority*. Writing systems are normally based on representation of units and combinations belonging to a corresponding spoken language. To these four basic considerations may be added: (v) *Learning priority*. 'It is entirely possible to learn a foreign language without knowing anything of the way it is written ... On the other hand, it is next to impossible to learn *only* to read and write a foreign language' (Moulton 1970:14).

These arguments were already available to linguists in the nineteenth century: the problem is that from a Saussurean point of view they are the wrong arguments. They are all 'external' linguistic arguments. That is to say, they are based on empirical generalizations of various kinds about human intellectual and cultural development. As such, they are in no sense 'principles of semiology'. Thus they are quite irrelevant, for example, to the semiological problem of whether in cases where spoken and written signs co-exist they may function as complementary components of a single system. No semiological principle is posited in the *Cours* which rules out *a priori* the existence of 'mixed' semiological systems. In fact, the section on semiology ([32-5]) nowhere lays down any specific criteria for the identification of a sign system.

What Saussure needs, ideally, is a semiological principle which will allow him to demonstrate, deductively, the dependence of writing on speech: and this will have to be a general principle which simultaneously determines the same relationship for any independent sign system S_1 and a dependent system S_2. This will presumably be part of a theory of implicational relations which allows the semiologist to say under what conditions any given sign system presupposes another given sign system. But all that, for Saussure, lies in the domain of the future science of semiology. He is simply forced to assume in advance the availability of the result which the *Cours* will take for granted. That is why the *Cours* very meticulously avoids the more obvious linguistic arguments for according priority to spoken language, and is careful to treat the relationship between spoken and written forms as a semiological relationship, not a historical or cultural one.

What would be quite unwarranted is to treat Saussure's reticence as obliviousness to the semiological problem. It had already been raised in the nineteenth century by scholars far less theoretically astute than the author of the *Cours*. Murray, for example, in the Preface to the first volume of the *Oxford English Dictionary*, accepts that in 'the natural order of language ... speech comes first, and writing is only its symbolization' but points out that a word like *gaseous* 'reverses the natural order' because it belongs essentially to writing. Such words do not have a spoken form in the same sense as the words of colloquial speech: 'for "pronunciation" anything passes muster which suffices to recall the written symbol in question; just as any reading of a mathematical formula passes muster, if it enables an auditor to write down the formula again' (Murray 1888: xi). Now what Murray regarded as a reversal of 'the natural order', and hence a problem for the lexicographer, would be for Saussure a reversal of semiological dependence, and hence a problem for the semiologist. That there will be problems of this order in semiology is evident from various remarks in the chapter which the *Cours* devotes to writing; in particular on *la tyrannie de la lettre* ([53]) and on the case of Chinese, where Saussure surprisingly concedes that writing constitutes *une seconde langue* ([48]). Even in this latter example, however, the word *seconde* implies a relationship of semiological dependence between two separate systems.

For Saussure's argument about the 'object' of linguistics, what matters is that writing is a separate system, albeit semiologically dependent on *la langue*. Since linguistics, conceived of as the science of *la langue*, does not even embrace the study of *l'écriture* except insofar as that may be necessary to establish evidence about *faits de langue*, it can hardly propose to undertake the more general study of the postulated human 'sign faculty' underlying *all* sign systems. That would be the province not of linguistics but of semiology. Thus there is no contradiction in Saussure's admitting that the human 'sign faculty' is our natural *faculté linguistique par excellence*, but at the same time maintaining that the study of this natural faculty does not fall within the scope of linguistics.

The importance of these arguments has gone virtually unnoticed in later Saussurean exegesis. They form an essential link between two superficially unrelated Saussurean theses; one about the relationship between speech and writing, and the other about the relationship between linguistics and semiology.

The way the case is argued appears at first sight to make a concession to the view that a science is – or should be – concerned with the investigation of natural phenomena. What Saussure is apparently concerned to defend is the proposition that linguistics, on the contrary, has to address itself first to the investigation of a cultural phenomenon (*la langue*) if it is to proceed to establish itself as a science. The arguments he deploys fall into two groups. On the one hand, there are arguments derived from our inability to identify immediately the 'natural' basis of human speech. On the other hand, there are arguments derived from the consideration that even if such a basis could be identified, what matters is the cultural implementation of our natural linguistic abilities, since they would otherwise lie fallow.

In order to clarify Saussure's position, let us suppose for a moment that human beings had a rather different vocal apparatus, which served no other purpose than speech (being physiologically independent of the organs for breathing, mastication, swallowing, etc.). Let us also suppose that Broca had discovered in the brain a localized control system specialized exclusively for the operation of this physiologically independent vocal apparatus. Let us even suppose that human beings were born with two sets of ears, one receiving just the output of the vocal apparatus and the other receiving any other audible signals. Finally, let us suppose that in pathological cases where there was any impairment of this articulatory-cum-auditory system, the patient in question was recognized as linguistically deficient: in other words, as having no alternative mode of linguistic expression or comprehension available. Thus, for example, impairment of the system would entail corresponding impairment of writing or reading. Let us, in short, take literally the much invoked metaphor of a 'language organ', and imagine that human beings clearly had such an organ – just as clearly as, for instance, they have eyes to see. Now what, in this hypothetical situation, would Saussure's stance be?

The answer has to be that the putative author of the *Cours* is then apparently faced with a choice. One alternative is that linguistics thereby becomes a science with two distinct branches: one branch, the psycho-physiological, studying the general workings of this hypothetical language organ, and the other branch, the cultural, studying its various products in different social and historical circumstances. The other alternative is that one of these two branches of study is relegated to the province of some other science, and the term *linguistics* is restricted to the other. Now what Saussure seems to urge is that, irrespective of terminology, a science of language can in no way ignore the centrality of languages as cultural phenomena. Furthermore, this centrality is logical rather than merely empirical. In other words, it would be so even if speech happened *not* to be the natural form of human linguistic expression. We cannot (logically) engage in linguistic activity at all unless there exist languages for us to use. And no language comes ready-made, supplied by Nature. No wonder Broca gets short shrift from Saussure. The case, in other words, is a subtly presented *reductio ad absurdum* of the notion that linguistics might be one of the natural sciences (a subdivision of neurophysiology, for instance). 'It is no absurdity to say that it is *la langue* which gives language what unity it has' ([27]).

To sum up, then, the Saussurean strategy for linguistics is based upon three propositions accepted without serious question: (i) that languages are systems of (non-natural) signs, (ii) that there are non-linguistic systems of signs, which human beings are capable of creating and using, and (iii) that linguistics is not concerned, except incidentally, with semiologically dependent systems, such as writing. Saussure at no point attempts to justify these three propositions in any detail; but all three are individually and collectively essential to his position.

Just how essential can be seen if we eliminate them one by one. A theorist who rejects (i) can have no common ground with Saussure, and must presumably find some alternative basis for linguistic analysis which either claims linguistic signs to be natural or else eliminates the need for a theory of the linguistic sign altogether. A theorist who rejects (ii), while accepting (i) and (iii), will be obliged to equate linguistics with semiology – a position clearly incompatible with Saussure's explicit distinction between the two. A theorist who rejects (iii) (that is, rejects the doctrine of the 'primacy of speech') but accepts (i) and (ii) presumably has two options open: either to maintain the 'primacy of writing', or else to treat spoken and written languages as autonomous and equipollent systems. The former option entails that pre-literate societies have to be treated as having no languages; and this is clearly quite unacceptable from a Saussurean point of view. The latter option leads straight to the paradox that in any given literate community there would be no linguistic relationship obtaining between the spoken and the written systems of signs. Thus, for example, it would from a linguistic point of view be merely fortuitous that written French and spoken French were both 'French', and that literate French people treat the two as systematically interrelated. This also is evidently unacceptable as far as Saussure is concerned. Finally, how about treating both spoken and written systems as alternative forms of the same *langue*? This possibility is also excluded for Saussure, who regards *la langue* as a system of bi-planar correlations, in which each unit on the plane of *signifiants* corresponds to just one unit on the plane of *signifiés*, and vice versa. Consequently writing and speech cannot belong to one and the same *langue*, since at least *two* sets of bi-planar correlations must be involved.

The Saussurean strategy for linguistics, it should be noted, and the arguments used in its support, although rejecting the availability of any natural basis for the classification of linguistic facts, in no way preclude the possibility that certain features of linguistic structure may be naturally determined (in the sense of being imposed by the nature of the general human 'sign faculty'). But since we do not know what, if any, these features are, we cannot make them the basis of classification for the purposes of a science of language.

* * *

The *Cours* has so far referred to *la langue* in very general terms as one (unidentified) part of language (*le langage*). The question which now inevitably arises in the reader's mind is, which part? Saussurean commentators have almost with one accord read the next section of the *Cours* as an immediate reply to this implicit question. Consequently, the remarks contained in §2 of Chapter III have been construed as supplying Saussure's basic definition of *la langue*. It is in the light of this supposed definition that all subsequent observations about *la langue* in later chapters have been interpreted. Likewise, it is in the light of this definition that various charges of inconsistency or incoherence in Saussure's views have ultimately been brought to court. What §2 offers, however, turns out to be merely the first in a series of progressive reformulations, in the course of which all the key technical distinctions of Saussurean linguistics will be introduced. The series begins with the distinction between *langue* and *parole,* and attempts first of all to situate that distinction in the context of a general model of communication.

The section begins by inviting the reader to consider a typical act of speech, in which two hypothetical interlocutors, A and B, are linked in what Saussure calls the 'speech circuit'. This circuit involves a chain of connexions between the brains, vocal organs and ears of the two persons in question. According to the 'speech circuit' account, what happens when, for example, A says something to B is that certain concepts in A's brain trigger or activate corresponding sound patterns in A's brain (*images acoustiques*) which in turn trigger certain movements in A's vocal apparatus, which in turn cause certain sound waves, which then eventually stimulate B's ears. This aural stimulation, being relayed to B's brain, triggers there the appropriate sound patterns, which in turn trigger the corresponding concepts. If B replies to A's utterance, an exactly similar chain of events will be set in motion in the opposite direction, going from B's brain to A's. Thus A might ask 'What time is it?' and B might reply 'Six o'clock'. That exchange, according to Saussure's model, would occupy just one complete lap of the speech circuit.

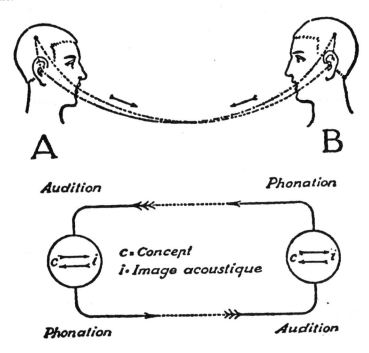

This simple picture seems at first sight clear enough: and to make assurance doubly sure, the text of the *Cours* includes an illustration with dotted lines and arrows tracing the hypothetical pathways connecting the two talking heads of A and B, and a diagram in which the speech circuit is shown laid out like the plan of a model railway.

The initial clarity of this picture is unfortunately blurred by various subsequent observations which may have misled Saussurean commentators. The first is the remark on p. [30] which appears to identify *la parole* with the 'executive' section of the circuit. The second is the remark on p.[31] claiming that *la langue* can be localized in that section of the circuit where sound patterns are associated with concepts; but this is followed immediately by the statement that *la langue* is the social part of language, and 'external to the individual' ([31]).

The impression created is that Saussure is trying to construe the distinction between *langue* and *parole* in a diversity of ways simultaneously. Hjelmslev (1942) argues that if *parole* is identified with execution it cannot also be identified with the individual – as distinct from the social – part of language. 'Every execution' objects Hjelmslev (1942:41) 'is not necessarily individual ... Everything which is individual is not necessarily an execution ...' This apparent inconsistency in Saussure leads Hjelmslev to set aside the distinction between *langue* and *parole* and replace it by a distinction between the abstract system of linguistic contrasts (*schéma* in Hjelmslev's terminology) and its social implementation (*usage*). Others have agreed that the various criteria which the *Cours* invokes in distinguishing *langue* from *parole* 'do not divide language in the same way and they thus leave much room for dispute' (Culler 1976:81). A useful survey of this 'room for dispute' and possible interpretations of Saussure's distinction is provided by Spence (1957, 1962), who finds that none is completely satisfactory and eventually concludes 'that scientific method in linguistics will be best served by the elimination from consideration of the duality between *langue* and *parole*' (Spence 1962:52). Since this distinction is usually taken to be the cornerstone of Saussure's theory, it is rather difficult to see what would remain of Saussurean linguistics without it.

Here, as in other instances, the editors of the *Cours* have been collared as whipping boys. 'The definition of the contrast *langue/parole* appears on p.38, whereas the problem of the *identity* of linguistic units is broached on p.249, and that of *valeur* on p.150. In other words, to reconstruct the Saussurean sequence of ideas, the reader must begin with Chapter 8 of Part Three (on 'Diachronic Units, Identities and Realities'), proceed to Chapters 3 and 4 of Part Two (on 'Identities, Realities, Values' and 'Linguistic Value'), thence to Chapter 1 of Part One ('Nature of the Linguistic Sign'), and eventually to Chapter 3 of the Introduction ('The Object of Study'), where the opposition between *langue* and *parole* should have been presented.' (Calvet 1975:20) If all this is necessary to understand Saussure's distinction, it is little wonder that reading Saussure has come to be regarded as requiring the expertise of a Talmudist.

Whether the text of the *Cours* actually contains all the inconsistencies of which Saussure or his editors are often accused is another matter. A careful reader will observe that the sentence in which *parole* is allegedly identified as 'execution' occurs in a passage comprising several paragraphs ([29-30]) devoted to explaining the origin of the 'social crystallization' which is necessary for the establishment of *la langue* in society. The relevant contrast here is between 'active' processes in the brain and 'passive' ones, and the term *exécutif* stands opposed to *réceptif*. Saussure's claim is that the individual plays no active part in this 'social crystallization' of *la langue*, but is merely the passive recipient of an accumulated fund of linguistic signs used in *la parole*. This proposition might, doubtless, be contested on various grounds: but what is more to the point is that it makes nonsense of Saussure's claim if he is also taken to be opposing *parole* to *langue* as execution to reception. What the *Cours* says here is that 'execution is never carried out by the collectivity' ([30]); but it might also have added, had it been relevant to the argument, 'and nor is reception either'. What John Smith hears, in that sense, is not heard by anyone else in the community; any more than what John Smith says is said by anyone else. There is no question of identifying what distinguishes execution from reception in the speech circuit with what distinguishes *parole* from *langue*. Execution and reception are both processes of *parole*, and once that is grasped the alleged incompatibility with the opposition of *parole* to *langue* as 'individual' to 'social' vanishes.

As regards the alleged inconsistency between treating *langue* as 'external' to the individual but nevertheless localizing it within one of the 'internal' sections of the speech circuit, any contradiction disappears once the point is taken that in order to function, according to Saussure, the processes of *parole* need access to *la langue*. Saussure's 'localization' of *langue* in the brain is the answer to the question of how and where this access occurs. Again the answer may perhaps be contested; but it does not contradict the notion that *la langue* is a social, supra-individual reality to claim that each person has an individual internal representation of it (any more than it would be contradictory to claim that each individual may reliably be guided by his or her own copy of the rules of a game in spite of the fact that the rules as such exist 'outside' the distributed set of copies, and indeed 'outside' any particular episodes of play).

The *Cours* is the first treatise on language to insist that speech communication is to be viewed as a 'circuit', and to attach any theoretical significance to the fact that the individuals linked by this circuit act in turn as initiators of spoken messages and as recipients of such messages. Later theorists sometimes used the Saussurean term *circuit de la parole* (e.g. Malmberg 1968) as if this emphasis on reciprocality were of no particular importance. However, the *Cours* is quite explicit on the matter: without two individuals capable of exchanging spoken messages, 'the circuit would not be complete' ([27]). Exactly what the implications of a 'circuit' are will be discussed at greater length below in connexion with Saussure's theory of communication (p.204ff.). Here it suffices to note three general points. First, by taking the speech-circuit model with its two talking heads as basic, Saussure makes it clear that *la langue* is a system which assumes face-to-face communication as the norm. This assumption reinforces the Saussurean distinction between *langue* and *écriture*: for writing is, archetypally, a system which makes the opposite assumption (that is, that the sender and recipient of the message are *not* in a face-to-face situation). Second, without the notion of a speech circuit there would be no explanatory force behind Saussure's account of how *la langue* accumulates as a collective *trésor* ([30]). Unless there were assumed to be an essential link in circuitry between the two capacities of speech-production and speech-comprehension, it would need a separate theory to explain why, for example, when A says 'Good morning' and B replies 'Good morning', either could recognize the other as having said 'the same thing'. But that recognition, for Saussure, is essential to *la langue* as a social institution. In other words, there would be no collective *trésor* at all if individuals were not able to recognize the circuit as being circuitous (namely, that B, by saying 'Good morning', is now 'returning' to A via the circuit the same verbal message as B heard A originally deliver). Without that minimal assumption, *la langue* in the Saussurean sense could not exist. Third, the Saussurean thesis of the duality of all linguistic phenomena ([24]) would collapse unless speech communication were essentially circuitous. Thus if it were possible to identify, for instance, the consonant *n* by articulatory criteria alone or by auditory criteria alone, then it would not be a *linguistic* phenomenon as such. This ties in with Saussure's later claims about the 'amorphousness' of sound ([64-5]). What makes this amorphous substance viable as a medium of communication is precisely that reciprocality which somehow enables participants in the speech circuit to recognize some of their own articulatory productions as equivalent to some of the auditory impressions they receive when listening to others. The 'mutual delimitation' ([65]) of minimum units of speech would otherwise be impossible.

* * *

The speech-circuit model deals with a specific subcategory of signs; namely, signs belonging to *la langue*. The following section of the chapter proceeds immediately to deal with the science of signs as a whole (*sémiologie*). At this point, attention shifts from the question 'What is *la langue*?' to focus once more on the question 'What is linguistics?'

Saussure's status as the founder of modern linguistics is unproblematic: but his status as founder of twentieth-century semiology is nothing if not paradoxical. On the one hand, this latter role seems to be undeniable if we are to judge by the number of subsequent semiological studies and works of semiological theory claiming Saussure directly or indirectly as their inspiration (Barthes 1964, Prieto 1966, Metz 1971, Toussaint 1978, Broadbent, Bunt and Jencks 1980, etc.). On the other hand, what the *Cours* says on the subject of semiology could hardly pass muster as a theoretical foundation for anything, for reasons which will be discussed below. Nevertheless, according to our currently received history of ideas, Saussure disputes with C.S. Peirce the palm for having established the possibility of a general 'science of signs'. Saussure's use of the term *sémiologie* is dated back to 1894 and Peirce's use of the term *semiotic* to 1897 (Lange-Seidl 1977: 13-14). As regards academic spadework for this new science, Peirce is acknowledged as having done more than Saussure: perhaps even too much. For to start by distinguishing, as Peirce did, no less than 59049 types of sign is arguably enough to strangle any science of signs at birth. Saussure at least did not do that.

Three passages in the *Cours* discuss questions concerning semiology. The longest of these constitutes §3 of the third chapter of the Introduction, immediately following the discussion of the speech circuit. Two later passages in the text add significant clarifications. One ([100-101]) is a paragraph contained in the important section dealing with the principle of the arbitrariness of the linguistic sign. The other is a brief remark ([149]) at the end of the chapter on '*Les entités concrètes de la langue*', where Saussure takes up the question originally raised on p.[33] as to what makes *la langue* a special type of semiological system. These three passages do not amount to more than a thousand words all told. An exiguous theoretical foundation if ever there was one; and, not surprisingly, one which has given rise to conflicting interpretations.

Eco claims that the essential difference between Saussurean semiology and Peircian semiotic is that the former is dependent on the concept of communication:

> the sign is implicitly regarded as a communicative device taking place between two human beings intentionally aiming to communicate or to express something. It is not by chance that all the examples of semiological systems given by Saussure are without any shade of doubt strictly conventionalized systems of artificial signs, such as military signals, rules of etiquette and visual alphabets. Those who share Saussure's notion of *sémiologie* distinguish sharply between intentional, artificial devices (which they call 'signs') and other natural or unintentional manifestations which do not, strictly speaking, deserve such a name. (Eco 1976: 15)

For Peirce, on the other hand, the subjects of semiosis are not human subjects but 'three abstract semiotic entities, the dialectic between which is not affected by concrete communicative behavior' (Eco 1976: 15). Prieto, however, draws a very similar distinction within Saussurean semiology itself, citing Buyssens as a representative of those Saussureans who treat semiology as dealing only with 'communication' and Barthes as a representative of those who treat semiology as dealing more generally with 'signification' (Prieto 1968: 93-4).

If Saussure's speech circuit is to be read as a theory of communication, that might appear at first sight to lend support to Eco's interpretation of the difference between Saussure's general science of signs and Peirce's. However, what Eco offers with the right hand is speedily removed by his left: for he concedes that his account of Peirce's semiotic 'could also fit Saussure's proposal'. Nevertheless, he claims that Peirce's account 'does not demand, as part of a sign's definition, the qualities of being intentionally emitted and artificially produced'. Hence Peirce's notion 'can also be applied to phenomena that do not have a human emitter, provided that they do have a human receiver, such being the case with meteorological symptoms or any other sort of index.' So Peirce's approach, unlike Saussure's, it would seem, does not 'reduce semiotics to a theory of communicational acts' (Eco 1976: 15-16). Thus whereas rings round the moon 'meaning' rain, or spots 'meaning' measles, would fall within the province of Peirce's general science of signs, they would be excluded from Saussure's.

Unfortunately, Eco's reading of Saussurean semiology is not supported by what the text of the *Cours* says. In the *Cours* we read of 'a science *which studies the role of signs as part of social life*' ([33]). It is difficult to see how this could exclude, for example, meteorological signs (particularly when weather forecasts are appended to daily news broadcasts as a regular feature of a communications system available in principle to every member of the linguistic community). It might even include the astrological signs taken as a basis for the so-called 'horoscopes' featured by popular newspapers and magazines. At the very least, it would have to include doctors' interpretations of their patients' symptoms. Unless we adopt a curiously narrow interpretation of which parts of life are 'social', presumably all three categories of sign – meteorological, astrological and medical – are 'part of social life'. Although there is no indication that Saussure was particularly interested in meteorological, astrological or medical signs, they are certainly not excluded from the province of semiology by what the *Cours* says. It is no doubt true that isobars are not signs until interpreted as significant; nor are conjunctions of heavenly bodies or spots on the skin. But, to repeat, all the *Cours* apparently demands is that this significance should play a role in *social* life. Consequently, if there is a distinction between Saussure's approach to a general science of signs and Peirce's, it can hardly be drawn at the point where Eco draws it.

Worse still, it seems to be a misreading of the *Cours* which is responsible for the suggestion that the Saussurean sign is defined by reference to communicative intentions. This is to confuse *faits de langue* with *faits de parole.* The communal institution (*la langue*) has no intentions. It merely provides linguistic resources to be utilized by individuals who *do* have communicative intentions. Nowhere in the *Cours* does intention enter into any definition of the sign, linguistic or otherwise.

Two points certainly remain unclear from Saussure's rather vague observations about semiology: just how general this general science of signs is to be, and exactly what signs, other than linguistic signs, fall within its province. But the fact that Saussure leaves these questions open is doubtless in part due to the consideration that, as in the case of linguistics ([20]), one of the tasks of semiology would be to determine its own limits and objectives as a science ([100]). All that can be inferred on the basis of the remarks in the *Cours* may be summarized as follows. 1. Semiology is envisaged as a human science and part of social psychology ([33]). Therefore it would exclude, for example, the study of animal communication. 2. Semiology is not restricted to the study of signs as opposed to the study of symbols ([100-101]). Nevertheless, one of its main tasks will be the analysis of the various human systems of signs which are, like the linguistic sign, arbitrary. 3. Linguistics will occupy a privileged position within semiology, by providing a model (*patron général*) for all semiological investigation ([101]).

Thus there is no doubt that Saussure's semiology falls far short of being a general science of signs in the sense later defined by semioticians like Charles Morris: it does not deal with 'signs in all their forms and manifestations, whether in animals or men, whether normal or pathological, whether linguistic or nonlinguistic, whether personal or social' (Morris 1964: 1). But it does correspond to at least one part of the science which Locke in the last chapter of the *Essay Concerning Human Understanding* baptizes with the Greek term *semeiōtikē*: 'the business whereof is to consider the nature of signs the mind makes use of for the understanding of things, or conveying its knowledge to others' (Locke 1706: 4.21.4). That correspondence certainly invites consideration: the two neologisms do not exhibit etymological parallels by coincidence. (Scholars doubt whether Saussure had ever studied Locke at first hand (de Mauro 1972: 381 n.11, Aarsleff 1982: 27): but the question is irrelevant to a reading of the *Cours.*) Furthermore, it makes sense not only of the privileged position assigned to linguistics, which a more general science of signs would have to reject, but also of Saussure's statement that the exact role of semiology is a matter for the psychologist. In other words, Saussure's general science of signs takes its place as part of an inquiry into what Locke described as 'the objects of our understanding' and a later generation of academics called 'cognition'. It deals specifically with those communally and communicationally developed instruments of the understanding which comprise the whole gamut of social signs.

This view of semiology nevertheless leaves certain problems unresolved; in particular, how to construe Saussure's notion of the privileged position accorded to linguistics as a semiological science. For Barthes, what Saussure had implicitly done was not establish linguistics as a branch of semiology at all, but rather establish semiology as an extension of linguistics; and Barthes proposed to redefine the relationship accordingly (Barthes 1964: 11). This 'reversal' of Saussurean priorities met with acrimonious criticism, and Barthes was accused of having 'perverted' Saussure's idea of semiology (Lange-Seidl 1977: 44 n.12). The case for and against Barthes' position is of less importance than the fact that the controversy itself highlights a genuine difficulty concerning Saussure's assumption of a special relationship between linguistics and semiology.

Even if, for the sake of argument, it were conceded that Saussurean linguistics would eventually fall into place as part of a more general science of social signs, it remains quite unclear why it should be a foregone conclusion that the more general science should take linguistics as its model. For this seems to presuppose in advance of any investigation that all sign systems human societies develop are structured along the same lines as *la langue*. The assumption already points ahead to a theoretical conflict. If there are sign systems to which the Saussurean analysis of *la langue* cannot be applied, linguistics must lose its priority as a model of investigation. Alternatively, any systems which resist the imposition of a linguistic model will be rejected as systems of signs. The conflict could only result in an exhibition of theoretical dexterity in accommodating the maximum number of social signs as analogues of the linguistic sign, and in controversy over membership of the general class of signs.

That is not all. An even more critical conundrum is posed by Saussure's conjecture ([149]) that what distinguishes *la langue* from all other semiological systems is the fact that its entities are not immediately 'given'. This suggestion ties in with the famous Saussurean dictum that where the study of language is concerned 'it is the viewpoint adopted which creates the object' ([23]). As Spang-Hanssen points out (1954: 103-4), there is another fundamental difficulty here. How can the notion that *la langue* is unique in this respect be reconciled with the idea that 'the language sign can to advantage be studied as a special example of arbitrary signs'? Or, more bluntly, how can one avoid the conclusion that 'the basis for a semiology in Saussure's sense' does not in reality exist? Spang-Hanssen goes on to suggest that post-Saussurean semiology can be analysed in terms of attempts to salvage whatever can be salvaged from this conceptual disaster. The possibilities are four in number:

(a)   that semiology is preserved as the designation for the study of
        language signs and other signs as far as these have common
        characteristics (e.g. as arbitrary signs as opposed to 'natural signs').
        In this case linguistics does not become a part of semiology, but
        language can be studied from a semiological aspect.
(b)   that semiology covers only the study of signs with the same formal
        properties as the language sign.
(c)   that semiology covers only the study of arbitrary signs which are not
        language signs.
(d)   that the designation is rejected.

(Spang-Hanssen 1954: 104)

Spang-Hanssen points to a division among Saussure's successors, arguing
that Buyssens (1943) opts for possibility (a), while Hjelmslev (1943) opts
for (b).

Firth thought that the view that linguistics must find its place among
the sciences as part of semiology was 'perhaps the most striking thing in
the whole of de Saussure's great work' (Firth 1935: 17); and that reaction
is an interesting one in view of the very many 'striking things' which the
academic world found in the *Cours*. What seems to have impressed Firth
was the implicit denial that the linguistic sign can be studied
scientifically as something *sui generis*. Identifying linguistics as a branch
of semiology, and claiming quite specifically that 'the laws which
semiology will discover will be laws applicable in linguistics' ([33]),
makes it quite clear that the linguistic sign is only one variety of a more
general phenomenon. This insistence connects in an important way with
Saussure's critique of the comparative and historical linguistics of the
nineteenth century. The connexion, once grasped, explains better than
anything else the rationale of Saussure's curiously inchoate appeal to a
future science of semiology.

The cornerstone of nineteenth-century linguistics had been the study
of sound change. At the same time, the study of sound change relied
almost entirely on the historical evidence of written forms. This placed
far too much emphasis on the 'wrong' things for Saussure's liking. The
interpretation of ancient texts was the province of philology: while the
sounds of speech were the province of the phonetician. Consequently, a
linguistics which continued to place the study of written texts and of
speech sounds in the forefront of its investigations would be reversing the
order of priorities necessary to establish its own scientific autonomy. To
re-orient linguistics in the right direction, however, it did not suffice to
identify *la langue* as a synchronic system, or to separate synchronic from
diachronic studies. For even if *la langue* were defined as a synchronic
system of vocal signs, the risk of ending up with linguistics as a minor
branch of physiology or acoustics remained.

The strategic dilemma was this. One obvious way of refocussing
attention towards the study of linguistic structure and away from the

study of speech sounds would have been to treat languages as abstract systems which could be expressed *either* in spoken *or* in written form. But this would merely promote the study of written texts again for a different reason, and perhaps run the even greater risk of rehabilitating the popular prejudice, virtually endemic in literate societies, of treating the written language as superior to the spoken. Nevertheless, a solution had to be found which would relegate study of the phonic side of language to its proper place. Saussure's way out is to treat the (vocal) linguistic sign as being on a par with other signs which are non-vocal, but which can nevertheless be assumed to be in some way comparable to the signs of *la langue*. Hence the postulation of a more general science of social signs, in which the linguistic sign is just *primus inter pares*. For there is otherwise no division of human communicational activities which will keep writing out of the picture as a natural and equal partner to speech. Semiology, then, is Saussure's answer to the twin problems posed by the status of writing and the status of sounds. Semiology demotes writing to the level of 'just another social sign system' (comparable to the Morse code, symbolic rites, etc.) at the same time as it demotes phonetics to the role of a merely ancillary discipline to linguistics. Two birds are killed with one theoretical stone.

Saussure therefore needs semiology for two reasons. First because, as argued earlier, he cannot do without the premiss that the relationship of *écriture* to *langue* is that of dependent to independent sign system. That already means drawing one post-dated cheque on his account at the semiological bank. But he will also need another, to cover his theoretical debts in treating the structure of *la langue* as independent of its phonic materialization. For that too cannot be demonstrated except on the assumption of certain semiological principles. Here we first encounter the most important hidden premiss of the *Cours* so far, which will turn out to play a crucial role in the fully developed Saussurean theory of *la langue*. This is the premiss that a sign system is adequately defined, from a semiological point of view, in terms of 'form' rather than 'substance' (which in practical terms means abstracting from the specific channel of communication involved). A linguistics which did not accept that premiss would be destined to be either a sub-science of phonetics or a sub-science of philology, or else some hybrid of the two. Semiology, for Saussure, is the way round the grim academic alternatives of leaping from the philological frying-pan into the fire of phonetics, or vice versa.

Critics of Saussure's strategy might well complain that this manoeuvre merely buys independence from philology and phonetics at the expense of mortgaging the future of linguistics to semiology. The Saussurean reply to this criticism would doubtless have been (i) that since semiology does not yet exist, this in practice means an independent status for linguistics, and (ii) that linguistics is in any case guaranteed in advance a privileged position within semiology which it lacks under the hegemony of any other science. That this latter guarantee is quite bogus matters far less for our reading of the *Cours* than the fact that it is offered. The offer shows perhaps more clearly than anything else exactly how the Saussurean answers to the questions 'What is *la langue*?' and 'What is linguistics?' are interdependent. For Saussure, since *la langue* is the 'object' of linguistics, the question of what we take *la langue* to be must merge with what we take – or want – linguistics to be.

CHAPTER IV

Linguistics of Language Structure and Linguistics of Speech

Having situated linguistics within a scientific hierarchy (by placing it under the superordinate, albeit hypothetical, science of semiology) the *Cours* proceeds in Chapter IV of the Introduction to distinguish between a linguistics of *la langue* and a linguistics of *la parole*. This serves to emphasize and supplement the rather sparse indications already given ([27-32]) concerning what belongs to *la langue* and what belongs to *la parole*. Again, the expository point is a subtle one: it is not until we come to consider how the study of language might in practice be conducted that certain intuited linguistic distinctions fall into place as part of a coherent whole. (Another exemplification of the Saussurean priority of 'viewpoint' over 'object'.)

For the first time it is made absolutely clear that the study of speech sounds does not fall within the linguistics of *la langue*. This is, in fact, merely spelling out what is already implicit in the way the relationship between linguistics and semiology has been described in the preceding chapter. Here, however, the statements are unequivocal. 'The vocal organs are as external to the language system as the electrical apparatus which is used to tap out the Morse code is external to that code' ([36]). And on the same page we find the first of the celebrated Saussurean linguistic analogies, comparing *la langue* to a symphony. The symphony has a reality 'which is independent of the way in which it is performed'. This analogy was later borrowed by American generativists in the 1960s to validate their own distinction between 'competence' and 'perform-ance' (Katz and Postal 1964: ix). (Saussure's use of the musical comparison is particularly apt, since his point here is about the status of sound-production. The distinction between competence and perform-ance, on the other hand, is a broader distinction, involving far more than phonetic or phonological considerations. The later use of the musical analogy thus offers an interesting example in the history of linguistics of a second-order metaphor: a metametaphor.)

Saussure's underlying rejection of the preoccupation with sound-change in nineteenth-century linguistics now comes out into the open. A quibble is voiced: 'One may perhaps object to regarding phonation as separate from the language system. What about the evidence provided by phonetic changes, coming from alterations in sounds as produced in speech?' ([36]). The objection is no sooner raised than dismissed with impressive finality. 'The language itself as a system of signs is affected only indirectly, through the change of interpretation which results' ([37]). The dismissal is indeed so summary that its full thrust is not obvious here. But that will be rectified later, in the section of the *Cours* which deals with diachronic linguistics. What Saussure is rejecting is a whole tradition of scholarship which assumed that linguistic evolution could in large measure be 'explained' by reference to sound changes, themselves 'explained' by reference to general physiological processes of articulation.

Linguistics, then, as the study of *langage* divides naturally into (i) a primary linguistics of *la langue, la langue* being 'social in its essence and independent of the individual', and (ii) a secondary linguistics of *la parole*, dealing with 'the individual part of language' ([37]). Several details about the way the distinction between *langue* and *parole* is now drawn may be noted. This reformulation is deliberately more specific than in the preceding chapter. For example, we find the phrase 'speech, including phonation' (*la parole y compris la phonation*). Why might there be any doubt as to whether phonation is included in *la parole*? Because previously the term *parole* had been used only with reference either to the circuit as a whole (*circuit de la parole*) or specifically to the 'executive' section of its psychological component ($c \rightarrow s$) ([30]). But the notion of execution is now being applied less restrictedly, and the entire process of phonation is described as 'the execution of sound patterns' ([36]). Furthermore, it is now clear that the processes of *parole* include also the transmission of sound waves; for the linguistics of *la parole* is described as a 'psycho-physical' study ([37]). (Perhaps a more exact, if clumsier, term would have been 'psycho-physio-physical': for there is no doubt that the intention is to include all three subdivisions of the circuit in *la parole*.)

Thus what previously might have seemed to be gaps, tensions or even contradictions in the exposition are now, at least temporarily, dealt with. *La parole* is 'individual' in the sense of being that part of *le langage* manifested in the processes of linguistic interchange between individuals. Its individuality requires a separate speech circuit which is in no sense part of *la langue*. *La langue* is 'social' in the sense of being that part of *le langage* which collectively subsumes any individual linguistic interchange, being utilized in and presupposed by it. Now that is a complex distinction, which cannot straightforwardly be given a definitional gloss in terms of cruder contrasts such as 'actual' vs.

'potential', or 'execution' vs. 'plan', or 'unique' vs. 'common', or 'token' vs. 'type', or 'extension' vs. 'intension'; *even though it remains true that such contrasts will be applicable to particular cases.* But the distinction between *langue* and *parole* is not itself reducible to any one or any combination of these contrasts, for reasons which the *Cours* now attempts to elucidate.

The elucidation takes a curious and arresting form ([38]). The reader is presented with two quasi-mathematical formulae. The formula representing *la langue* is:

$$1 + 1 + 1 + 1 \ldots = I$$

We then have another of Saussure's celebrated linguistic analogies as a gloss upon it: 'a totality of imprints in everyone's brain, rather like a dictionary of which each individual has an identical copy' ([38]). This seems to suggest that the Arabic figures on the left-hand side of the equation stand for particular copies which, however numerous, do not 'add up' to more than one lexicon (represented by the Roman figure on the right). Thus far it looks as if the two sides of the equation symbolize multiple 'tokens' (on the left) vs. a single 'type' (on the right). But this is then contrasted with the formula representing *la parole*:

$$1 + 1' + 1'' + 1''' \ldots$$

The semiology of this 'mathematical' contrast, although striking, has either escaped the attention of Saussurean scholars or else been misconstrued (as, for example, by Spence (1957: 19), who ignores the difference between Arabic and Roman numerals, and thus reduces the example to mathematical nonsense). The first point to note is that the second formula is not an equation. The second point to note is that the primes in the second formula are appended to Arabic numerals, each of which in the first formula stands for one person's representation of *la langue*. (It is ironical, given Saussure's views on writing, that the *Cours* here employs conventions of written symbolism to express linguistic distinctions for which *la langue* apparently has no structurally articulated counterparts.)

What these formulaic devices attempt to express is the fact that there is no direct correspondence between *faits de langue* and *faits de parole*. The correspondence is always mediated via individuals. Were it not for this crucial mediation, the relationship between *langue* and *parole* would be a simple relationship of abstraction. As it is, however, there is inevitably a double classification to be reckoned with (individual vs. social). In addition, the two classifications operate on different principles. Classification from the individual point of view treats speech acts in relation to each individual's linguistic experience $(1 + 1 + 1 + 1 \ldots)$. Classification from a social point of view generalizes across indefinitely many speech acts and indefinitely many individuals, ignoring their particularities. This explains why the priority as between *faits de langue* and *faits de parole* can be seen in different perspectives. A child could not acquire a language except through first having experience of particular acts of speech: the language is already 'there' to be acquired, but it is initially there only in the indirect mode of a finite number of acts of speech produced by particular individuals with whom the child comes into contact. Historically, too, the establishment of a language as the language of a particular community presupposes a finite number of acts of speech by a certain number of individuals. On the other hand, as an established social fact the language is not just a finite sum total of *faits de parole* involving a specific number of individuals: it is the unity (I) which makes an indefinite number of acts of speech (1 + 1' + 1'' + 1''' ...) by an indefinite number of individuals (1+ 1 + 1 + 1 ...) manifestations of one and the same language.

CHAPTER V

Internal and External
Elements of a Language

The opening sentence of Chapter IV of the Introduction makes the bold claim that by allocating to a science of *la langue* its essential role within the study of *le langage* 'we have at the same time mapped out linguistics in its entirety' ([36]). The reader may consequently be surprised to find that Chapter V does not proceed to elaborate this new Saussurean cartography by filling in the contours of a linguistics of *la langue* and a linguistics of *la parole*. Instead, it examines and apparently defends a more obvious division of language studies between 'internal' and 'external' matters. Under the latter, the *Cours* tells us, fall questions relating to: (i) 'the relations which may exist between the history of a language and the history of a race or civilization' ([40]), (ii) 'relations between languages and political history' ([40]), (iii) 'the literary development of a language' ([41]), and (iv) 'everything which relates to the geographical extension of languages and to their fragmentation into dialects' ([42]). In short, the whole range of historical, geographical and cultural factors which bear upon the life of the linguistic community.

The perplexing question which may immediately arise in the reader's mind is whether such matters can properly be the concern of linguistics at all, given the radical re-casting of the subject which Saussure has just proposed in Chapter IV. To add to the perplexity, there is the title of Chapter V: *Éléments internes et éléments externes de la langue*. For how can *la langue*, as described in Chapter IV, have 'external elements' at all?

It is possible to dismiss the latter puzzle simply by blaming Saussure's editors for an ineptly chosen chapter heading. One suggestion is that it should have read: *Eléments internes et éléments externes de la linguistique* (de Mauro 1972: 428 n.82). Even if we accept this emendation the first enigma remains, and is rendered even more enigmatic by two arguments put forward in the course of Chapter V.

1. Languages often borrow foreign words. But this does not mean that an examination of foreign sources is an essential part of the study of imported elements in the vocabulary of a language. For once a borrowed word takes its place in the linguistic system, it functions just like any other word: 'it exists only in virtue of its relation and opposition to words associated with it, just like any indigenous word' ([42]). 2. In certain cases, history can tell us nothing about the peoples who spoke certain languages or the circumstances under which these languages were spoken. 'But our ignorance in no way prevents us from studying their internal structure, or from understanding the developments they underwent' ([42]).

These two arguments by no means validate the treatment of 'external' topics as an essential or integral part of a science of linguistics. They are simply further arguments supporting the recognition of *la langue* as an autonomous object of study, and, specifically, the independence of a linguistics of *la langue*. Nothing could make the irrelevance of 'external' considerations to a linguistics of *la langue* more conspicuous than the analogy with the game of chess (the first of a number of chess analogies) on which Chapter V closes. Here we are told that the fact that chess came to Europe from Persia, or that chess pieces are made of ivory, are facts which are 'external'. Whereas the fact that there are only a certain number of chess pieces in a set is 'internal': for the number of pieces affects the 'grammar' of the game. Thus the criterion for distinguishing between 'external' and 'internal' factors is: 'Everything is internal which alters the system in any degree whatsoever' ([43]).

The formula that 'Everything is internal which alters the system in any degree whatsoever' is, however, in certain respects an unfortunate one. In the first place, it appears to state only a sufficient condition, whereas arguably the condition is intended to be both necessary and sufficient. Furthermore, in the form stated it lends itself to more than one interpretation. It might, for instance, be read as implying that everything which brings about a change in the system counts as an internal factor. But that could make the Roman Conquest, for example, an internal factor; which is a conclusion patently inconsistent with what was said about the linguistic role of 'major historical events' a page earlier. In the context of the chess analogy, we are presumably expected to read Saussure's formula as meaning: 'All (and only?) things which, if they were altered, would *ipso facto* alter the system, are internal'. Thus even though the migration of chess from Persia to Europe could have resulted in certain changes in the rules of the game, that would not count. For a game is not automatically altered by being exported from one country to another: and this would remain true even if, as a matter of historical fact, it happened that in all known cases the change from one country to another were accompanied by a change in the rules. Such changes would still be merely contingent; whereas to 'play chess' without pawns, for instance, *ipso facto* makes it a different game, irrespective of where it is played.

If Saussure's criterion is interpreted along these lines, that still leaves open the question of how to reconcile the distinction of Chapter V between internal and external linguistics with the distinction of Chapter IV between the linguistics of *la langue* and the linguistics of *la parole*. How exactly the two distinctions are related is not explained in the text: they are presented independently and we are left to draw our own conclusions. Why? It is perhaps difficult to avoid the suspicion that Saussure's editors themselves were not entirely clear about how the various parts of Saussure's programme fitted together. That suspicion might be reinforced if we happen to know that many years later Sechehaye published an article in which he rationalized the Saussurean programme as comprising three components: (i) a linguistics of *la langue*, (ii) a linguistics of *la parole*, and (iii) diachronic linguistics. According to Sechehaye, the second of these components is intended to play a mediating or linking role between the first and third (Sechehaye 1940: 7). But that simply leaves Saussure's 'external' linguistics nowhere. Two possible but awkward ways of construing this would be: either (a) that 'external linguistics', in spite of being so called, is just not a branch of linguistics at all, or (b) that somehow external linguistics is subsumed under or split among the three major branches. Sechehaye is silent on the matter: and the silence might be taken as echoing the original question the editors of the *Cours* appeared to leave unanswered.

There is, however, another way of making sense of this section of the *Cours*. Given that we have not yet been introduced to the distinction between synchronic and diachronic studies, which is later to play such an important part in Saussure's programme, it is possible simply to read both Chapters IV and V of the Introduction as jointly providing the foundation for that later distinction. On this view, the two chapters present not separate slices of the academic linguistic cake (that is, subdivisions of a programme for linguistics) but simply a demonstration of possible alternative ways of using one and the same conceptual knife. The knife in question is the concept of *la langue*. In other words, we here have a first gloss on the hitherto unexplicated claim of Chapter III that *la langue* provides a 'principle of classification' ([25]), and at the same time yet another reformulation of the distinction between *langue* and *parole*.

In support of this reading, it may be pointed out that the distinction between the two linguistics of Chapter IV is based on exactly the same principle as the distinction between the two linguistics of Chapter V. The linguistics of *la langue* appears to embrace just the same range of facts as internal linguistics does. In both cases we are concerned with what 'belongs to the system'. Does this mean, then, that 'external linguistics' is another designation for *linguistique de la parole*? On one level, the answer has to be 'yes': for at least two reasons. First, it is required by the internal logic of Saussure's own position. This treats *faits de langage* as divisible into just two classes: *faits de langue* and *faits de parole*. There is no third category of *faits de langage*, and hence no third 'branch' of linguistics. Second, every example Saussure gives of what falls under external linguistics constitutes in fact a particular grouping of certain *faits de parole*. Thus, to pursue the chess analogy, to say that chess came to Europe from Persia is simply a way of describing certain facts about where and when particular games of chess were played. To say that chess pieces are made of ivory is a way of describing certain other facts about games actually played. These are all matters which relate to the *parole* of the game of chess. And these are the examples Saussure gives of external factors. Had these games been played elsewhere and in a different chronological succession, or had they been played in countries where ivory was unknown, then historians of chess might be telling us that chess was imported into Persia from Europe and that chess pieces were traditionally made of tin. Saussure's point is that *faits de langue* are not of this order, any more than the rules of chess are generalizations about the past history of playing chess.

Why, then, confuse the issue by suggesting two terminologically different distinctions? The answer to this question takes us back once again to the Saussurean dictum about viewpoints creating objects. External linguistics may indeed be concerned in the final analysis with the same set of phenomena as a linguistics of *la parole*: that is to say, its ultimate *matière* may be the sum total of acts of speech. What distinguishes external linguistics, however, is the fact that its classifications are based on considerations drawn from history, geography, etc., and not on considerations drawn from an analysis of speech processes. On that level, the terminological contrasts of Chapters IV and V correspond to two different objects of study. But in both cases, it is *la langue* which emerges as the *fundamentum divisionis*.

CHAPTER VI

Representation of a Language by Writing

Writing is first of all mentioned in passing in Chapter III of the Introduction of the *Cours* and described in somewhat curious terms as the 'tangible form' of the *images acoustiques* of *la langue*. The limited number of elements in any *image acoustique*, we are told, can be represented by a corresponding number of written symbols. Writing is thus able to 'fix' linguistic signs in 'conventional images' ([32]). These considerations about the nature of writing are introduced as part of an argument designed to show that *la langue* is no less concrete than *la parole*, and that linguistic signs are not mere 'abstractions'. The evidence provided by writing is held to demonstrate this fact. For whereas writing can record every relevant element of a given linguistic sign, not even a camera could record in every detail the elements involved in the corresponding act of *parole* ([32]). As an argument this is not immediately convincing (to say the least) and it has been suggested that it originated with Saussure's editors. There is no evidence that it featured in the Geneva lectures (de Mauro 1972: 425 n.70). A more interesting question than its ultimate intellectual sponsorship, however, is how it would fit in with the Saussurean thesis about writing set out in Chapter VI of the Introduction. This question will be taken up below.

The next reference to writing in the *Cours* occurs in the section on semiology, where it is made evident that writing is to be distinguished from *la langue*, since writing is listed among various examples of comparable systems of 'signs expressing ideas' ([33]). From this it is already clear that from a Saussurean point of view written signs are signs in their own right, and do not owe this status to their connexion with speech. Whether or not this is because the term *écriture* is acknowledged as covering systems of musical and choreographic notation, together with other non-linguistic forms of recording, does not emerge at all clearly from the text at this point. For reasons which will be discussed shortly, it seems doubtful whether Saussure can afford many concessions to the broader interpretation of the concept of writing.

Ecriture in Chapter VI of the Introduction certainly refers specifically to graphic systems devised for linguistic purposes. The first section of this chapter reaffirms that writing is not part of the 'internal system' of *la langue*, but explains why the study of writing is nevertheless essential for the linguist. 'Languages are mostly known to us only through writing', and even in the case of our native language the written form constantly intrudes ([44]).

The opening sentence of §2 reaffirms more explicitly the point already made on p.[33]. *Langue* and *écriture* are 'two separate systems of signs'. Furthermore, the sole reason for the existence of the latter is to represent the former. More explicitly still: 'The object of study in linguistics is not a combination of the written word and the spoken word.' Linguistics is concerned only with the spoken word ([45]). This deliberate emphasis on separating writing from speech raises an interesting question: why is such conspicuous reiteration necessary? The point, after all, was by no means new. It had been a commonplace in nineteenth-century linguistics (Paul 1890: 660) and for a long time earlier. So it cannot be regarded as one of the novel theoretical moves associated particularly with Saussure.

If Saussurean scholars have been somewhat slow to probe this question that may be because they take at their face value the reasons the *Cours* gives for insisting on the non-linguistic status of writing. 'As much or even more importance is given to this representation of the vocal sign as to the vocal sign itself' ([45]). Popular misconceptions abound concerning the effect of writing on the development of the spoken language ([45-6]). Even distinguished linguistic scholars such as Bopp and Grimm failed to distinguish clearly between letters and sounds ([46]). The *Cours* suggests four factors accounting for the unwarranted 'prestige of writing': (i) the permanence and solidity of the 'graphic image', (ii) the greater clarity of visual images as compared with auditory images, (iii) the importance of the literary language in a literate society, and (iv) inconsistencies between pronunciation and spelling ([46-7]). But none of this rather superficial discussion goes any way towards justifying the theoretical claims which lie at the heart of Saussure's treatment of the relationship between writing and *la langue*. Instead, the chapter moves swiftly on to the rather dogmatic account of systems of writing in §3.

There are only two basic kinds of writing, according to the *Cours*. These are: (i) ideographic, and (ii) phonetic ([47]). The classic example of ideographic writing is Chinese, each word being written as a simple sign bearing no relation to pronunciation. Phonetic systems of writing, on the contrary, do relate to pronunciation. They are either syllabic or alphabetic, the latter representing 'the irreducible elements of speech'

([47]). The *Cours* admits that it is also possible to have 'mixed' systems of writing: that is to say, partly ideographic and partly phonetic ([47]). Having drawn up this simple classification of writing, Saussure says no more about ideographic and 'mixed' systems but proceeds to concentrate on phonetic systems, and more particularly still on the European alphabet. Such an alphabet in principle provides the means for a 'rational' representation of *la langue*: but in practice we find many discrepancies between spelling and pronunciation. In the following section, §4, Saussure examines the reasons for these discrepancies. They are: (i) that *la langue* evolves, while spelling remains fixed ([48]), (ii) that an alphabet designed for the representation of one language may be borrowed to represent another, for which it is less well adapted ([49-50]), and (iii) that etymological preoccupations may affect spelling ([50]). Finally, there are some discrepancies which are just bizarre and unexplained ([50]). The results of the discrepancies are detailed in §5, with examples from French, German, English and Greek. These examples show to what extent 'writing obscures our view of *la langue*' ([51]). Worse still, 'the tyranny of the written form' may even modify *la langue* itself, through the introduction of erroneous pronunciations modelled on spelling ([53]).

What is remarkable throughout the whole of Chapter VI is that nowhere in this relatively detailed discussion of writing is any attempt made to offer a serious argument in support of the two highly controversial theses which it presents. Both theses are based on the two 'hidden' premises already identified which postulate certain semiological relations between systems of signs. In this chapter it becomes abundantly clear why Saussure needs these premises. For he is committed to arguing not just that writing is a semiologically secondary system, derived from speech, but that *écriture* is actually a semiological 'representation' of *langue*. This thesis is closely connected with Saussure's earlier claim that it is possible to study the linguistic structure of those languages which are available to the linguist *only* through written sources. Why does he insist on this? Because otherwise he would be obliged to conclude that in the case of dead languages a study of *la langue* ('the social product stored in the brain' ([44]) is impossible in principle. In other words, most of the work done by the Indo-Europeanists of Saussure's own generation would have to be excluded from linguistics. The iconoclasm of the *Cours* is not as extreme as this: it implies merely that the Indo-Europeanists had inextricably confused synchronic and diachronic analysis, consequently failing to put either on a firm theoretical foundation.

Here Saussure is accepting and trying to deal with the theoretical consequences of the kind of Neogrammarian position taken by Paul, who had claimed that writing is not language, that 'it is in no way an equivalent for it' (Paul 1890: 663), and furthermore that as far as the linguist is concerned writing 'always needs to be rendered back into speech before it can be dealt with' (Paul 1890: 661). The weakness of the Neogrammarian position was that in practice the proclamation of conjectural 'sound laws', worked out *ad hoc* and mainly on the basis of textual evidence, was substituted for a general theory of the relationship between speech and writing. This, from a Saussurean point of view, was to put the cart before the horse. It is Saussure's doctrine of 'sound types', to be considered in the following chapter, which will explain in detail how a 'rendering back into speech' of written evidence is in principle possible. But such an explanation would be still-born without the theoretical underpinning provided by Saussure's thesis concerning the representational function of writing.

To appreciate how much hangs on this question of the relationship between writing and *la langue*, it suffices to examine what Saussure's position would be on any alternative assumption. Suppose, for example, the assumption were that writing represented solely *la parole*. Now according to the *Cours*, not even a camera can capture all the details of an act of *parole* ([32]). (If, as has been suggested, the remarks about writing on p.[32] are an editorial interpolation, it is nevertheless an interpolation which fulfils a valid and valuable role: for it at least provides an otherwise missing reason for distinguishing between the problem of representing *parole* and the problem of representing *langue*.) It would follow that writing, by definition, as an attempt to capture the facts of speech is an intrinsically imperfect form of representation. To determine in any particular case, therefore, how reliable a system of writing is, it would be necessary to compare it with the actual data of *parole*. But these data are precisely what the linguist does not have access to in the case of dead languages. Likewise, if it is supposed that writing is partly a representation of *langue* and partly a representation of *parole*, then without access to the data of *parole* it becomes impossible to determine which graphic features represent what. Finally, if it is supposed that writing represents neither *langue* nor *parole*, its value as evidence for the linguist is in any case reduced to nil. None of these options will suit the purposes of Saussure, who requires the assumption that certain forms of writing are in principle optimal representations of *la langue*, and the only practical problem is to detect and allow for those lapses from optimal representation which the passage of time and similar factors have brought about.

The second Saussurean thesis about writing is more specific; namely, that an 'ideal' alphabet would give the 'ideal' representation of the *image acoustique*, in the sense of a one-one correspondence between letters and the units of the *image acoustique*. Without this idealization, obviously, there is for Saussure little point in discussing the accuracy or inaccuracy of systems of alphabetic writing. On the Saussurean scale of values, alphabetic writing ranks above syllabic and ideographic systems, precisely because only alphabetic writing mirrors – or can in principle mirror – faithfully this aspect of the composition of the linguistic sign. An ideographic system could certainly provide separate symbols for the word 'cat' and the word 'dog': but it would not necessarily mirror anything at all about the *image acoustique* – not even whether these two words were identically pronounced or differently pronounced.

Saussurean commentators have failed to examine the tension between this specific thesis of 'alphabetic idealization' and the more general thesis that writing represents *la langue*. It may well be this tension which explains the rather summary treatment accorded in the *Cours* to the whole question of writing. The difficulty can be pinpointed by means of a hypothetical example. Suppose a language has two separate systems of writing, one ideographic and the other alphabetic. The ideographic system has different ideograms for the words 'cat' and 'dog'. However, these two words, let us suppose, are identically pronounced, and hence the alphabetic system does not distinguish between them. The example is not an unfair one, since Saussure goes so far as to say that in the case of Chinese, writing is 'a second *langue*' ([48]), and mentions that when confusion arises in conversation a Chinese may 'refer to the written form in order to explain what he means' ([48]). This concession itself is the Achilles' heel of Saussure's position on writing. For once it is admitted that writing may independently represent an idea or a thing without thereby representing any *image acoustique*, the general thesis that writing represents *la langue* is in tatters: and *a fortiori* the special thesis that alphabetic writing represents the *signifiant* of the linguistic sign.

There is one fleeting indication that the author of the *Cours* recognized the vulnerability of this Achilles' heel and endeavoured to protect it. In the remarks on ideographic writing we are told that the ideogram 'represents the entire word as a whole, and hence indirectly the idea expressed' ([47]). The fleeting indication is the word 'indirectly'. Saussure cannot allow the possibility that writing *directly* represents ideas. But he is caught here in a dilemma arising from his central doctrine that *la langue* is a simple bi-planar system, in which units on both planes are determined solely by bi-planar interrelations. Granted that an ideogram does not represent the *image acoustique* at all, there is no way in which it represents 'the entire word as a whole', and therefore no way in which it only 'indirectly' represents the idea expressed. One might just as well claim that at the same time the ideogram represents the *image acoustique* 'indirectly'. But that would be too obviously to beg the whole question of *what* it is that graphic symbols represent, and why an alphabetic system should be held to represent the *image acoustique* 'directly' (which presumably means, *inter alia*, a representation independent of *la parole*).

CHAPTER VII

Physiological Phonetics

The final topic treated in the Introduction to the *Cours* is phonetics. In view of what Saussure has said in the immediately preceding chapter concerning the relationship between writing and speech, his problem here is to steer a none-too-straightforward course between dismissing the study of articulatory processes *per se* as belonging to a linguistics of *la parole*, and admitting that without it the linguist would be in no position to interpret written sources as evidence bearing upon *la langue*. The compromise offered is that physiological phonetics is an 'auxiliary science' which sets linguistics free from reliance on the written word ([55]), and from the graphic illusions which would otherwise beset it ([56]). This compromise, at the same time as acknowledging that movements of the vocal apparatus are not part of *la langue* ([56]), makes it clear that *la langue* nevertheless relies on contrasts between the auditory impressions derived from phonation ([56]).

Critics have claimed to detect a contradiction between the views on phonetic transcription expressed in §2 of Chapter VII and the views on sound as the material substrate of *la langue* to be found in later passages in the *Cours*. This is because they have taken the principle of phonetic transcription enunciated on p.[57], which lays down the requirement that transcription should 'provide one symbol for each unit in the sequence of spoken sounds', to indicate Saussure's commitment to a belief in a 'natural' segmentation of *la chaîne parlée*. According to de Mauro (1972: 431-2 n.105):

> Saussure here seems to be convinced that it is possible to devise an 'unambiguous' phonetic transcription ... based on a prior analysis of the 'speech chain' into its successive 'elements', and the classification of these segments solely on the basis of phonetic criteria. This conviction would be well founded if, in contrast with what Saussure demonstrates elsewhere, physio-acoustic phenomena did have any capacity whatever or any reason whatsoever to group themselves into distinct classes, and if there were divisions of a physio-acoustic nature within phonic sequences ... But this is

a view contradicted primarily and absolutely by Saussure's pages on the intrinsically amorphous nature of phonic substance ([155f.]).

It is undeniable, as de Mauro goes on to point out, that the phonetician can produce a number of different classifications of speech sounds and a variety of segmentations of a given sound sequence, depending on the phonetic criteria selected as a basis for the analysis. In this sense, there are no unique or ultimate phonetic analyses given by Nature. What is questionable is whether Saussure ever implies that there are and, in particular, whether his pronouncements about phonetic transcription are in fact in conflict with his claims about the 'amorphousness' of sound. The Appendix which follows Chapter VII sets out a system of phonetic classification for speech: but there is no claim that it is the only possible classification. What is claimed for the system, rather, is that its principles provide a 'natural basis' ([63]) and a 'natural starting point' ([64]) for the linguist's study of speech sounds. The 'naturalness' resides in the fact that, unlike certain other phonetic systems, this is a system based jointly on articulatory and auditory criteria. Why is this 'natural'? Because, we are told, that is the principle on which human speech perception in fact works. 'We cannot tell articulatorily where one sound ends and another begins ... It is the sequence the ear hears that enables us immediately to detect when one sound is replaced by another ...' ([64]). Now Saussure offers no physiological or experimental evidence in support of this claim: but that is a different matter. What is quite clear is that the claim itself does not deny the possibility of more than one way of analysing and classifying phonetic data. His system is an amplification, in short, of the point made previously in Chapter III about the duality of linguistic phenomena. 'One cannot divorce what is heard from oral articulation. Nor, on the other hand, can one specify the relevant movements of the vocal organs without reference to the corresponding auditory impression' ([24]). This is where the 'amorphousness' of sound is given due recognition: it remains an undifferentiated continuum until subjected to the conjoint discriminations provided by the articulatory and auditory processes of speech. The discriminations have to be conjoint because, taken separately, an articulatory sequence is as 'unanalysable' as the corresponding auditory sequence ([64-5]).

A different question again is whether we should read Saussure as being committed to the proposition that in speech there is a basic, universal (language-neutral) differentiation of the amorphous phonetic continuum. Relevant to this are his remarks in praise of the primitive Greek alphabet. 'Each *son simple* is represented by one symbol, and conversely each symbol invariably corresponds to a *son simple*' ([64]). But this principle, 'which is both a necessary and a sufficient condition for good transcription' ([64]), was a principle 'not grasped by other nations, and consequently their alphabets do not analyse sound sequences into constituent auditory units' ([65]). Saussure cites as deficient in this respect the Cypriot syllabary and the Semitic system of representing consonants only. It is certainly very easy to construe this comparison as implying that the Greeks had discovered a fact of nature about human speech which had eluded other literate civilizations. Is it possible, on the other hand, to treat these remarks as pointing out merely that not all literate peoples manage to analyse what would nowadays be called the 'phoneme system' of their own language? There are various reasons for regarding such a reading as implausible. In the first place, the observations about the Greek alphabet occur in a chapter devoted to phonetics, which has already been quite unequivocally described as a merely 'auxiliary' discipline, concerned with *faits de parole* as distinct from *faits de langue*. For Saussure: 'It is true that if no *langue* existed the movements of the vocal apparatus would be pointless. None the less, these movements are not part of *la langue*, and an exhaustive analysis of the processes of phonation required to produce every auditory impression tells us nothing about *la langue*' ([56]). In the second place, nowhere in this chapter (or elsewhere in the *Cours*) do we find a discussion of the possibility that the same sound sequence might be analysed differently by speakers of different languages – a *topos* nowadays reiterated *ad nauseam* in introductory manuals. This is a point Saussure never makes in spite of the fact that it is eminently 'Saussurean'.

A third consideration is the way Saussure defines the minimum unit of speech as 'an aggregate of auditory impressions and articulatory movements, comprising what is heard and what is spoken, one delimiting the other' ([65]). More explicitly still, 'a combination such as *ta* will always comprise two units, each occupying a certain temporal segment' ([66]). There is no mention at all of the possibility that *ta* in different languages might be treated as comprising different units. Thus there appears to be no room in Saussurean phonetics for the hypothetical Cypriot who claims that *ta* is just one sound (because clearly the Cypriot syllable is a single unit), or for the hypothetical Semite who claims that *ta* is just one variety of the single consonant *t* (because clearly the Semitic root is a combination of consonants). Both these claims would be objectively 'wrong' for Saussure. In short, the Saussurean *linguistique de la parole* envisages a universal set of 'irreducible' phonetic units or 'sound types', of which the number is limited. (This again fits in with Saussure's evident wish to allow the possibility of engaging in an analysis of *la langue* for dead languages accessible only through written sources. Otherwise, no concession at all to nineteenth-century linguistics would be possible. But if the number of 'sound types' is universal and limited, and if writing systems are sufficiently advanced to 'represent' them, the possibility remains open. All the linguist analysing Greek or Latin has to do is decide which of the universal 'sound types' are represented by which letters in the Greek and Latin alphabets. Since the inventory is limited, an analysis should be possible, always provided that the available written evidence is internally consistent.)

Fourth, it would be an anachronism to attribute retrospectively to Saussure any more 'modern' view of the phoneme. His approach to identifying the minimal units of speech is what would nowadays be called 'physical', as opposed to either 'psychological' or 'functional' (Fudge 1970). Not only that, but Saussure's is a very primitive variety of 'physical' theory. It is not the more sophisticated 'family of related sounds' of Daniel Jones, but rather the crude 'physiological alphabet' concept of Max Müller. Saussure, indeed, would doubtless have approved Müller's contempt for 'too much nicety' in phonetics and his insistence that all the linguist needs is to acquire 'a clear conception of what has been well called the *Alphabet of Nature*'. Müller wrote (1864: 165-6):

> If we have clearly impressed on our mind the normal conditions of the organs of speech in the production of vowels and consonants, it will be easy to arrange the sounds of every new language under the categories once established on a broad basis. To do this, to arrange the alphabet of any given language according to the compartments planned by physiological research, is the office of the grammarian, not of the physiologist.

In a similar vein, Saussure sees no problem of 'discovery procedures' for the linguist in identifying the sound units of an unfamiliar language: 'after analysing a considerable number of sound sequences from a variety of languages, the linguist is able to recognise and classify the units involved' ([66]). Just a question of professional experience, it would seem.

Such expertise is possible only on the assumption that Nature has provided for the exercise of *la langue* an instrument of very limited capacity (namely, the human vocal apparatus) constructed in a way which can be studied independently of its utilisation by this or that particular linguistic community. Consequently, the problem of 'rendering back into speech' the evidence of writing is analogous to the problem confronting a musicologist who has to interpret various forms of musical notation, but knows in advance that the melodies in question were all designed to be played on a pipe of which the entire constructional details are independently available. The musicologist, given this problem, will doubtless proceed on the assumption that an 'ideal' musical notation is one which indicates as simply and unambiguously as possible the different fingering positions corresponding to the various notes which the pipe is capable of producing. In addition, it might perhaps be assumed that the more musically sophisticated the civilization the closer its musical notation will tend to approximate to an ideal one-one correspondence between symbol and finger position (always allowing for a small number of discrepancies to be explained by reference to particular historical and cultural circumstances). In this complex of musicological assumptions, nothing precludes the possibility that different musical communities may have developed quite different musical scales, even though the instrument used for musical *parole* is identical. The musical analogy just outlined is nowhere suggested in the pages of the *Cours*, but it makes good sense overall of the various pronouncements in the *Cours* about the relationships between linguistics, phonetics and writing.

Was Saussure perhaps a more 'advanced' musicologist than this simple analogy suggests? It is sometimes implied by Saussurean scholars that a kind of pre-Prague-School concept of the phoneme as a purely differential unit within a system of phonological oppositions (irrespective of its exact pronunciation) is already in germ in the precocious *Mémoire sur le système primitif des voyelles* of 1879. If this is so, then it is fair comment to add that in the thirty-odd years between the publication of the *Mémoire* and the publication of the *Cours* germination had still not occurred. For nowhere does the Saussure of the *Cours* supply what a present-day reader would regard as an explicit and unequivocal distinction between minimum units of phonetic analysis and minimum units of phonological analysis. What will be found instead are various remarks which might lead us nowadays to expect that Saussure is about to formulate the very definition of the phoneme we anticipate. But a search for such a definition itself in the pages of the *Cours* is a search in vain.

Is this a lacuna in the *Cours*? Does Saussure's linguistics actually need a 'structural' definition of the phoneme? It may doubtless be regarded as heretical by some Saussureans to suggest that it does not, and that therefore it is quite gratuitous to suspect Saussure of failure to realize and explicate the phonological possibilities inherent in his own structuralism. But that is because modern intellectual fashions favour theories which are completely self-contained, as distinct from being merely free of internal contradictions. It is perfectly possible, on the other hand, to read Saussure as allowing that a human *faculté de langage* which presides over the culturally determined patterns of bi-planar correlation between sounds and concepts will 'naturally' (that is, biologically) choose certain modes of physiological articulation, irrespective of the particular circumstances of cultural history. It will not fall within the province of linguistics to *explain*, but merely to grasp these modes of articulation. For theoretical purposes, consideration of the connexion between the cultural facts and the biological facts may be indefinitely postponed through insisting on a series of 'intermediate' levels. But by the same token, the connexion might just as well be recognized as soon as convenient. It makes no theoretical difference; and considerations of intellectual 'economy' favour the latter strategy. In any semiological study, as defined by Saussure, there will come a point at which the possibility of semiological contrasts is restricted by or coincides with a certain range of physiological possibilities, if semiology is a human science. (How does the motorist distinguish between a 'red' traffic light and a 'green' one?) But the precise level at which that restriction is encountered is irrelevant. Clearly, there will be more or less naive conceptualizations of the interface between the cultural and the biological, as well as more or less sophisticated ones. The author of the *Cours* may well nowadays sound as if he is offering a fairly naive version. The interesting point to observe is however we read the *Cours*, it is clear that we are intended to treat linguistics as an investigation which is – to adopt a convenient Irish formulation – 'practicable, if only in theory'. At the time the *Cours* was published, it would have been academically impolitic, to say the very least, to draw the dividing line between the theoretically practicable and the theoretically impracticable in such a way as to exclude from a scientific linguistics the study of the languages of antiquity. The Classics were still the backbone of European education. The possibility of a 'scientific' study of Greek and Latin could be made more plausible by reducing the gap between the cultural and the biological aspects of language than by widening it. It is no matter for surprise that in the *Cours* we find the gap as narrow as it is.

APPENDIX

Principles of Physiological Phonetics

Saussure's linguistics is certainly not a phonetically based linguistics. Bloomfield said contemptuously of the phonetics in the *Cours* that it was 'an abstraction from French and Swiss-German which will not stand even the test of an application to English' (Bloomfield 1923). A more important point to make might have been that Saussure's phonetics is not in any serious sense phonetics at all, but merely an attempt to justify an alphabetic conceptualization of the *image acoustique*. Saussure comes close to conceding this when he remarks at the very beginning of Chapter VII: 'If we try to dismiss the written form from our mind, and do away with any visual image altogether, we run the risk of being left with an amorphous object which is difficult to grasp. It is as if someone learning to swim had suddenly had his cork float taken away' ([55]). The Appendix to the Introduction provides an example of the kind of cork float which Saussurean linguistics still assumed to be available. Although it does not advertise itself as a transcription system, in fact that is what it is. Its details do not matter a great deal, and will therefore not be discussed at length here. For purposes of Saussurean theory, any number of alternative systems would have served the turn just as well. That is why the editors – rightly – relegated it to an appendix.

The specific system of phonetic analysis adopted is based in part on notes from an earlier course of lectures given in 1897 ([63]) supplemented by a descriptive framework borrowed from Jespersen ([67] n.2). Its minutiae are irrelevant to the main linguistic issues with which the *Cours* is concerned. Thus, for example, the adoption of a classification of sounds by aperture ([70]ff.), in preference to the more usual classification by point of articulation, has no theoretical significance whatsoever. Articulatory and auditory phonetics have in any case moved a long way since the turn of the century. The main thing which is relevant to a present-day reading of the *Cours* is how its treatment of phonetics affects the theoretical coherence of Saussure's position, and this has already been discussed in connexion with Chapter VII.

Only one or two further points need be added in the present context. The division of the subject into two parts, one comprising an inventory of individual 'sound types' and the other a 'combinatory phonetics' of the speech chain, is obviously significant in relation to Saussure's 'second principle' of linguistics: the linearity of the *significant* ([103]). It also has certain implications for his treatment of sound change, which needs to be able to count classes of sound types and positions in the speech chain as 'naturally' given (that is to say, determined by purely physiological criteria) in order to claim (i) that phonetic evolution operates quite independently of *signifiés* and of linguistic structure in general, and (ii) that the developments formulated as 'sound laws' are in fact isolated, one-off events with no systematic properties ([132-4]).

Although phonetics is for Saussure merely 'an ancillary science to linguistics' ([77]), he is willing to concede that in certain cases it can help the linguist solve genuinely linguistic problems: for example, the much debated question of Proto-Indo-European sonants ([79]). He also seems willing to concede that there may be phonological universals in language which are to be explained by reference to purely phonetic factors ([79]).

Finally, it may be worth noting that Saussure's recognition that languages are not free to adopt just *any* linear combination of sound types as a *significant* (because of articulatory restrictions: [78-9]) in no way infringes his doctrine of the arbitrariness of the sign ([100-2]). Arbitrariness is a question of the relationship between a particular *significant* and a particular *signifié*: it has nothing to do with the range of the possible inventory of *significants* available.

PART ONE
General Principles

CHAPTER I

Nature of the Linguistic Sign

By the end of the Introduction, Saussure has presented the reader with a preliminary conceptual framework within which to situate general questions about language and the study of language. The basis of this framework is a broad distinction between *faits de langue* and *faits de parole*. These two classes combine to make up the totality of *faits de langage*. Linguistics as a science, according to Saussure, deals with nothing else. It does not include, except incidentally, the study of writing or of other modes of linguistic expression than the spoken. It does not claim to deal with language as a specific human mental faculty (if indeed any such faculty exists). As between *faits de langue* and *faits de parole*, a science of language will give priority to the former. But nothing has so far been said in detail about what exactly *faits de langue* are or how they may be investigated, other than that they are facts of a social and supraindividual character, which are nevertheless implicated in the individual acts of speech which constitute the sum total of human linguistic activity. Having established this framework in outline, the *Cours* now proceeds to lay down what the title of Part I calls 'General Principles' ([97]). The first chapter of Part I considers the nature of the linguistic sign, and in particular its duality.

Later commentators on the Saussurean linguistic sign principally focussed their attention on one or other of the features which Saussure posits as its fundamental characteristics: 'arbitrariness' and 'linearity'. Just how these characteristics are best interpreted for purposes of Saussurean linguistics will be discussed below. The former in particular has been the subject of prolonged controversy, which still continues. (Toussaint 1983. A bibliography of this controversy down to 1964 is given in Engler 1962 and 1964.) Concentration on this much-debated issue has meant, unfortunately, that an even more basic problem about the Saussurean linguistic sign has been virtually ignored. It is this more basic problem, however, which ultimately gives rise to precisely the difficulties which critics have encountered in trying to give a satisfactory interpretation to the Saussurean notion of arbitrariness. This is the problem, quite simply, of identifying which elements Saussure claims are 'combined' in the duality of the linguistic sign, and making sense of how they are thus 'combined'. On these issues the picture which the *Cours* initially presents is simple and dramatic, rather than perspicuous.

The reader, by now accustomed to the style of presentation typical of the *Cours*, will not be surprised to find the opening paragraphs of the chapter ([97-8]) devoted to explaining what linguistic signs are not. Signs are not, we are told, dualities which comprise pairings of names with things named (for instance, the name *tree* with a botanical specimen or specimens). The sole feature of this 'nomenclaturist' misconception which Saussure concedes not to be erroneous is its dualism: that is, its recognition of the linguistic sign as a bi-partite unit ([98]). For Saussure too the linguistic sign is bi-partite; but apparently a bi-partite entity of quite a different kind from the nomenclaturist's sign.

Saussure's attack on nomenclaturism in the *Cours* has been compared, not unreasonably, to Wittgenstein's in the *Philosophical Investigations* (Wittgenstein 1958: §1ff.). It is certainly interesting that both Saussure and Wittgenstein use an attack on nomenclaturism as a way of introducing a view of language which is – or purports to be – entirely antithetical to the nomenclaturist position. It is all the more interesting in that Wittgenstein, as far as is known, had never read Saussure, and neither Wittgenstein nor Saussure was drawing upon any earlier antinomenclaturist tradition. Wittgenstein chose to attack specifically the 'Augustinian' picture of language (Baker and Hacker 1980), which is an ancient and prototypical example of nomenclaturism. But Saussure's target is less clearly defined: and Saussure's objections are not Wittgenstein's.

According to the *Cours*, the nomenclaturist theory of the linguistic sign is open to many objections, but only three of these are specified ([97]). First, nomenclaturism presupposes that ideas exist 'ready made' in advance of names. Second, it fails to make clear whether names are vocal or mental entities. Third, it implies that the link between name and thing is a 'simple' one, which is not the case. These objections are so cryptic that it is by no means easy to judge exactly what target they are aimed at. Is Saussure attacking the Biblical account of the origin of names? (There is a manuscript note which refers to the story of Adam in Genesis: de Mauro 1972: 439-40 n.129.) Or is he attacking some philosophically more sophisticated theory? All the *Cours* says is that, 'for some people' a language 'reduced to its essentials, is a nomenclature' ([97]).

More perplexing than the deliberate vagueness is this curious trio of indictments. For they do not, either individually or collectively, adequately identify the essentials of the thesis apparently under attack. Is it, for instance, an essential feature of nomenclaturism to leave open the question of whether names are vocal or mental? (Why, it might be asked, is this an important question anyway? Why cannot a name be both vocal and mental? Does one interpretation exclude the other?) Presumably a nomenclaturist who held, for whatever reason, that names are not vocal but mental would *ipso facto* not incur Saussure's criticism on that score. Is it essential for the nomenclaturist to hold that the relationship between name and thing is a 'simple' relationship? On the contrary, a commonly held nomenclaturist view going back via the medieval *modistae* to Aristotle (Harris 1980: 34ff.) maintained that names serve to signify things only indirectly, by way of concepts. Again, is the notion that ideas exist 'ready made' essential to the nomenclaturist? Is not the nomenclaturist's commitment rather to the proposition that things exist 'ready made'? Is it not the tree which the nomenclaturist regards as given by Nature, rather than our idea of what a tree is? In short, it seems possible to be a nomenclaturist and yet escape scot free on all three of Saussure's charges. The reader cannot fail to see that there is something very odd about this.

The oddity, as so often in the *Cours*, becomes less odd than at first sight appears if one bears in mind the probability that what is implicitly under attack here is not a philosophical thesis as such but the way nineteenth-century linguistics had made use of this thesis. The clue is provided for the attentive reader by the discrepancy between Saussure's claim that nomenclaturism pairs names with things and the immediately following objection that this involves supposing that 'ideas' are given in advance; whereas the objection one might expect is, rather, that it involves supposing that 'things' are given in advance.

Saussure's objection has to be read against an intellectual background where it was commonplace to claim that linguistics was 'scientific' precisely inasmuch as the linguist could 'prove' that, for example, French *arbre* was a direct descendant of Latin *arbor*. Part of the proof would be that *arbre* and *arbor* were both names of the 'same thing'. The framework of nineteenth-century linguistics had been built on etymologies which validated countless correlations such as that between *arbre* and *arbor* by tacit reference to the assumption that one could establish whether or not a word had changed its meaning by determining whether or not the thing it designated had remained the same. (This was not a necessary condition for etymological identity, nor even a sufficient condition; but conjointly with conformity to regular patterns of sound change it yielded a sufficient condition.) The point Saussure is making is that even if trees have not changed in any significant respect between Caesar's day and Napoleon's, and even if the thing designated by the word *arbor* is the same as the thing designated by the word *arbre*, this does not mean that there has been no change of meaning *unless we also assume that identity of things designated guarantees identity of ideas* (as Aristotle, for one, appears to have maintained, to judge by *De Interpretatione* I: '... the mental affections themselves, of which words are primarily signs, are the same for the whole of mankind ...'). Unless one accepts this Aristotelian assumption, which in effect guarantees that *arbor* and *arbre* 'mean the same' (granted the botanical invariance of trees) the semantic part of the linguist's etymological theory collapses. It lacks any way of proving that *arbor* and *arbre* have the same meaning. For identity of things referred to does not entail sameness of meaning (a point Frege had made in 1892, but which Saussure, who had almost certainly never read *Über Sinn und Bedeutung*, seems to have arrived at independently).

Once we see that Saussure's attack on nomenclaturism is an indirect attack on his linguistic predecessors (just as Wittgenstein's was an indirect attack on his philosophical predecessors), we also see that the three objections to nomenclaturism formally tabled in this chapter of the *Cours* are nothing other than counterparts to three claims which Saussure is committed to maintain against one widespread nineteenth-century view of the linguistic sign. The first of these is the most important, and is that the constitutive elements of the linguistic sign are not physical but mental. 'The linguistic sign links not a thing and a name, but a concept and a sound pattern' ([98]).

It is at this point ([99]) that the *Cours* proposes the introduction of the technical terms *signifiant* (= sound pattern), *signifié* (= concept) and *signe* (= *signifiant* + *signifié*) to avoid any potential misunderstanding arising from the way the word *signe* is commonly used. Ordinarily, says Saussure, the French word *signe* ('sign') designates solely the *image acoustique*. This is a surprising claim, which it seems difficult to justify. It takes far more metalinguistic subtlety than lay language-users have much time for to draw a careful distinction of the kind Saussure insists on between the 'sound' of a word in the sense of its *image acoustique* and the 'sound' of a word in the sense of the associated acoustic phenomena. In any case, the French word *signe*, like the English word *sign*, is much more generally employed in connexion with various forms of visual communication than to designate any mental correlate of the spoken word. More unfortunately still, having drawn this somewhat question-able distinction between the allegedly lay use of the term *signe* and its proposed technical use in linguistics, Saussure more than once in the *Cours* fails to follow his own terminological recommendation, and slips back into the 'non-technical' usage which he has previously rejected. (An example occurs in the very next chapter, p.[109].)

At this crucial point in the *Cours* where the new 'technical' concept of the linguistic sign is introduced the reader is given surprisingly little help towards understanding it. The only example offered is the Latin *arbor* ('tree'), and this is a particularly Delphic example. The diagrams ([99]) by means of which the *Cours* supposedly spells out the relationship between the *concept* and the *image acoustique* of *arbor* are especially problematic. The difficulty is that *arbor* can be interpreted in at least two ways; either lexemically or morphologically. That is to say, the written form *arbor* (Saussure never tells us how it is pronounced) can be taken to stand either for an item of Latin vocabulary (in the sense in which the conventional dictionary lists items of vocabulary) or, more specifically, for a particular word-form, the nominative singular in the paradigm of a certain Latin noun. These are two quite different linguistic units. Is this an example of false disingenuity which the reader is expected to see through? Does it deliberately blur the distinction between lexicology and grammar? Or does Saussure simply fail to recognize that the 'combination' of *signifiant* with *signifié* is not quite the simple bi-partite correlation which the diagrams suggest?

It is worth looking at the diagrams on p.[99] with these questions in mind, since this is a point on which the authenticity of the text of the *Cours* has been seriously questioned (de Mauro 1972: 441, n.132). It appears that the third diagram has been added by the editors, together with the arrows in all three diagrams.

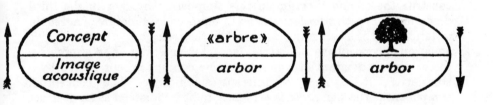

According to de Mauro (loc.cit.) we have here an example of how a minor editorial intervention may have quite serious consequences. The editors are also responsible for describing Latin *arbor* as a 'word' (*mot*), and for the observation that the two elements in a sign are 'intimately linked and each triggers the other'. The result, claims de Mauro, is that 'the reader has the impression that for Saussure the *signifiant* is the vocable, the *signifié* is the image of the object, and that each recalls the other, just as the nomenclaturist maintains. Thus we slide towards a concept which is the diametric opposite of Saussure's.'

How far is this criticism justified? One way of assessing it is to see how the reader would fare if the allegedly misleading additions were simply removed. This would leave the first two diagrams (without arrows), the status of *arbor* unexplained, and no comment on the connexion between the *image acoustique* and its corresponding *concept*. Now in certain respects this simple version makes interpretation easier; but in other respects more difficult. There is no longer any occasion for puzzling over the relationship between the second and third diagrams, because the third diagram has disappeared. On the other hand, the removal of the arrows and of the comment about the link between *image acoustique* and *concept* leaves something of a lacuna between this account of the linguistic sign and the account which the previously presented speech-circuit theory of *la parole* apparently demands, where concepts were said to trigger sound-patterns and vice versa ([28]). (These 'vertical' arrows come up for discussion again in the chapter on *La valeur linguistique* ([158ff.]), where they are distinguished from 'horizontal' arrows linking one sign to another.) Finally, and perhaps most importantly, in this simplified version the Latin example is identified as a linguistic unit solely by means of pairing an orthographic form (*arbor*) with a French translation ('arbre').

The net result is to shift the balance on p.[99] in favour of a lexemic interpretation of *arbor*; for *arbor* and *arbre* appear to stand to each other as lemma and gloss respectively in an imaginary bilingual dictionary or 'mental lexicon' somewhere in the speaker's brain. The function of the third diagram now becomes clear: in effect, it warns the reader *not* to construe the second diagram in this simplistic way. For in the third diagram the French translation *arbre* is replaced by a picture of a tree. In isolation, such a diagram would doubtless suggest a rather naive equation of concepts with pictorial mental images; but as an alternative to the second diagram in which the same concept is represented by a translation, it assumes a different significance. The conceptual component of the sign *arbor* is evidently to be understood as an abstract 'meaning' which can be mentally interpreted in various ways, both verbal and visual.

So far, then, it seems that in Saussure's technical sense the linguistic sign *arbor* is to be construed simply as a mental combination of a certain sound pattern with a certain meaning. At this stage the reader has been told nothing about the internal relationship of the *signifiant* to the *signifié*, and it is this omission which makes *arbor* an unfortunate example to have chosen. If *arbor* is to be construed as representing a morphological form rather than a lexeme, would one not expect its conceptual component to include not only the notion 'tree' but also the notions 'nominative' and 'singular'? The fact that these notions are missing altogether from the account of the *signifié* presented on p.[99] raises a legitimate doubt in the reader's mind as to whether grammatical notions count as concepts at all in Saussure's sense. In fact, they do: but this does not become clear until later in the *Cours*. (On the basis of what is said in §3 of Chapter III on *La linguistique statique et la linguistique évolutive* it will be retrospectively evident that the 'full' Saussurean analysis of *arbor* treats it as a combination of stem plus a 'zero' sign: but we are not given this more sophisticated analysis on p.[99], since the ground has not yet been prepared for it.)

The explanation for this rather unsatisfactory expository strategy is presumably as follows. At the point in the text where *arbor* is introduced to exemplify the Saussurean theory of the linguistic sign, the prime concern is seen as being to ensure that the reader does not unwittingly identify the two components of this bi-partite unit with the 'names' and 'things' recognized by the nomenclaturist (who here represents the erroneous view accepted in nineteenth-century linguistics). This is why a typically nomenclaturist example is taken (the 'name' *arbor*) and explicitly re-interpreted in a Saussurean manner. To this end, the third diagram giving a pictorial version of the *signifié* on p.[99] deliberately utilizes again the same 'tree picture' as originally appeared on p.[97] to illustrate the misguided nomenclaturist pairing of 'name' and 'thing'. The intention is doubtless to emphasize that the difference between the nomenclaturist theory of the sign and the Saussurean theory of the sign is *not* a difference over what a tree is (or, *mutatis mutandis*, any other 'thing'). What distinguishes the two theories on this particular issue is solely and simply that whereas the 'tree picture' in the nomenclaturist diagram stands for a tree, the corresponding 'tree picture' in the Saussurean version stands for a concept of a tree (which is not just an internal visual image, as the equivalence between the second and third diagrams shows).

In short, the text of the *Cours* here attempts (not altogether successfully) to disabuse the reader of two possible misconceptions simultaneously. One misconception is that the bone of contention between Saussure and the nomenclaturist has something to do with the extent to which speakers' linguistic concepts are a true reflection of things in the external world: on the contrary, it has nothing at all to do with that. The other misconception is that speakers' linguistic concepts are just private pictorial images of corresponding things in the external world. (Exactly what linguistic concepts are, however, will not be fully explained until the chapter on *La valeur linguistique*.)

The expository price paid for this decision to emphasize at the outset just the main parallels and contrasts between two possible archetypes of a theory of the linguistic sign (one archetypally 'wrong' and the other archetypally 'right') is expensive. For it leads directly to the various uncertainties and difficulties of interpretation noted above. This expense is only justified if we grasp that the main thrust of the *Cours* at this point is to dissociate itself from certain 'built in' assumptions about language which a university student of linguistics who had followed the established curriculum of comparative and historical studies in the early years of the present century might be expected to have acquired. The picture such studies project is that the 'scientific' approach to language reveals mankind's linguistic activity over the centuries as a slow but continuous process of developing new sets of vocal labels for a basic universe of 'things' antecedently given by Nature (and subject to only marginal cultural additions, discoveries or reclassifications). This is what Saussure calls the view of languages as 'nomenclatures'. Saussurean linguistics proposes to reject this view entirely, except – and the sole exception is an important one – insofar as it endorses the idea that languages are bi-planar systems and the linguistic sign is bi-partite.

One reason why the exception is important is that later critics claimed that this retention of a bi-planar analysis of language was Saussure's great mistake. Instead of championing bi-partition, he should have opted for tri-partition. Rather than insisting that the meaning of a word was in the mind, and not in the external world, he should have recognized that language involves a triangular relationship between, for example, (i) the word *arbor*, (ii) the botanical tree, and (iii) the mental concept 'tree'. This is the gist of the anti-Saussurean position first taken by Ogden and Richards in their book *The Meaning of Meaning* (1923) and subsequently endorsed by others. According to critics of this school, Saussure correctly perceived the inadequacy of the old 'name-and-thing' model of the linguistic sign, but wrongly supposed that the simple solution was to transpose both terms of this duality into the mental sphere. (Hence an *image acoustique* coupled with a *concept*.) Thus, far from solving the problem of the linguistic sign, Saussure simply perpetuated an old error in a new disguise.

'How great is the tyranny of language over those who propose to inquire into its workings,' say Ogden and Richards, 'is well shown in the speculations of the late F. de Saussure, a writer regarded by perhaps a majority of French and Swiss students as having for the first time placed linguistics upon a scientific basis' (Ogden and Richards 1923: 4). This attack on Saussure is placed right at the beginning of *The Meaning of Meaning*, thus ironically emulating the Saussurean strategy of beginning with the demolition of a linguistic Aunt Sally. All Saussure succeeded in accomplishing as a theorist, according to Ogden and Richards, was (by his definition of *la langue*) 'inventing verbal entities outside the range of possible investigation' (Ogden and Richards 1923: 5). The fatal and irremediable flaw was that Saussure's theory of signs 'by neglecting entirely the things for which signs stand, was from the beginning cut off from any contact with scientific methods of verification' (Ogden and Richards 1923: 6). It might perhaps be noted at this point that if Ogden and Richards had been writing fifty years later they would doubtless have levelled exactly the same criticism against those proponents of generative linguistics who, like Saussure, make a theoretical virtue out of 'neglecting entirely the things for which signs stand'.

Saussure's fatal omission Ogden and Richards proposed to remedy by including a 'referent' in their celebrated triangular model of the sign (Ogden and Richards 1923: 11):

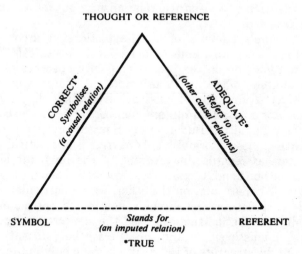

According to defenders of Saussure, on the other hand, any attempt to remedy the supposed omission from Saussure's theory of the linguistic sign, by 'adding' a third component, simply reveals a failure to understand Saussure's position (de Mauro 1972: 439 n.129). The conflict between these two attitudes towards the Saussurean view of the essential duality of linguistic signs is important for a reading of the *Cours*. How are we to construe Saussure's deliberate exclusion of the fact that the *prima facie* reason for the existence of the linguistic sign *arbor* is that speakers feel some social necessity or desirability for a word referring to trees (and, similarly, of other 'names' for 'things')?

There are very divisive issues involved here. Ullmann (dismissed by de Mauro (1972: 439 n.129) as a follower of Ogden and Richards) makes the point that there is nothing fundamentally new in the Ogden and Richards 'triangle': it is a reversion to the medieval scholastic dictum '*vox significat mediantibus conceptibus*' (Ullmann 1962: 56). Furthermore, in Ullmann's opinion the Ogden and Richards 'triangle' offers, from the point of view of the linguist, 'both too little and too much'. It offers too little because it 'seems to neglect the speaker's point of view' (Ullmann 1962: 37). On the other hand, it offers too much because 'the referent, the non-linguistic feature or event as such, clearly lies outside the linguist's province' (Ullmann 1962: 56). The reasons Ullmann gives for this exclusion, however, reveal his fundamental lack of sympathy with (or failure to comprehend) the Saussurean duality of the linguistic sign. Ullmann says: 'An object may remain unchanged and yet the meaning of its name may change for us if there is any alteration in our awareness of it, our knowledge about it, or our feelings towards it.' This Saussure would never have said. So Ullmann ends up by restricting the linguist's attention to a bi-partite relationship; but for reasons Saussure would not have endorsed.

That Saussure's analysis of the linguistic sign *arbor* (unlike the nomenclaturist's account) finds no place for the botanical 'thing' we call a tree is no reflection on the professional incompetence of linguists in botanical matters. There is, in principle, no reason why the linguist should not try to find out, if need be, everything the botanist knows about trees. Botanists, after all, are members of linguistic communities, no less than linguists. But from a Saussurean point of view the acquisition of endless information about trees is linguistically irrelevant. What matters as regards the meaning of the linguistic sign *arbor* is neither, on the one hand, the totality of what the Romans knew, believed or felt regarding trees; nor, on the other, which particular types of tree happened to grow in the Roman empire. What counts is how, conceptually, the Latin language used the sign *arbor* to contrast with other Latin linguistic signs. And this is essentially an 'internal' matter pertaining to the structure of Latin. It has to do only indirectly with the 'external' botanical facts, or with such knowledge of botany as the Romans possessed. Thus when Saussure's diagram offers *arbre* as a conceptual 'translation' of *arbor*, it implies neither that what the French mean by *arbre* the Romans meant by *arbor*, nor that botanical classifications have remained invariant for two thousand years; but merely – and more basically – that the relationship between the Latin *signifiant* and *signifié* in the case of *arbor* is of the same order as that between the French *signifiant* and *signifié* in the case of *arbre*.

*   *   *

The relationship between *signifiant* and *signifié*, the *Cours* tells us, is 'arbitrary'. This is not presented as a mere generalization, but as a 'principle': indeed, 'the first principle' of linguistics ([100]). It is necessary to insist on this point at the outset, if only for the reason that much subsequent criticism of the Saussurean concept of arbitrariness seems to be predicated on the misguided assumption that whether or not a sign is arbitrary is a matter to be resolved by simple observation of the facts (possibly with the tacit help of etymology). No one, says Saussure, disputes the arbitrariness of the linguistic sign ([100]). Perhaps some of his critics took this as a rash challenge which could easily be quashed by the simple expedient of proceeding to dispute it.

More serious is the fact that Saussure initially supports the thesis of arbitrariness by invoking examples and arguments which appear to be ultimately inconsistent with his own theory of the sign. Citing the fact that different languages have different terms for the same thing (French *bœuf*, German *Ochs*, [100]) is a blatantly nomenclaturist argument, particularly since the first section of this chapter has just been devoted to explaining why the internal *signifié* of a linguistic sign is not to be confused with the external thing which the sign may be the name of. On the face of it, therefore, interlinguistic disparity of nomenclature could not possibly be a relevant consideration for Saussure: or if it is, then it undermines his own case.

One explanation that has been offered for this apparent contradiction is that the editors of the *Cours* clumsily incorporated at this point an example originally given in an early lecture, before the introduction of the terms *signifiant* and *signifié* (de Mauro 1972: 443, n.137). Once again, this rescues Saussure at the expense of his editors, who are implicitly accused of overlooking a glaring inconsistency in the text. If we allow that the editors may have been a little less obtuse than this explanation would suggest, there is an alternative. It is that insistence on arbitrariness as a 'principle' of linguistics (and the word *principe* is used no less than five times on this page of the *Cours*) is to be understood as meaning that we are dealing with a truth which has to be recognized irrespective of one's own theoretical position. Thus we should take the *bœuf/Ochs* example as showing that even on a nomenclaturist view of the sign it has to be admitted that the connexion between the two parts of the sign is arbitrary. This gives point to the remark which immediately follows the example: that 'no one' (sc. not even a nomenclaturist) disputes the principle. Indeed, from a nomenclaturist point of view the principle is even more obvious than from a Saussurean point of view. But then, as Saussure goes on to observe, 'it is often easier to discover a truth than to assign it to its correct place'. The nomenclaturist, in other words, may well recognize that the bi-partite relationship is arbitrary, but fails to see what consequences for linguistics follow from this truth.

Similar considerations would explain why Saussure bothers to deal specifically with the straw 'counterexamples' of onomatopoeia and exclamations ([101-2]), which in fact do not endanger his own theoretical position in the least. The point is that these cases do not conflict with the principle of arbitrariness however interpreted. There may well be a natural connexion between the call of a cuckoo and the names of that bird in various languages. Likewise there may be a natural connexion between an exclamation and a cry of pain, fear, etc. But these connexions, far from supporting a 'naturalist' theory of the linguistic sign, serve as indirect evidence against such a theory by making all the more conspicuous the difficulty of explaining the general relationship between the two parts of *any* linguistic sign as determined non-arbitrarily. Onomatopoeic words and exclamations are not even for Saussure exceptions which prove the rule. The natural connexions to which they bear witness are contingent, not essential. There is no sense in which the cuckoo had to have a name which echoed its characteristic call, or exclamations had to mimic natural cries.

Thus far, then, the principle of arbitrariness is presented as acceptable and accepted, no matter which particular theory of the linguistic sign a linguist adopts. All this means is that there is simply no plausible basis for an alternative principle of non-arbitrariness, whether we are nomenclaturists, Saussureans, or adherents to any other theoretical approach. The agreement, in other words, is purely negative. But the question now arises: if we look at linguistic phenomena from a specifically Saussurean point of view, how is the notion of arbitrariness to be construed in positive terms? Where do the implications of arbitrariness begin to differ as between Saussurean and non-Saussurean theories of the sign?

Certain critics of Saussure evidently believed that for Saussure the notion 'arbitrary' simply stood opposed to the notion 'necessary': hence they attacked what they took the Saussurean position to be by asserting that even within the framework which Saussure himself proposed it had to be admitted that the connexion between *signifiant* and *signifié* was 'necessary'. Rebutting such criticisms, Bally (1940) saw that any attack along these lines simply misconstrues what the *Cours* says on the subject. If by 'necessary' is meant that language-users have no choice but to accept the connexion, or that the connexion is psychologically imperative, the *Cours* already concedes this ([101]). Clearly, linguistic arbitrariness for Saussure has nothing to do with *la parole*, and it is in retrospect astonishing that linguists could have read this into it. On the other hand, what the *Cours* says in no way runs at cross purposes to the logic which claims that there *must* be (necessarily) a certain connexion between a given *signifiant* and its *signifié* if it is to be accepted that the two are not independently definable. This, again, Saussure would readily concede. On such points as these the debate over the arbitrariness of the linguistic sign shows all the standard features of a *dialogue des sourds*.

Bally himself saw in Saussure's notion of arbitrariness (versus non-arbitrariness) nothing more than a version of the traditional Greek distinction between *phusei* and *thesei*, already drawn in Plato's *Cratylus* (Bally 1940: 202). This identification, however, was in turn seen as rather naive by other Saussurean commentators (de Mauro 1972: 442-3, n.137). Certainly it seems curious, if no more is meant by 'arbitrary' than is already covered by Greek *thesei*, that the *Cours* does not make the obvious reference to *Cratylus* or some other classical text, but instead gives credit to Whitney (of all people) for recognizing this feature of the linguistic sign ([110]). That would be rather like Russell congratulating Whitehead on recognizing seven as a prime number.

One reason why Saussure would not have been happy with the terms in which the debate between linguistic 'naturalists' and 'conventionalists' was formulated in the Western tradition is obvious enough. The conventionalists were fond of relying on the argument that words can be arbitrarily changed. An early example of this occurs already in *Cratylus* (384 D) where Hermogenes urges Socrates to accept that 'whatever name you give to a thing is its right name; and if you give up that name and change it for another, the later name is no less correct than the earlier, just as we change the names of our servants; for I think no name belongs to any particular thing by nature ...' With Hermogenes' conclusion Saussure would certainly have agreed; but equally certainly not for Hermogenes' reasons. Saussure is quite categorically opposed to the notion that an individual has the power to alter any linguistic sign as an element of *la langue* ([31],[101],[104 ff.]). He explicitly rejects the idea that arbitrariness has anything to do with individual whim. 'It must not be taken to imply that a signal depends on the free choice of the speaker' ([101]).

Less obvious, perhaps, is that for Saussure the linguistic sign does not depend on the communal choice of the collectivity either. This is why Whitney's concept of arbitrariness is singled out for mention. According to Saussure, Whitney (rightly) stressed the fact that the linguistic sign was arbitrary 'in order to emphasize that a language was nothing other than a social institution' ([110]). But for Saussure this concept of 'arbitrariness' is not radical enough. To link arbitrariness with the status of *la langue* as a social institution still suggests that what is 'arbitrary' stands simply opposed to what is naturally determined. In this weak sense of 'arbitrary' all social institutions, as cultural artifacts, are 'arbitrary'. Saussure wishes to go much further than this. He says that Whitney failed to see that the arbitrary character of *la langue* fundamentally distinguishes it 'from all other institutions' ([110]). This is a surprising and very important claim, and demands a criterion of linguistic arbitrariness which goes considerably beyond the weaker and more usual interpretations.

The essential difference for Saussure, it seems, lies in the fact that other social institutions (political, religious, legal, economic, etc.) deal with things which are already interconnected, directly or indirectly, in a variety of non-arbitrary ways. Hence these links in large measure determine in advance the structure of the institution. With *la langue*, however, this is not – *and could not be* – the case. The materials *la langue* operates with – sound and ideas – are not naturally connected at all (that is, externally to the connexions imposed by *la langue* itself). Features which may seem arbitrary in other social institutions are only so at a very superficial level. Saussure evidently thought this point so obvious as not to need illustration: but the kind of example he would doubtless have given is the apparent 'arbitrariness' of the market price of a commodity. It may seem arbitrary that a pound of potatoes should cost five pence (perhaps yesterday it cost less; perhaps another greengrocer charges six pence, etc.). But this superficial arbitrariness of the price is not comparable to the profound arbitrariness of the linguistic sign *soeur*. For in the case of *soeur*, (i) it would make no difference to the linguistic transaction (the act of *parole*) if the word for 'sister' were not *soeur* but *zoeur*, or *soeuf*, or *pataplu* ..., whereas it makes a fundamental difference to the commercial transaction whether the price of a pound of potatoes is five pence, or ten pence, or a thousand pounds. (For the commercial transaction hinges essentially on the possibility of implementing that equation between price and commodity.) Furthermore, (ii) although five pence may for various reasons seem a rather arbitrary price for that particular pound of potatoes, nevertheless the price structure operative in the greengrocery market as a whole is determined by economic factors which are far from arbitrary, and the price of potatoes is related more or less 'rationally' to other prices, both inside and outside the market. In the case of *soeur*, on the other hand, not only is there no linguistic 'reason' why the word for 'sister' should be *soeur* rather than *zoeur, soeuf*, etc., but its relations to other words are 'irrational' too, and the same is true for all French words. (Exceptions to this the *Cours* will later deal with under the head of *arbitraire relatif*.) So while it may seem that a particular price is arbitrary, it is not true that prices *as such* are arbitrary; but in the linguistic case, not only are particular words arbitrary, but words *as such* are arbitrary.

Soeur, therefore, is profoundly arbitrary both in that there is no reason 'external' to the social institution of *la langue* why the sound sequence *s-ö-r* should function as a *signifiant* at all; and also in that, given that it does so function, there is no 'internal' structural reason why it should function as the *signifiant* of the concept 'sister'. This 'double arbitrariness', as we might call it, Saussure sees as having no parallel in any other social institution. Other institutions are structured in ways which more or less directly reflect the 'external' social purposes which they serve and the material exigencies which they are called upon to deal with. Not so *la langue*.

Linguistic arbitrariness for Saussure, then, is not just a question of the rose by any other name smelling as sweet (true though that may be), nor just a question of the unexpected variety of ways different languages handle common features of human experience (true though that may be too). If that were all there were to arbitrariness, *la langue* would not differ along this dimension, except perhaps in degree, from other social institutions. But *la langue*, claims Saussure, is arbitrary in a unique way. The absence both of external and of internal constraints on the pairing of particular *signifiants* with particular *signifiés* means that for any given language the choice of actual signs (e.g. *soeur*) from among the range of possible signs (*zoeur, soeuf, pataplu* ...) is entirely unconstrained. This absolute freedom to vary 'arbitrarily' is the fundamental reason Saussure will adduce for the remarkable diversity of human languages and the no less remarkable susceptibility of languages to quite revolutionary structural changes. Other social institutions are not free to vary in this way because changes in their case (economic, legal, political, etc.) have immediate material consequences for the members of society. Thus although *la langue* is a social institution – and in certain respects the very archetype of a social institution – its arbitrariness gives it a structural autonomy vis à vis society which would be unthinkable (and incomprehensible) in the case of any other established social institution.

* * *

Saussure's second 'principle of linguistics', that of the linearity of the *signifiant*, has attracted considerably less comment and debate than the principle of arbitrariness, although the *Cours* tells us that both principles are equally important. The consequences of linearity are 'incalculable' and 'the whole mechanism of *la langue* depends upon it' ([103]). In view of this forthright statement, it is curious that Saussure's commentators have not inquired rather more closely into what the *Cours* means by 'linearity'. Perhaps they were disarmed by the casual remark that the principle of linearity 'is obvious, but it seems never to be stated, doubtless because it is considered too elementary' ([103]). This remark, at least, endorses the suggestion put forward above that what Saussure means by a 'principle' of linguistics is a truth about language so basic that all linguists must accept it in some form or other before they can even begin to agree or disagree about the right theoretical approach to the subject. On one level, the whole intellectual ingenuity of the *Cours* is devoted to showing how just two such principles, trivial or commonplace as they may appear, are all that are needed to provide the entire theoretical basis for a science of language (provided they are rightly interpreted).

Why these two principles in particular? (The *Cours* never claims that there are no other basic truths about language.) Godel (1964: 53) suggests that the first principle in effect provides Saussure's definition of the general term *signe* (since the term *symbole* ([101]) is reserved for communicational devices which incorporate a non-arbitrary element), while the second principle provides a corresponding definition of *signe linguistique*. Thus linguistic signs would be identified, on the basis of Saussure's two principles, as the class of signs having linear *signifiants*:

arbitrariness	−	+	+
linearity	+ −	+ −	+
	symbole	*signe*	*signe linguistique*

At the same time, this would automatically situate linguistics in its appropriate place within the wider discipline of semiology.

If this scheme correctly represented the definitional structure of Saussure's terminology, it would provide a very compelling answer to the question posed by Saussure's selection of 'principles', and also explain the order in which they are ranked. (The *Cours* never indicates why arbitrariness is the first principle, and linearity the second.) Unfortunately, although neat, this solution will not do. To correspond to Saussure's definitions, the second principle would have to appeal to something other than linearity. There is no specific claim in the *Cours* that only linguistic *signifiants* are linear, and to uphold this as a matter of definition would be to foist on Saussure a very odd concept of 'linearity'. But then, in spite of assurances in the *Cours* that this second principle is obvious and elementary, it is by no means clear exactly what Saussurean linearity entails.

Lepschy (1970:49) distinguishes two questions relating to linearity which the *Cours* leaves in obscurity. One is a question about linearity 'within' the *signifiant* and the other about linearity 'between' *signifiants*. As regards the former, the Saussurean principle of linearity has been criticized by those phonologists (Jakobson 1962: 419-20, 631-58) who construe Saussurean linearity as 'one-dimensional' in the sense of excluding simultaneous contrasts. This is equated with a failure on Saussure's part to recognize that phonemes are units composed of co-occurring distinctive features. (Thus although the *signifiant* of *soeur* comprises the linear sequence of sounds *s-ö-r*, each of these three units is itself a non-linear complex of specific phonetic features which combine to distinguish it from other units. Therefore at this level the principle of linearity is held to be invalid.) Against this charge, Saussure has been defended on the grounds that it involves anachronistically reading back into the *Cours* a post-Saussurean concept of the phoneme, and that in any case Saussure's principle of linearity applies to syntagmatic relations 'between' *signifiants*, not to the internal composition of the individual *signifiant* (de Mauro 1972: 447-8, n.145). It has also been argued in defence of Saussurean linearity that no phoneme combines distinctive features from the same dimension simultaneously (Ruwet 1963).

Here one suspects another Saussurean *dialogue des sourds*. The *Cours* nowhere rejects the notion of phonic complexity in the units of the speech chain, and the articulatory diagrams and tables given in the Appendix to the Introduction in substance already provide the basis for an elementary phonology of distinctive features. So it is quite gratuitous to interpret Saussure's principle of linearity as implicitly denying that the elements of *s-ö-r* are further analysable contrastively in phonetic or phonological terms. Nor, consequently, is there any need to leap to Saussure's defence by claiming that the principle of linearity was never intended to apply 'within' the *signifiant*. On the contrary, unless it does apply 'within' the *signifiant* the reader is hard put to it to make sense of the quite explicit terms in which the principle is introduced in the *Cours*. We are told that *le signifiant* (not *les signifiants*) occupies a certain temporal space (*une étendue*) which is measured in just one dimension: it is a line ([103]). Even more specifically, the elements (*éléments*) of these auditory *signifiants* 'are presented one after another; they form a chain' ([103]). Again, it is not a question of a sequence composed of *signifiants* as indivisible units but a sequence of elements of *signifiants*. This is quite simply a reiteration, in other words, of one of the basic points already made in the Appendix to the Introduction concerning the nature of the speech chain. Furthermore, the putative counterexample to the principle of linearity which Saussure raises and rejects in the final paragraph of this section is the phenomenon of syllabic stress. The example would scarcely make sense if linearity were only a principle which applied to the syntagmatic relationship between one *signifiant* and the next, but did not apply to the speech chain *in toto*.

Lepschy's second question, concerning linearity 'between' *signifiants*, simply falls if we take the principle of linearity as applying to the speech chain as a whole. (There were never two questions in the first place, but a single principle which has been doubly misunderstood.) In other words, if the speech chain itself is linearly structured then *a fortiori* syntagmatic sequences of *signifiants* are linearly structured, given that each *signifiant* is located in just one continuous linear segment of the speech chain. This is precisely what the *Cours* itself later assumes ([146ff.]), thus confirming the interpretation of the principle of linearity here proposed. On p.[170] we are told that words enter into relationships based on linearity, since the linearity of *la langue* precludes the possibility of pronouncing more than one thing at a time. Now this feature of relations between words could hardly be presented as one of the 'consequences' ([103]) of linearity if linearity itself were defined *ab initio* as a sequential relation between *signifiants*. One might then just as well dispense with linearity altogether and simply enunciate as a more general principle the impossibility of two or more signs occurring simultaneously. Why Saussure does *not* opt for this move brings us to the nub of the theoretical problem.

In what sense do *signifiants* enter into temporal or quasi-temporal relations? In what sense do the elements of a *signifiant* have such a relationship to one another? The *Cours* is quite adamant about the temporal character of linearity. *Le signifiant, étant de nature auditive, se déroule dans le temps seul et a les caractères qu'il emprunte au temps* ([103]). There is no indication that Saussure's reader is here expected to subscribe to a recondite metaphysics of time: it is time of the lay, common-or-garden, minutes-and-seconds variety that the *Cours* is talking about. So we cannot equate linearity with the more abstract concept of ordering. (There are many kinds of ordering other than temporal sequence.)

Various remarks in the laconic §3 of Chapter I may perhaps have misled commentators concerning the level at which Saussure envisages the *signifiant* as linear. One is the initial observation: the *signifiant* 'being auditory in nature' ... etc. This suggests that linearity somehow follows from the auditory character of the *signifiant*, or is intrinsic to the use of sound as a medium. (Saussure never mentions music; but most musicians would be surprised to be told that music, being auditory in nature, is confined to simply linear configurations.) Another potential source of confusion is the comparison in the next paragraph between auditory and visual signs. Again, one can easily read this as implying that the distinction between linearity and non-linearity is in some way related to the different modalities of sensory perception. This is particularly puzzling, since the comparison seems at first blush not to support very convincingly the thesis of auditory linearity. (Just as a visual signal may rely on the capacity of the human eye to distinguish, say, the simultaneous employment of vertical and horizontal contrast, may not an auditory signal likewise rely on the capacity of the human ear to discriminate the simultaneous utilization of pitch contrasts and amplitude contrasts?)

A third easily misinterpretable comment is the observation about syllabic stress, already referred to above. 'For example, if I stress a certain syllable, it may seem that I am presenting a number of significant features simultaneously. But that is an illusion. The syllable and its accentuation constitute a single act of phonation. There is no duality within this act, although there are various contrasts with what precedes and follows' ([103]). The reference to a 'single act of phonation' immediately seems to lend colour to the suspicion that there is some confusion here between the act of *parole* and the structure of the *signifiant*. For a single act of phonation entails nothing about the duality or otherwise of the linguistic elements thus given vocal expression. But critics who argue that Saussure is wrong because emphatic stress should be treated as a separate meaningful element (Henry 1970: 90-1) are missing the point here. It is open to Saussure to treat emphatic and non-emphatic pronunciations of the 'same word' as different *signifiants*, just as he treats liaison and non-liaison forms ([147]).

It is by no means necessary to interpret these various comments in the *Cours* as associating linearity exclusively with the fact that speech relies on sound. Saussure is here contrasting the linear nature of a spoken signal with the non-linear nature of alternative ways of conveying the same or a similar message: for instance, by means of ships' flags. In the case of speech, he argues, the distinction between stressed and unstressed syllables is not a matter of additional contrasts in a different dimension from linearity. A signal like a flag, on the other hand, will normally use more than one dimension of contrast simultaneously: for instance, contrasts in the size of particular configurational elements, their shape, number, relative position, colour, etc. There is no way all these contrasts can be construed as one-dimensional: whereas in the case of speech the single dimension of linearity will accommodate all the discriminations between structurally distinct elements which it is necessary to make. The phenomenon of stress will be construed not as an 'extra' element superadded simultaneously, but as a syntagmatic contrast between elements in linear succession. (Saussure never explains how to deal with intonation, but presumably it will have to be along the same lines, in order to conform to the principle of linearity.) Critics who have argued that the evidence of emphatic stress shows the *signifiant* to be not linear but 'bilinear' (Henry 1970: 91) have simply got it wrong. There is no double linearity (as there is, for example, in the case of choral music) because stresses in sequence do not contrast significantly with one another independently of the syllables thus stressed.

It might seem nevertheless that the trouble with Saussure's second principle is that it does confuse questions of *parole* with questions of *langue*. The messages transmitted via the speech circuit clearly take time to formulate and deliver. The sounds A utters are uttered as a temporal succession, and reach B's ear as a temporal succession of stimuli. But are not these facts of temporal transmission *faits de parole*? Everyone agrees, presumably, that if the message A sends to B includes the word *sœur* then it will be possible to measure (in milliseconds) exactly how long it took A to pronounce it, exactly how long the initial sibilant was, etc. But it does not follow from all this that the *signifiant* of the word *sœur* comprises a determinate number of consecutive phonological units, any more than the fact that it takes a certain length of time for a football to be kicked past a goalkeeper entails that the score (e.g. 'Blackpool 1: Manchester United 0') comprises a determinate sequence of sub-scores. (?'Blackpool ½: Manchester United 0'). Nor does it help matters to point out that since Blackpool cannot score two goals at once, the final score 'Blackpool 3: Manchester United 0' must mean that the Manchester United goalkeeper was beaten on three chronologically separate occasions. These occasions belong to the *parole* of a particular match, and its unfolding in time as a series of episodes of play.

Similarly, if A utters the sentence 'The cat sat on the mat', there is no doubt that the word *mat* will be uttered later than the word *cat*. But again this is a feature of an act of *parole*. It does not follow that it is automatically a feature of *langue*. A builder is obliged to construct a house by laying bricks in a certain temporal sequence because he cannot lay them all simultaneously. Nevertheless the spatial relations of the various parts of the completed house are what ultimately count, and not the chronological order in which the builder carried out the construction work. These analogies, however, perhaps suggest a plausible reason why linearity is more important in the case of speech than in the case of building or football. If we interchange the utterance of the words *cat* and *mat* a different sentence necessarily results. Likewise an internal change of the sequence of consonants and vowels in a word will produce either a different word or a non-word. In the case of the house, on the other hand, it will make no difference whether the kitchen was completed before the living room, or vice versa. Nor does it make any difference to the result of the football match in which order the goals were scored. Languages, in other words, make significant use of variations in word-order and in the syntagmatic succession of elements. Is this why Saussure selects linearity as the most basic feature of the *signifiant*?

It is at first very tempting to think that something like this must be the right answer. But further reflection leads one to doubt it. The fact that languages utilize the linearity of the *signifiant* contrastively in various ways is a contingent fact. It consequently cannot provide any ultimate justification for erecting linearity into a 'principle' of linguistics. From a Saussurean point of view, languages would still be languages even if free word-order were universal and words themselves were invariably monosyllables with a fixed structure which never contrasted in respect of the internal order of consonants or vowels. The rationale behind the Saussurean principle of linearity goes much deeper.

Trying to understand the principle of linearity takes us back to the question of what is meant by the Saussurean *image acoustique*: for originally we were given to understand that a *signifiant* is nothing else ([99]). We might even reformulate Saussure's second principle accordingly as that of *linéarité de l'image acoustique*. The term *image acoustique* itself is among the most enigmatic in the vocabulary of Saussurean linguistics. It perhaps suggests a combination of visual representation and acoustic content (cf. the application of the expression *visible speech* to sound spectrograms) as if the brain stores spectrograms rather than sounds. From the function of the *image acoustique* in the Saussurean speech circuit, however, it seems clear that its role is that of a 'mental representation' of some kind which is deemed to play a part both in the speaker's capacity to execute the appropriate motor programme required to utter the sounds desired *and* in the hearer's capacity to identify the auditory impressions received by the ear as those corresponding to a given concept. Now two questions which a sceptic might wish to ask immediately are: (i) why should there be any one 'mental representation' answering to this description? and (ii) even if there were, how could this mental representation occupy a temporal space, be measurable in just one dimension, etc.? In other words, what could possibly be meant by the claim that the mental representation (*image acoustique*) itself is linear (Henry 1970: 89)?

The first of these questions seems already to have occurred to Saussure's editors. Their unhappy footnote on the term *image acoustique* ([98]) bears witness to their anxieties on this score. They point out that language users presumably need a mental representation of muscular patterns of articulation as well as of auditory patterns (as the commentary on the original speech-circuit diagram ([28]) also concedes). Their explanation is that for Saussure the *image acoustique* is 'above all the natural representation of the word as *fait de langue virtuel*, independently of any actualization in speech. Hence the articulatory aspect of the word may be taken for granted, or relegated to a position of secondary importance in relation to its *image acoustique*.' This editorial comment unfortunately turns a mere lacuna into an outright incoherence. In the first place, there is no sense at all in our taking the *image acoustique* as a mental representation so abstract that it gives no information whatever about the actualization of the word in *la parole*: if that were so, there would be no point in calling such a representation an *image acoustique*. In the second place, if indeed the *image acoustique* does capture characteristic auditory properties of the spoken word, then it is more than just the representation of a *fait de langue virtuel* (for the same reason that if we represent the bishop in chess by an image which shows the characteristic shape of the bishop's mitre, we are doing something other than merely representing information about the role of the piece in the game: we are showing how it may be visually identified on the chess board). In the third place, if the *image acoustique* is something quite separate from the representation of an articulatory motor programme, it becomes impossible to see how it can fulfil the dual role assigned to it in the model of the speech circuit.

As regards the second question, it is difficult to refuse to admit the force of the objection. It can hardly be a 'mental representation' which has the property of linearity. Henry (1970: 89) cites in this connexion the way Saussure contrasts visual *signifiants* with auditory *signifiants* ([103]), but fails to point out that this comparison involves a tacit extension of the meaning of the term *signifiant*. (A flag, for example, can hardly be said to have an *image acoustique*.) So by the time Saussure's second principle is introduced, we are apparently dealing with a more generalized notion of the *signifiant*: it is now a mental representation including information of any sensory modality appropriate to the signalling system in question. That, however, does not dispose of the sceptic's point. Henry insists that the notion of a temporal chain is appropriate if referring to the sounds actualized in *la parole*; but inappropriate if referring to the *empreinte psychique* of *la langue*. Admittedly, he argues, the representation of *arbor* has to be a representation of *arbor* and not of *orarb*: in that sense, it must respect the order of constituent elements. But there is no question of temporal priorities in a representation which takes the form of an *aperception en bloc*, and he refers to certain types of motor aphasia which appear to involve precisely an inability to 'translate' information stored in non-linear form into the correct linear sequences (Henry 1970:89).

Whether the relevant modality is auditory, visual, or any other, the mental representation itself should not have attributed to it properties which are those of the items represented. (Whereas it makes perfectly good sense to say that Smith's idea of a triangle includes the information that triangles have three sides, it would be absurd to say that Smith's idea had three sides.) Now unless we read Saussure as indeed being guilty of this very confusion, there must be an alternative way of interpreting his second principle of linguistics.

The problem, in short, is to find a reading which simultaneously acquits Saussure both of the incoherence to which his editors' explanation of the *image acoustique* condemns him, and of the category mistake to which he is committed by a literal interpretation of the linearity of the *signifiant*. A solution of sorts is possible if we are willing to accept that for Saussure the key theoretical role of the *signifiant* is to integrate an account of the structure of the cognitive system (*la langue*) with a step-by-step account of the activity (*la parole*) through which the system is put to work. The combination implicit in this cognitive-cum-mechanical role means that to the *signifiant* are attributed whatever properties *both* these functions demand. Now linearity is totally irrelevant to the function of the *signifiant* as part of the cognitive system, but highly relevant to its mediation between system (*langue*) and activity (*parole*). In other words we can interpret Saussure's second principle as an elliptical way of saying: 'the semiology of linguistic systems demands that information about the significant ordering of certain features in *parole* be available for purposes both of encoding and of decoding the signal'. Whether this information is actually stored separately for auditory and articulatory operations, or how many distinct forms of 'mental representation' are involved, is no concern of Saussure's whatsoever. He merely simplifies by subsuming all this under a characterization of the *image acoustique*.

Thus Saussure's two principles correspond to two quite different ways of looking at *la langue*: in one case as supplying the system needed for a unique form of cognition, and in the other case as supplying the mechanism needed for a unique form of activity. From the cognitive point of view, the structure of *la langue* is seen as pairing sounds with concepts in a way which owes nothing to any independent connexions between sounds and things in the external world: hence the principle of arbitrariness. From the viewpoint which sees language as an activity, on the other hand, the way *la langue* is put to work is seen as reflecting the fact that all human activities in the external world take place in time: hence the principle of linearity. But from this latter point of view it is quite irrelevant whether the linguistic sign is arbitrary or not: the mechanism of *la parole* would operate in just the same way in any case. Saussure's two principles, in other words, provide yet another illustration of how the viewpoint selected creates the linguistic object.

By formulating the antithesis between these two principles – one denying and the other admitting an involvement of linguistic structure with the structure of the external world – the *Cours* makes the most profound revolution in grammatical theory since Port Royal. Whether Saussure correctly identified this involvement and its linguistic consequences is a different question, and a full answer to it would necessarily go far beyond the scope of a commentary on the *Cours*. It suffices here to note that Saussure's theory of language does assume that it is precisely the extent and modality of this involvement, as expressed in his two principles, which determine how language functions.

This high-level philosophical antithesis is not the whole story, however. There is a more practical academic reason why a single Saussurean principle of linguistics will not suffice, and why not *any* two principles will do either. The criterion of arbitrariness alone provides the linguist with no basis for a method of identifying and classifying linguistic signs, since in itself it does not distinguish signs from sequences of signs. Nor would the distributional principle that linguistic signs cannot co-occur help in this respect, basic though it may be. Something further is needed if linguistics is to have an analytic method. It is a mark of Saussure's brilliance as a theorist that he reduces this 'something further' to a single principle to complement his principle of arbitrariness (which he will need in any case, since without it linguistics could hardly be an autonomous discipline). To call this principle 'linearity', however, was arguably an unhappy choice of terminology. Arguably too, the explanation which treats linearity as being in some sense a 'temporal' feature of linguistic structure is quite specious. Speech is certainly an activity which has a temporal dimension: but no more so and no less so than every other human activity. The idea of time as a single continuous 'line' being drawn at uniform speed in the same direction is itself a sophisticated concept which relies on a spatial metaphor. It is also at odds with other and possibly less restrictive ways of conceptualizing time (Henry 1970: 80).

On the other hand, speech is by no means the only human activity to exhibit properties of the kind which Saussure wishes to attribute to the *signifiant*. These properties are the basic properties of single catenary articulation: for this is what Saussurean linearity essentially amounts to. No other types or features of linearity are taken into consideration in the theoretical use Saussure makes of the *signifiant*. The most revealing remark about linearity in the whole of the *Cours* is that the linearity of the spoken word becomes manifest when speech is set down in writing and 'a spatial line of graphic signs is substituted for a succession of sounds in time' ([103]). In other words, spoken language is articulated as a single, linked succession of discrete elements: it constitutes a chain. If this is assumed to be the case, then by combining both Saussurean principles linguistics is immediately provided with a method of analysis, which will consist basically of segmenting any given catenary sequence by determining which arbitrary sets of consecutive elements in that sequence could constitute single *signifiants* and which could not. (This is in fact the method later described in detail on pp.[146 ff.].)

It now becomes apparent that what underlies both of Saussure's principles is another – and perhaps the most fundamental – 'hidden premiss' of Saussurean linguistics. It is the premiss that the spoken word is 'invisibly' organized on exactly the same lines as the 'visible' organization of the written word. This premiss in turn relies on a particular theory about writing (namely, the theory that the alphabetic system provides not merely a flexible convention for writing but a 'true' description of the constitution of the spoken word). Once this is tacitly accepted, all that is required is a plausible inventory of universal phonic units corresponding to alphabetic letters. (The *Cours* has already supplied these fixed 'sound types' in the first chapter of the Appendix to the Introduction.) It then becomes unnecessary to give any further argument for linearity. By the same token, it becomes superfluous to offer any further case for arbitrariness. For just as a random string of letters is not meaningful unless it 'spells' a word, so 'sound types', which are *ex hypothesi* meaningless, do not concatenate into meaningful sequences other than those for which *la langue* provides a *signifié*. What was initially meaningless cannot by a mere chaining process, in itself equally meaningless, become automatically meaningful. Thus both arbitrariness and linearity spring conceptually from a single source. It is a source which subtly infuses Saussurean linguistics, in spite of lip-service paid to the primacy of speech, with all the latent scriptism of a pedagogic tradition in which writing was taken as the model to which language must – or should – conform.

CHAPTER II

Invariability and Variability
of the Sign

The chapter which the *Cours* devotes to '*Immutabilité et mutabilité du signe*' ([104-13]) is more often skipped than studied carefully. This may well be because it is seen as functioning merely as a bridge between the opening chapter of Part I, which explains the initial Saussurean conception of the linguistic sign, and the discussion of the distinction between synchronic and diachronic linguistics, which is about to be broached in Chapter III. Consequently, de Mauro suggests, the attention of Saussurean scholars has been diverted from it because they have been 'hypnotised' (de Mauro 1972: 448 n. 146) by the apparently far greater theoretical import of what immediately precedes and what immediately follows. To this one might add that it is a chapter which contains a curious mixture of points which sound as if they are labouring the obvious and points which sound rather too cleverly contrived. Neither variety brings out the best in a reader. The first impression is that a rather dull but necessary lecture for undergraduates has been livened up by throwing in a few academic rhetorical flourishes.

The formal structure of the chapter is also deceptively banal. The first half deals with factors which tend to maintain a linguistic *status quo*, while the second half deals with factors which tend to promote change. But the underlying argument by no means corresponds to this simple bi-partition: it is marshalled in a rather complicated way which obliges the reader to leap back and forth from one section to the other in order to follow it. The organization of the chapter is consequently unsatisfactory. Clearly, the overall plan of the *Cours* demands that, having thus far examined the linguistic sign purely from the point of view of its constitution and internal structure, there should now be some general discussion of the linguistic sign in relation to the linguistic community. This is needed to pave the way for the next theoretical move, which will be the absolute separation of synchronic from diachronic relations. Too much is sacrificed, however, to this transitional purpose. The thematic division between stability in the first part and change in the second part of the chapter is evidently intended to foreshadow the coming dichotomy between synchronic and diachronic. But however neat or aesthetically pleasing this may be, in the end it unnecessarily obscures an important part of the rationale behind that dichotomy.

Neglect of the main points this chapter makes is one of the main reasons, according to de Mauro, for the prevalence of a false view of Saussure. The author of the *Cours* is erroneously cast in the role of apologist for an abstract, 'anti-historical' linguistics, which would treat languages as static systems cut off both from their own past and from their social conditions of existence in the present. Such a view is refuted decisively, in de Mauro's opinion, by the evidence of this one chapter, which demonstrates Saussure's 'profound awareness of the historical necessity of the sign' and of the 'radical historicity of linguistic systems' (de Mauro 1972: 448, n.146).

True as all this may be, there is a risk that by over-reacting against sheer ignorance or subsequent distortions of Saussure's ideas it may retrospectively put the emphasis in the wrong place. The chapter is about language in a historical perspective: that much no one would deny. It is unlikely, however, that any linguist would devote a whole chapter of a book to establishing credentials which no contemporary reader would dream of questioning in the first place. Saussure's objective is a different one. The chapter makes more sense if we read it not as an endeavour to validate the historicity of the linguistic sign (which Saussure's contemporaries would have taken for granted without any prompting from Saussure) but as an attempt to show how very problematic – contrary to contemporary assumptions – that notion is. It is no coincidence that the problems of historicity which Saussure merely raises here, hinting at them rather than laying them out in full detail, are precisely the problems to which Saussure's fully developed theory of language will provide quite novel answers. Therefore it is worth while trying to reconstruct Saussure's argument in a more direct form, as it might have appeared if the bi-partite structure of this chapter, adopted for extraneous expository reasons, had been abandoned. In outline, Saussure's case might then have been put as follows.

Historicity manifests itself potentially in two ways: (i) stability over time, or (ii) change over time. At first sight, the linguistic sign appears to qualify under both criteria, since Indo-European historical linguistics apparently provides us with many examples of words remaining unchanged for long periods, but also with many examples of words undergoing change. In both cases, however, a careful examination of the question reveals unsuspected difficulties.

If the linguistic sign is arbitrary, and if languages are social institutions, it would seem to follow that a linguistic sign ought to be alterable at will. But, on the one hand, no individual has any power to alter either *signifiant* or *signifié*. On the other hand, in cases where it appears that a linguistic sign has altered (Latin *necare* 'to kill' > French *noyer* 'to drown' [109]) it can hardly be claimed that the linguistic community made a collective decision to alter it. Should we conclude, therefore, that history shows that the linguistic sign is not arbitrary after all? Or perhaps that languages are not, after all, social institutions?

Evidently, the *Cours* is committed both to the proposition that the linguistic sign is arbitrary and also to the proposition that *la langue* is a social institution. The latter proposition, however, is left in considerably deeper obscurity than the former. What exactly is meant by an institution? Nowhere in the *Cours* does Saussure define the term. The three examples of other institutions cited in this chapter on p.[110] ('customs', 'laws' and 'clothes') are not particularly helpful. However, there is a reference on the same page to Whitney and to Whitney's insistence on the arbitrary character of linguistic signs in order to 'emphasize that a language is nothing other than a social institution'. It would seem reasonable, therefore, to take as a point of departure Whitney's general definition of an institution as 'the work of those whose wants it subserves' (Whitney 1867: 48). However, the passage in which Whitney proposes this definition goes on to say of the institution of language:

> it is in their [sc. those whose wants it subserves] sole keeping and control; it has been adapted by them to their circumstances and wants, and is still everywhere undergoing at their hands such adaptation; every separate item of which it is composed is, in its present form ... the product of a series of changes, effected by the will and consent of men ...

'Every separate item' presumably includes, for Whitney, every single linguistic sign. Now this is a proposition which Saussure is loath to accept, as is made clear at the very beginning of §1 of this chapter. For Saussure, the community has no more power to alter a relationship between *signifiant* and *signifié* than the individual has. It cannot 'exercise its authority to change even a single word. The community, as much as the individual, is bound to its language' ([104]). Linguistic change is not a question of successive generations altering the linguistic contract, for there is no linguistic contract to be altered: a language is imposed on its speakers, not agreed to by them. History itself, for Saussure, shows this to be the case. 'At any given period, however far back in time we go, a language is always an inheritance from the past' ([105]).

This in turn, however, merely generates a new puzzle, which is the opposite of the first one. For if the connexion between a given *signifiant* and a given *signifié* is arbitrary, and speakers have no power to change it either individually or collectively, why, once established, does it not remain unchanged? Why did not the verb *necare* 'to kill' remain as it was? Alternatively, if we admit both (i) that the verb *necare* did as a matter of historical fact change (to French *noyer*), and (ii) that this change was not 'by the will and consent of men', have we not seriously undermined the thesis that the linguistic sign is arbitrary? (For it would seem that there must be forces at work controlling the linguistic sign which are 'natural', or at least not within institutionalized jurisdiction.) Thus, whichever way we look at the matter, history seems to make a mockery of the most basic premises it is reasonable to lay down concerning human language.

The problem, then, is how to reconcile the facts which history tells us about various languages with the theoretical assumptions of the arbitrariness and the institutionality of the linguistic sign. Saussure's response is twofold. It involves questioning (i) whether it is correct to assume that because *la langue* is a social institution it functions in the same way as other social institutions, and (ii) whether the notion of historicity is properly applicable to the individual linguistic sign. These two questions are interwoven throughout the discussion presented in Chapter II, but for present purposes it will be clearer to deal with them separately.

Whereas Whitney tends to equate linguistic arbitrariness with institutionality, or more exactly, to see arbitrariness as a consequence of institutionality, for Saussure this misses a crucial point. Whitney, says Saussure, 'did not go far enough' ([110]). Whitney failed to see that historical continuity and historical change present problems for a theory of the linguistic sign which have no parallel in the case of other social institutions. For other institutions 'are all based in varying degrees on natural connexions between things' and 'exhibit a necessary conformity between ends and means' ([110]). (Saussure's example here is that the clothes we wear, although 'arbitrary' in many respects, nonetheless exhibit a fundamental conformity to the natural configurations of the human body.) An institution bound by no necessary conformities whatsoever is in a unique and curious position. As an institution it combines simultaneously extremes of intrinsic stability and intrinsic instability. Since the connexion between a *signifiant* and *signifié* is arbitrary, that is the best of all reasons why it should remain stable: for nothing can be gained by altering it. At the same time, an arbitrary connexion is more vulnerable to change than any other. For there is nothing to be gained by keeping it either: any other sign would do just as well. A language is thus an institution which is 'intrinsically defenceless' ([110]) against change. This is true even of artificially created languages like Esperanto ([111]).

Saussure is arguing, then, that *la langue* is the unique case of a social institution in which the nature of the institution itself, being based on an arbitrary relationship, is equally conducive to variance as to invariance.

(This will clearly have two practical implications for linguistics which are not pursued in this chapter. One will be that why a linguistic sign remains unchanged over time needs just as much explaining as why it changes. The other is that the particular reasons for both stability and change become, in individual instances, extremely elusive. For in the end no one can demonstrate, because of the arbitrary nature of the linguistic sign, that it matters one way or another what the fate of any particular sign is. Historical reasoning which involves tracing chains of cause and effect consequently becomes even less straightforward in the case of *la langue* than in the case of social institutions based on natural relations.)

Now the nature of the difficulty is not just practical but, beyond a certain point, conceptual. It calls in question the whole lay concept of 'history', which is not geared to dealing with arbitrary relationships. The lay concept demands a contrast between invariance and change over time: without that, historicity becomes meaningless. But arbitrary relationships have precisely the characteristic that, within their given domain, substituting *y* for *x* makes no difference: the result is equivalent in all relevant respects to leaving *x* as it was. That is just what arbitrariness means. There is thus a profound conflict between arbitrariness and historicity. Arbitrariness demands at some level an equivalence between change and *status quo*, whereas historicity constantly demands an opposition.

If we read Saussure's argument in this way, it is evident that on one level the linguistic sign, being arbitrary, remains untouched and untouchable by history. Its historicity – if the term is appropriate – is of a quite different order from the historicity which pertains to other social institutions. That would also explain why in the second half of this chapter Saussure takes such meticulous pains to avoid using terms like 'change' and 'alteration' of the linguistic sign itself, but prefers instead the cumbersome circumlocution 'a shift in the relationship between *signifié* and *signifiant*' ([109]). The implication of this, evidently, is that historical factors in the lay sense may affect *signifié* or *signifiant* (or both separately): but not the sign as such. Changes in the pronunciation or in the meaning of words occur for various reasons totally unconnected with the relationship which binds any particular pronunciation to any particular meaning. That relationship, having itself no physical correlate in the world of historical time, is something on which historical forces are powerless to act. But they do act on linguistic communities. Thus it is the role of the linguistic community to provide the anchorage which links a system of arbitrary signs to the operation of historical processes. This is the significance of the diagram on p.[112]:

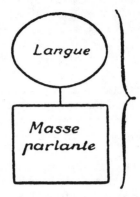

The sole unit of historical significance in linguistics is not the language alone but the language plus the linguistic community.

Even more important, as will become apparent later, is the emended diagram on p.[113], which adds the arrow of time to the bond between the community and its language. 'When this is taken into account, the language is no longer free from constraints, because the passage of time allows social forces to be brought to bear upon it' ([113]).

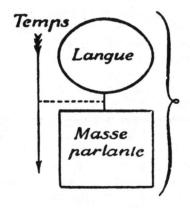

La langue, then, is the unique case of a social institution based on a relationship which simultaneously promotes stability (by making variation pointless) and facilitates change (by offering no resistance). That this single feature of the linguistic sign should give rise to two apparently conflicting tendencies might at first sight appear mysterious: but that is because the tendencies conflict only when seen in the perspective of history. What is an opposition in historical terms may be an equivalence in a semiological perspective. Thus, paradoxical though it may seem, 'variability and invariability are both, in a sense, characteristic of the linguistic sign' ([109]).

This conclusion evidently worried Saussure's editors enough for them to add a footnote of their own defending Saussure's assignment of these seemingly contradictory characteristics to the linguistic sign, and reassuring the reader that it is 'intended simply to emphasize the fact that a language changes even though its speakers are incapable of changing it' ([108] n.1). But this is merely to reiterate rather lamely what has already been said in the first part of the chapter. There is a further and much sharper point to Saussure's oxymoron which the editors' apologetic gloss misses entirely. The notion of linguistic change as it applies to *individual signs* also implies absence of change. In other words, change is conceived of as continuity, not as discontinuity. And this in turn presupposes what Saussure calls 'the survival of earlier material' ([109]) in the sign. (Three examples are provided on pp.[109-110]: Latin *necāre*, German *dritteil*, and Anglo-Saxon *fōti*.) Now if 'survival of earlier material' is a *sine qua non*, as it would appear to be, (for otherwise the lay concept of history would recognize an instance not of change but of complete disappearance) then it seems that the sign must be a linguistic unit conceived of as able to remain 'the same' in certain respects at the same time as becoming 'not the same' in others. Hence simultaneous variability and invariability must be a property of the linguistic sign as such.

This may at first sound like a hackneyed reworking of some ancient Greek paradox. As usual with Saussure, however, the target is not a philosophical but a linguistic theory: in this case, the entirely inadequate theory of linguistic change projected by the work of the comparative and historical philologists. It has been said of Whitney, for example, that 'his notion of historical processes, and hence methods of investigating them, depends on individual items in a language, at all structural levels, rather than on some a priori notion of structure' (Silverstein 1971: xv). But much the same could be said of a whole era of linguistic scholarship. When Whitney writes (1867: 54-5):

> Language is made up of signs for thought, which, though in one sense parts of a whole, are in another and more essential sense isolated and independent entities. Each is produced for its own purpose; each is separately exposed to the changes and vicissitudes of linguistic life, is modified, recombined, or dropped, according to its own uses and capacities.

he is expressing a doctrine of linguistic change which was to be taken to its logical conclusion by others and summed up in Gilliéron's famous anti-structuralist aphorism: *chaque mot a son histoire* ('every word has its own history'). The nineteenth century had seen nothing problematic at all in the notion of a word 'surviving' over the centuries, irrespective of its incorporation at different times into different linguistic systems (as if one were dealing with the historical continuity of a physical object, or some analogue thereof). Why this will not do is a question Saussure will return to again in his discussion of panchronicity ([134-5]). How to replace this inadequate notion by a more satisfactory concept of historical continuity in language is a problem which will occupy much of the remainder of the *Cours*. Its ultimate solution will involve the fully-fledged structuralist theory of *valeurs linguistiques*. A first step will be the establishment of the dichotomy between synchronic and diachronic relations, to which the *Cours* now turns.

CHAPTER III

Static Linguistics and Evolutionary Linguistics

The programmatic conclusion towards which this chapter steadily progresses throughout its nine sections is stated unequivocally in the two final sentences ([140]):

> *Synchronic linguistics* will be concerned with logical and psychological connexions between coexisting items constituting a system, as perceived by the same collective consciousness.
> *Diachronic linguistics* on the other hand will be concerned with sequences of items not perceived by the same collective consciousness, which replace one another without themselves constituting a system.

It is interesting to examine the strategy Saussure deploys in order to lead up to this conclusion, but at the outset it may be useful simply to contrast the position which this conclusion represents with the kind of position against which Saussure is implicitly arguing.

Hermann Paul, for example, in his *Principien der Sprachgeschichte* had distinguished between descriptive grammar (which at first sight corresponds to Saussure's 'synchronic') and historical grammar (which at first sight corresponds to Saussure's 'diachronic'), but maintained nevertheless that this did not demand a difference of perspective within linguistics. For Paul, in the scientific study of language only a historical perspective is valid.

> What is explained as an unhistorical and still scientific observation of language is at bottom nothing but one incompletely historical, through defects partly of the observer, partly of the material to be observed. (Paul 1890: xlvi-xlvii)

Paul held that it was impossible to describe scientifically even one state of a single dialect without tacitly relating forms to one another on a historical basis.

If we compare, for example, the different significations of a word with each other, we attempt to establish which of these is the fundamental one, or to what fundamental signification, now obsolete, they point. If, however, we define a fundamental signification from which the others are derived, we lay down a historical fact. Indeed, we cannot even assert that related forms are derived from a common basis without becoming historical. (Paul 1890: xlviii)

Paul concludes:

And so I cannot conceive how anyone can reflect with any advantage on a language without tracing to some extent the way in which it has historically developed. (Paul 1890: xlviii)

This is as good an example as one can find of a position which is diametrically opposed to Saussure's.

For Saussure, Paul's single 'historical' point of view which embraces states as well as changes (Paul 1890: 8) is theoretically incoherent. It fails to recognize that relations between co-existing linguistic items are logically and psychologically of a quite different order from relations between chronologically successive linguistic items. This difference, apparently so simple in principle, nevertheless turns out to involve unexpected difficulties. Chapter III shows Saussure attempting to grapple with some of them, in the context of working towards the statement of a rational 'scientific' programme for linguistics.

The first step in §1 prior to the introduction of the terms *synchronique* and *diachronique* is the observation that all 'sciences which involve the study of values' (*valeurs*) are obliged to distinguish between an 'axis of simultaneity' and an orthogonal 'axis of succession' ([115]). This is the first mention of a technical term (*valeur*) which will assume a key position in Saussure's fully elaborated linguistic theory. What exactly values are in this sense is not yet explained, but already Saussure proclaims in advance that '*la langue* is a system of pure values, determined by nothing else apart from the temporary state of its constituent elements' ([116]). The system of values is thus allocated unequivocally to the axis of simultaneity, which concerns 'relations from which the passage of time is entirely excluded' ([115]).

Even in this respect, however, Saussure claims that *la langue* is not quite like any other system of values. Since the linguistic sign is arbitrary, the separation between the axis of simultaneity and the axis of succession is more absolute than in other cases.

Insofar as a value, in one of its aspects, is founded upon natural connexions between things (as, for example, in economics the value of a piece of land depends upon the income derivable from it), it is possible up to a point to trace this value through time, bearing in mind that it depends at any one time upon the relevant system of contemporary values. However, its connexion with things inevitably supplies it with a natural basis, and hence any assessment of it is never entirely arbitrary. There are limits upon the range of variability. But, as we have already seen, in linguistics these natural connexions have no place. ([116])

For the reader, this caveat about the special status of linguistic values, although it ties in with the point made in the preceding chapter that *la langue* is unique as a social institution in virtue of being based entirely on non-natural connexions, cannot fail to make the notion of *valeurs* initially all the more perplexing. If it is possible to trace changes in the value of a piece of land over the years, why is it not possible to trace changes in the meaning of a word over the years? On the other hand, if indeed this is not possible in the case of language, why does the axis of simultaneity intersect at all with the axis of succession (as shown in the diagram on p.[115])? For intersection presumably implies that at least one item may be situated on both axes.

Instead of answering such queries immediately, §1 leaves them pending and proceeds to a discussion of terminology. 'Historical linguistics' is rejected in favour of 'evolutionary linguistics' or, better still, 'diachronic linguistics'; while 'static linguistics' and 'synchronic linguistics' are proposed as designations of the science of 'linguistic states' (*états de langue*). In view of Saussure's explicit refusal to accept the implications of the usual term 'historical linguistics', it is quite remarkable how readily later commentators assumed that this was at bottom merely a terminological quibble, and that Saussurean diachronic linguistics was just historical linguistics under a new academic title. Bloomfield (1923) even went as far as to gloss Saussure's term *linguistique diachronique* as 'historical linguistics' and identified its subject matter as being sound changes and analogical changes 'such as are recorded in our historical grammars'. Evidently a case of *plus ça change*.

Bloomfield was by no means an exception. His profound incomprehension of Saussure's distinction between synchronic and diachronic relations demonstrates strikingly just how difficult it was in the 1920s for an eminent linguist trained in the traditional philological approach to his subject to realise that Saussure was not just re-affirming (in a novel terminology, to be sure) the assumptions which had for so long underwritten the discipline of language studies. For Bloomfield, evidently, Saussure was saying nothing very different from what Hermann Paul had already said some thirty years earlier when distinguishing between descriptive grammar and historical grammar. Saussure's disclaimers are simply ignored and his reasons for rejecting the equation 'diachronic = historical' are not challenged but passed over in silence. It is all the more important to appreciate what these reasons are.

The first reason given ([116-17]) is that the terms 'history' and 'historical' not only fail to mark the distinction Saussure intends to draw by opposing 'synchronic' to 'diachronic', but actually conflate that distinction. For 'history', as commonly understood, includes not only facts pertaining to states but also facts pertaining to evolutions. The typical error of 'historical linguistics' for Saussure was a failure to distinguish these two orders of facts, and consequently a pervasive tendency to describe linguistic states in evolutionary terms and linguistic developments in static terms.

The second reason, however, is the more important: that juxtaposing descriptions of successive *états de langue* is not a way of studying languages along the temporal axis. In order to study linguistic phenomena along this axis of succession, 'it would be necessary to consider separately the factors of transition involved in passing from one linguistic state to the next' ([117]). This is exactly what Saussure's predecessors had failed to do. The same point will be reiterated even more forcefully in the *Cours* at the beginning of Chapter VII of Part II, where we find the blunt, uncompromising statement that in Saussure's view there is no such thing as 'historical grammar' ([185]). Now since the crowning achievement of language studies in the nineteenth century had been working out the details of the 'historical grammar' of the various Indo-European languages, and since, as Bloomfield (1923) put it,

> Outside of the field of historical grammar, linguistics has worked only in the way of a desperate attempt to give a psychologistic interpretation to the facts of language, and in the way of phonetics, an endless and aimless listing of the sound-articulations of speech.

it is small wonder that an outright rejection of historical grammar might have seemed so blasphemous to linguists of Bloomfield's generation that they could hardly bring themselves to believe that this was the message of Saussurean linguistics.

Seeking to avoid this heretical conclusion at all costs, they doubtless misread the rider which immediately follows the dismissal of 'historical grammar' ('What is called 'historical grammar' is in reality simply diachronic linguistics' [185]) as affirming an equation between diachrony and history. Nothing could make more complete nonsense of Saussure's earlier refusal to accept that equation on pp.[116-17]. The point of the remark on p.[185], as its context makes clear, is to deny that there is any grammar over and above synchronic grammar: the changes between one grammatical system and its successor or successors in time are not themselves part of grammar. To put the point in terms of Saussure's chess analogy, any move which changes one state of the board into another state of the board belongs to neither state ([126]). For Saussure, 'diachronic grammar' would be a contradiction in terms. What, in his view, distinguishes so-called 'historical grammar' from 'descriptive grammar' is that the former mistakenly incorporates facts which rightly belong to diachronic linguistics.

In §2 of Chapter III Saussure develops this critique of 'historical linguistics' further. 'Historical linguistics' fails to describe *la langue* as it exists here and now for the language user, who neither knows nor needs to know anything about the past history of elements in a present *état de langue*; and it is in any case unscientific because it adopts no single, consistent point of view. 'It would be absurd to try to draw a panorama of the Alps as seen from a number of peaks in the Jura simultaneously' ([117]). But this is the kind of enterprise historical linguistics engages in. Furthermore, exclusive concentration on linguistic changes results in an atomistic approach in which *états de langue*, insofar as they are recognized at all, 'are considered only in fragments and very imperfectly' ([118]). In these respects nineteenth-century 'historical linguistics' is inferior to traditional grammar which, for all its shortcomings, adopted a 'strictly synchronic' programme ([118]). 'Having paid too much attention to history, linguistics will go back now to the static viewpoint of traditional grammar, but in a new spirit and with different methods' ([119]).

In §3 the reader is presented with analyses of a number of examples of linguistic change (French *décrépit*, Germanic noun plurals, French word stress, Slavic case distinctions) in order to illustrate that the contrast between synchronic and diachronic points of view 'is absolute and admits no compromise' ([119]). Although there may be an intimate connexion between diachronic process and resultant synchronic system, the two remain independent. 'The reason for a diachronic development lies in the development itself. The particular synchronic consequences which may ensue have nothing to do with it' ([121]). 'The language system as such is never directly altered. It is in itself unchangeable' ([121]). Diachronic changes affect individual elements of a system only. 'It is as if one of the planets circling the sun underwent a change of dimensions and weight: this isolated event would have general consequences for the whole solar system, and disturb its equilibrium' ([121]). This analogy alone perhaps sums up better than anything else Saussure's objections to 'historical linguistics'. By treating languages as continuously evolving 'historical' systems, it is intrinsically incapable of distinguishing between changes and their consequences. As a result, it achieves no level of explanation at all. To pursue Saussure's analogy, there will be neither an explanation of what happened to the planet, nor an explanation of what happened to the solar system (in both cases because what happened to the planet will be 'historically' indistinguishable from what happened to the system, the one being treated as part of the other).

By this point in the chapter it is already clear that one of the theoretical consequences of drawing an absolute distinction between synchronic and diachronic relations is that linguistics will require a concept of 'system'. For diachronically related items do not belong to any system, whereas synchronically related items do. But how exactly is the concept of a synchronic system to be construed? It is here that the theoretical difficulties attendant upon the apparently simple differentiation of synchronic from diachronic relations begin to emerge.

In §4 three analogies are suggested. The first compares the difference between diachrony and synchrony to the difference between a three-dimensional object and its two-dimensional projection. 'Studying objects, that is to say diachronic events, will give us no insight into synchronic states, any more than we can hope to understand geometrical projections simply by studying, however thoroughly, different kinds of object' ([125]). The second analogy compares the difference between diachrony and synchrony to the difference between a longitudinal section of the stem of a plant and a cross-cut of the same stem. 'The longitudinal section shows us the fibres themselves which make up the plant, while the transversal section shows us their arrangements on one particular level. But the transversal section is distinct from the longitudinal section, for it shows us certain relations between the fibres which are not apparent at all from any longitudinal section' ([125]). The third analogy is the celebrated comparison with chess. The difference between diachrony and synchrony is compared with the difference between the sequence of moves in a game of chess and the successive states of the board which result therefrom.

The appositeness of the chess analogy for Saussure is evidently that it emphasizes more clearly than either of the two preceding analogies the autonomous systematicity of the *état de langue*. 'In a game of chess, any given state of the board is totally independent of any previous state of the board. It does not matter at all whether the state in question has been reached by one sequence of moves or another sequence. Anyone who has followed the whole game has not the least advantage over a passer-by who happens to look at the game at that particular moment. In order to describe the position on the board, it is quite useless to refer to what happened ten seconds ago. All this applies equally to a language, and confirms the radical distinction between diachronic and synchronic' ([126-7]). As Saussure acknowledges, 'in chess, the player *intends* to make his moves and to have some effect upon the system. In a language, on the contrary, there is no premeditation. Its pieces are moved, or rather modified, spontaneously and fortuitously' ([127]). This, claims Saussure, is the only respect in which the comparison is defective. But this is not quite true. The analogy also limps in various other respects. In the first place, there is an equivocation between states of the board and states of the game. Except in the context of a game, there is no 'state of the board'. But the state of the game is not defined solely by the state of the board. The state of the game is as much a question of missing pieces as of the relative positions of the chessmen present on the board. The passer-by of

Saussure's example will 'read' the state of the game in the light of the knowledge that there is a characteristic structure to the development of games of chess: and this, presumably, it is not in Saussure's interest to concede in the case of languages. In any case, the state of the game is not to be identified with the state of the board alone. Saussure's passer-by will also need to know at least one piece of information which cannot be inferred from the state of the board; namely, whose move it is next. Again, there is no linguistic analogue. In the second place, a move in a game of chess *by definition* alters the state of the board. This is quite independent of any *intention* on the part of the player. But it is far from clear that anything analogous holds in the linguistic case; for Saussure will hardly wish to concede that synchronic states and diachronic changes are defined interdependently. Thus, for example, a consonant change which resulted in no new homophonies or grammatical syncretisms would leave the number of linguistic signs 'in play', their values and their synchronic relations unaltered. It would be like altering the shape of certain pieces on the board in some identical and trivial way which still left them distinguishable from other pieces without affecting the position of any one of them. But in chess that would not count as a move. In the third place, possible states of the board and possible moves are alike governed by the rules of chess, which exist independently of the course of any particular game. It is the rules, ultimately, and not the state of the board, which determine the values involved. Saussure does not see this as a defect in his analogy, because he claims that such rules 'fixed once and for all, also exist in the linguistic case: they are the unchanging principles of semiology' ([126]). Later, on p.[135], a slightly different line is taken, and the constancy of phonetic change (which could hardly be a 'principle of semiology') is instanced as a general linguistic law. But none of this will save the analogy. No unchanging principles governing games in general, or even board games in particular, determine the rules of chess. With the same board and the same pieces, it would be possible to devise many other games than the one we call 'chess'.

It is this third disanalogy which is in the end more devastating than any other for Saussure's comparison between *la langue* and chess. For it affords no way of delimiting the system which identifies a given *état de langue* along the axis of simultaneity other than by reference to rules which would simultaneously delimit all possible *états de langue* which might precede or follow. This is a problem for Saussure because, as §7 will subsequently make clear, he is committed to denying the validity of any 'panchronic' point of view where *la langue* is concerned. The upshot is that although the comparison with chess in this chapter carries the whole burden of clarifying Saussure's concept of a linguistic 'system', in the final analysis it does so at the expense of apparently posing a quite intractable problem for the linguist, who is left to find some way of describing the state of the game before knowing what the rules are.

Nothing in §5 makes this problem seem any less intractable. On the contrary, it becomes even more so with the important qualifications to the concept of synchrony which this section introduces. Synchronic and diachronic studies, we are told, are not on an equal footing. The former take precedence over the latter. Indeed, the linguist who takes a diachronic point of view 'is no longer examining *la langue*, but a series of events which modify it' ([128]). The methods of synchronic and diachronic linguistics will differ in two major respects. First, there is a difference in perspectives, and hence in methods. 'Synchrony has only one perspective, that of the language users; and its whole method consists of collecting evidence from them' ([128]). Diachronic linguistics, on the other hand, has two perspectives. 'One will be *prospective*, following the course of time, and the other *retrospective*, going in the opposite direction' ([128]). In the second place, diachronic linguistics does not need to confine itself to the study of sequences of items belonging to the same language: it may, for example, trace sequences of forms going back from French to Latin and to Proto-Indo-European. Synchronic studies, by contrast, cannot cross linguistic boundaries in this way. Furthermore, 'the object of synchronic study does not comprise everything which is simultaneous, but only the set of facts corresponding to any particular language. In this it will take into account where necessary a division into dialects and subdialects. The term *synchronic*, in fact, is not sufficiently precise. *Idiosynchronic* would be a better term ...' ([128]).

Here we have two quite crucial modifications to the concept of synchrony: so crucial that in certain respects they force a new interpretation of the original distinction between the synchronic and the diachronic. Hitherto the proposed basis of that distinction has been purely temporal: hence the actual terms *synchronic* and *diachronic*. Now, however, there is a retreat from temporality. Diachronic studies will include, in appropriate cases, the comparison of coeval signs (French *est*, German *ist*): for 'in order to justify comparing two forms, it is sufficient that there should be some historical connexion between them, however indirect' ([129]). So the scope of diachronic studies expands to include not merely historical sequentiality but historical relatedness, irrespective of sequentiality. At the same time, the scope of synchronic studies is restricted. It does not embrace everything which is simultaneous, but only signs which belong to the same linguistic system (whether language, dialect or sub-dialect). Thus, terminologically, it hardly suffices to replace *synchronic* by *idiosynchronic*, as Saussure proposes. What is needed in order to do terminological justice to this new contrast would be to drop the pair *synchronic* and *diachronic* altogether and replace them by the pair *idiosystemic* and *phylogenetic*. In spite of signs of hesitation, the *Cours* clings nevertheless to *synchronic* and *diachronic*: and in so doing lays itself open to a serious charge of inviting potential confusion.

More serious still as a theoretical issue, however, is the consequence of this shift away from the original contrast of axes ('simultaneity' vs. 'succession'). It complicates beyond measure the question of delimiting the 'linguistic system', and at the same time promotes this question to a position of central importance for the now misnamed study of 'synchrony'. For patently it will be no less grave an error to conflate facts pertaining to co-existing but separate idiosynchronic systems than to conflate facts pertaining to diachronically successive systems. Mistaking one such system for a co-existing one emerges as the synchronic counterpart to the historical mistake of failing to distinguish one *état de langue* from its predecessor. This shift from the synchronic to the idiosynchronic forces Saussure to face up to a new problem for linguistic theory.

By what criteria are idiosynchronic relations to be recognized? The *Cours* offers only one answer: by the criteria which make the linguistic system a social reality for its users. It now becomes apparent why in the preceding chapter Saussure had insisted that 'in order to have a language there must be a *community of speakers*' ([112]). This is not quite the banal platitude it at first appears to be. It is, in fact, a theoretical requirement for treating any *état de langue* as an objectively identifiable system. Otherwise, it would be open to the individual investigator to adopt whatever criteria seemed subjectively appropriate, and this would be no basis for establishing the status of linguistics as a science. The theoretical role of the linguistic community, therefore, is to provide the guarantee that the idiosynchronic system is not merely an abstraction invented by the linguist.

By what criteria, then, does the linguistic community recognize idiosynchronic relations? That, presumably, is for the linguist to find out. But how does the linguist identify the members of the linguistic community? Doubtless by their collective use of the same linguistic system. It is at this point that Saussure, in effect, draws the boundary of linguistic theory. The idea of idiosynchrony would be vacuous if not supported by reference to the collective consciousness: but the idea of a collective consciousness is not further explicated in the *Cours*. Probing it simply leads us straight back to the idiosynchronic system. It is thus the interlocking of these two ideas which will provide the theoretical keystone for the conceptual framework of Saussurean linguistics.

Already, however, the analogical explanation of systematicity has opened up certain awkward questions for a linguistics which proposes to treat synchronic and diachronic relations independently. The chapter now turns to deal provisionally with these. The most important is the question already hinted at in the analogy between *la langue* and the game of chess: the question of linguistic 'laws'. The question is awkward for Saussure because the chess analogy inevitably suggests a rather different programme for linguistics than the one Saussure proposes to offer. Consequently he now has to retract or at least limit the possible implications of that analogy. It is a task which proves unexpectedly difficult, and he makes rather heavy weather of it.

In §6, Saussure distinguishes between possible synchronic laws and possible diachronic laws, and gives examples of each. All, as it happens, concern phonetic facts, and all the illustrations are from Latin or Greek; but the implications are clearly meant to have general applicability. More important than the examples, however, is the premiss of Saussure's argument: 'any social law has two fundamental characteristics: it is *imperative* and it is *general*' ([130]). The term 'law' is here to be understood 'in its legal sense' ([134]). The question, according to Saussure, is simply whether so-called linguistic 'laws' of the synchronic or the diachronic type satisfy these two conditions.

Synchronic 'laws' do not satisfy the conditions, Saussure argues, because they are 'general, but not imperative' ([131]). By denying their 'imperative' character is meant not that speakers are not obliged to conform, but that '*in the language* there is nothing which guarantees the maintenance of regularity on any given point' ([131]). What Saussure means by a synchronic 'law' is, in fact, a generalization which holds for a given *état de langue*: for instance, the law determining which syllable in a Latin word bears the primary stress (this being regularly predictable on the basis of the number of syllables, length of the vowels, etc.). That this Latin stress law was not 'imperative' Saussure regards as proved by the fact that it altered in the course of time. No such pattern, however well established, is immune from change. Saussure's conclusion is that so-called synchronic 'laws' are not laws at all.

A parallel conclusion is reached concerning diachronic 'laws' also, on the ground that they fail to satisfy the second of the two conditions. Although imperative, they are not general. 'One speaks of a law only when a set of facts is governed by the same rule. In spite of appearances to the contrary, diachronic events are always accidental and particular in nature' ([131]). Saussure goes to some lengths to justify this latter claim. He takes it as obviously true in the case of semantic change: the fact that the French word *poutre*, meaning 'mare', eventually came to mean 'beam, rafter' is an isolated fact, to be explained by factors which affect no other item of French vocabulary. In cases of morphological and syntactic evolution, however, there might seem to be examples of general changes: for instance, the disappearance at a certain period of Old French nominative forms. But Saussure rejects this counterexample on the ground that in the more or less simultaneous disappearance of so many forms we see 'merely multiple examples of a single isolated fact', namely the disappearance of the Old French nominative case. This 'only appears to be a law because it is actualised in a system' ([132]). The same applies to so-called 'phonetic laws'. These affect many words simultaneously: but this is because the words in question all contain the particular sound which undergoes the change. Thus 'however many cases confirm a phonetic law, all the facts it covers are simply manifestations of a single particular fact' ([133]).

According to Saussure, then, neither synchronic 'laws' nor diachronic 'laws' are laws at all, although for different reasons in the two cases. What is the reader to make of this? It is certainly among the least convincing passages in the *Cours*. In the first place, Saussure's premiss that all social laws are both imperative and general is ill suited to his argument. If 'imperative' is glossed by saying, as Saussure does, that such a law 'demands compliance', this must mean that individuals subject to a social law have no option but to accept it. Failure to comply will entail sanctions or potential sanctions of some kind. In the linguistic case, however, Saussure denies that this is what is meant, and points out that 'laws' such as those determining word stress are subject to change. In that sense, synchronic 'laws' do not have to be kept. But this is to give a different sense to the term 'imperative' and, worse still, a sense in which few if any social laws are imperative either. Nor is it clear that diachronic laws are 'imperative' in one or other of these two senses, although Saussure claims that they are. The condition that social laws must be 'general' is scarcely any more satisfactory, since Saussure explicates 'generality' as 'covering all cases, within certain limits of time and place' ([130]). But in this sense of 'generality', a social law is on no different footing from any linguistic law which can be shown to 'cover all cases, within certain limits of time and place'. The dismissal of diachronic laws on this ground is thus question-begging. Saussure here needs either a different reason for refusing to accept diachronic laws, or else a stronger criterion of 'generality'.

Saussure's particular counterarguments dealing with morphological and phonetic change involve what amounts to special pleading. To count the disappearance of many Old French nominative forms as a single diachronic fact – namely, the disappearance of the nominative case itself – comes oddly from a theorist who elsewhere argues not only that the linguistic system as such is unchangeable ([121]) but also that grammatical cases are 'abstract entities' based on relationships between signs ([190]). For if the disappearance of a whole grammatical case (as distinct from the disappearance of the various individual forms) is not an example of diachronic change in a grammatical system, it is difficult to see what conceivably could be. Hence either Saussure's generalization that linguistic changes never directly affect the system as such must have exceptions; or else it acquires the status of an axiom. Either way, there are theoretical problems which the *Cours* makes no attempt to deal with. Again, if grammatical cases are abstract entities, their existence or non-existence must depend on the presence or absence in the system of contrasts between many individual signs which mark the grammatical distinction in question. For in Saussurean linguistics, it is the individual sign which is the basic 'concrete entity' of *la langue*. Nowhere does the *Cours* lay the ground for claiming that it is possible for whole sets of independent 'concrete entities' to be abolished at one stroke because of a single 'abstract' change at some higher level of linguistic organization. This would run counter to the whole Saussurean concept of linguistic articulation and to the doctrine of *valeurs*.

To appreciate the point, it is essential for the reader to realize (although the text of the *Cours* never makes this clear) that the Old French system included a variety of declensional types, of which at least the following six are usually recognized.

	Singular	Plural
Nominative	*murs*	*mur*
Oblique	*mur*	*murs*
Nominative	*pere*	*pere*
Oblique	*pere*	*peres*
Nominative	*porte*	*portes*
Oblique	*porte*	*portes*
Nominative	*flor(s)*	*flors*
Oblique	*flor*	*flors*
Nominative	*cuens*	*comte*
Oblique	*comte*	*comtes*
Nominative	*cors*	*cors*
Oblique	*cors*	*cors*

In other words, this is not one of those examples where the maintenance of a grammatical distinction depends on a single consonantal or vocalic contrast, and where consequently a single sound change affecting the consonant or vowel in question may obliterate the distinction. If in Kalaba all noun plurals are distinguished from their singulars solely by the addition of the suffix -*a*, it follows that if final vowels fall at some stage in the history of the Kalaba language, henceforth singular forms and plural forms will be phonetically identical. Such a change Saussure would not describe as the 'disappearance of the Kalaba plural': far from it, for that would be the kind of mistake made in 'historical grammar' by failing to distinguish between changes and consequences of changes. The fact that the later *état de langue* in Kalaba has no distinction between singular nouns and plural nouns would be a synchronic consequence of a phonetic change having nothing to do with Kalaba grammar.

How, then, are we to make sense of Saussure's claim that in Old French it was the nominative case which disappeared (as distinct from any particular sound or affix)? The implication seems to be that for Saussure 'nominative case' was a *signifié* in Old French, which happened to be shared by a large number of *signifiants*. Furthermore, it seems we must understand that just as a sign may drop out of the language because, by reason of phonetic change, its *signifiant* disappears (as in the hypothetical case of Kalaba final -*a*), so there are cases in which a sign may drop out of the language because its *signifié*, for reasons of semantic change, disappears. What happened to the Old French nominatives would then fall under this latter head. Saussure, in short, appears to envisage a parallel between the operations of phonetic change and the operations of semantic change, which could result in similar synchronic consequences for a later *état de langue*. An earlier grammatical distinction might be lost for either of two quite distinct reasons: (i) because phonetic change 'accidentally' obliterated the relevant differences between forms, or (ii) because semantic change obliterated the relevant conceptual differences.

The trouble with this, as an interpretation of Saussure's use of the Old French example, is that it makes the theoretical difficulty for Saussure even more acute. In the first place, the facts do not warrant a claim that the nominative case *as such* disappeared from Old French. For if 'nominative case' is a semantic concept, then it is possible to argue that (i) it still survived, but was expressed in a different form (by contrasts of word order, instead of by nominal flexions), and (ii) it survived in the pronoun system, which still distinguishes morphologically between nominatives (*je, tu, il*, etc.) and obliques (*me, te, le*, etc.). In the second place, processes of semantic change are manifestly not like processes of phonetic change in any case. There is a world of difference between, say, the 'disappearance' of a final vowel (which may or may not be of morphological significance) and the 'disappearance' of a concept (that is, of a Saussurean *signifié*).

While it seems reasonable in certain circumstances to invoke the disappearance of one *signifié* to explain the fate of an individual sign (because a linguistic community no longer needs a word for something it ceases to have occasion to talk about) it is far from clear that it makes sense at all to invoke the disappearance of one *signifié* to explain the disappearance of a whole series of different phonological forms. What would the sociolinguistic mechanism for such a change be? It clearly could not be parallel to, say, the process by which gradually phasing out the manufacture of thimbles might eventually lead to an *état de langue* in English which had no word *thimble*. That is perfectly comprehensible. One can even imagine that the obsolescence of certain types of activity or craft (for instance, sewing) might lead to the obsolescence of a whole vocabulary associated with it (*thimble, needle, stitch,* etc.). But that is not quite the same as suggesting that the forms of the words *thimble, needle, stitch,* etc. would automatically be eliminated in a linguistic community which did not have the concept of sewing. For that presupposes that the meanings of the words *thimble, needle, stitch,* etc. are all necessarily defined by reference to sewing. Now the *Cours* offers very little in the way of specific proposals about topics in semantics: but what it does say does not suggest that Saussure's theory of the linguistic sign is committed in advance to some form of componential semantics. Consequently the *signifié* 'thimble' could well survive in the absence of the *signifié* 'sew', and the *signifiant* [θimbl] could well survive too. Saussure here fails to reckon with a fundamental asymmetry between attributing the loss of a semantic distinction to sound change and attributing the loss of a formal distinction to semantic change.

Saussure's argument concerning sound change itself is no less deeply flawed. One of his own examples (the fall of final stops: **gunaik→gúnai, *epheret→éphere, *epheront→épheron*) will suffice to illustrate why. If such a change affects a number of sounds ([k], [t], etc.) which, according to Saussurean phonetics, belong to different 'sound types', and if the sounds in question are all and only those meeting certain specifiable conditions (final stops), it must be self-contradictory to claim that the change is not 'general' under the definition of generality which Saussure demands for social laws. Such a change is, in fact, exactly parallel to the introduction of a new social law which affects all and only members of a certain specified class or inhabitants of a certain specified area. It is not a question of rejecting Saussure's claim that 'words themselves are not directly subject to phonetic change' ([133]). Even if true, this is quite irrelevant to the argument: for social laws are not (usually) instituted for specific individuals either. Jones and Smith may not be 'directly subject' to changes in legislation, in that the law does not name them specifically or single them out for special treatment: but they are subject to it nevertheless if they qualify under whatever general provisions the new legislation makes, and irrespective of whether they are or are not the only members of society who happen to qualify. *Mutatis mutandis,* the same applies to words. The fact that the fall of final stops is a sound change which leaves untouched words which did not have final stops in the first place is no reason for denying its 'generality'. The case would be quite different if a random selection of words with final stops were subject to the change. But in that case, *pace* Saussure, there *would* be an argument for saying that certain words only were 'directly subject' to the change in question.

It is difficult not to conclude that §6 is a tactical mistake from beginning to end. It takes back clumsily the very explanation the chess analogy offered just previously. For if linguistic 'laws' are not really 'law-like' after all in the way the rules of chess are, or in the way social laws in general are, then the original analogy was worthless. We are left with *états de langue* which are *not* like states of the chess board, since the patterns they conform to lack the force of laws. This certainly explains why it is no part of the Saussurean programme for linguistics to concern itself with the establishment of a set of general linguistic laws which, like the rules of chess, simultaneously explain both states and changes, and their interrelations, in all conceivable cases. But the price paid for this retraction is a heavy one. For we are once again left without an explanation of what is meant by the systematicity of an *état de langue*.

Although §6 is a tactical blunder, it is not a strategic catastrophe. Saussure's theoretical position is perfectly defensible if the defence is managed less clumsily. What Saussure ought to have argued may be summarized as follows. 1. There are no synchronic laws. For although *la langue* is a social institution, there is nothing corresponding to a legal system which exists precisely *in order to* impose certain patterns of behaviour in the community. 2. There are no diachronic laws either. For *la langue* is not like those social institutions in which the transition from a prior state to a subsequent state is regulated. *La langue* has nothing corresponding to social 'laws of inheritance', or to the rules for moves in chess, which regulate the transition from one state of the board to the next. 3. Apparent counterexamples to the absence of synchronic laws are illusions arising from the regularities observable in *parole*. 4. Apparent counterexamples to the absence of diachronic laws are illusions arising from the fact that, retrospectively, series of unconnected changes give the appearance of a reorganization of the system. Thus the so-called 'disappearance of the Old French nominative case' is a diachronic misdescription or oversimplification of a whole series of separate events affecting particular forms or sub-groups of forms. With a defence conducted along these lines, Saussure's rejection of both synchronic and diachronic laws would be more secure.

Next, an alternative possibility is explored. Why cannot a science of language establish panchronic laws which relate to languages as the laws of nature relate to events in the physical world? Because, §7 argues, although it is possible to generalize about universal features of language (for example, that phonetic changes constantly occur), where specific linguistic facts are concerned 'there is no panchronic point of view' ([135]). Any concrete fact amenable to panchronic explanation could not be part of *la langue*. For example, the French word *chose* may be distinguished synchronically from other words belonging to the same *état de langue*, and diachronically from words in earlier *états de langue* (for instance, from Latin *causa*, from which it is etymologically derived). But there is no independent panchronic means of identifying it. The sounds šǫz may be considered panchronically in themselves: but the sounds as such do not constitute the word *chose*. 'The panchronic point of view never gets to grips with specific facts of *la langue*' ([195]). This is, obviously, another Saussurean reformulation of the charge already brought against 'historical linguistics': we cannot study 'the word' (whether it be *chose* or any other) as a continuously evolving entity with a life-span of two thousand years: for the simple reason that no such entity exists. All we can do is examine a number of different synchronic entities which do exist, and the separate diachronic changes which connect them. The 'panchronic' error, in other words, is another version of the 'historical' error. It is a mistake to imagine that there could be some more general perspective on language which would take in both synchronic and diachronic facts simultaneously.

§8 proceeds to give various exemplifications of the error, in the form of conflations between synchronic and diachronic facts. For years, says Saussure, 'linguistics has muddled them up without even noticing the muddle' ([137]). By unscrambling this muddle, one can arrive at a 'rational' programme for linguistic studies, which the table in §9 ([139]) summarizes;

$$
\text{Langage} \begin{cases} \text{Langue} \begin{cases} \text{Synchronie} \\ \text{Diachronie} \end{cases} \\ \text{Parole} \end{cases}
$$

As an essay in general linguistic theory, Chapter III can hardly be counted an unqualified success. It is a patchwork of examples and partial analogies, tacked together by rather tenuous threads of reasoning. But this patchwork quality itself demonstrates how unexpectedly difficult it is to argue for the apparently simple thesis which Saussure advances. It shows that it is one thing to grasp that the linguistic relationship between French *chose* and Latin *causa* must be of a quite different order from the linguistic relationship between French *chose* and French *chien*, but quite a different thing to supply a satisfactory theoretical framework which accommodates that difference. What emerges above all is that the programmatic separation of these two orders of relationship requires a concept of linguistic systematicity which it is far from easy to explicate when the signs involved are defined in terms of an arbitrary connexion between form and meaning. It is this major task of explication which is now to be tackled in Part II of the *Cours*.

PART TWO
Synchronic Linguistics

CHAPTER I

General Observations

The aim of general synchronic linguistics is announced straight away as being 'to establish the fundamental principles of any idiosynchronic system, the facts which constitute any *état de langue*' ([141]), and this will include not only the properties of the sign already discussed in Part I, but everything usually called 'general grammar' ([141]). This opening formulation raises the question of what the precise relation is between idiosynchronic system and *état de langue*. If the preceding chapter of the *Cours* had given the impression that there was little if any difference between the two, this equation is immediately called in question by what now follows.

The reader is told that (notwithstanding the analogy drawn in the previous chapter with a cross-cut through the stem of a plant) an *état de langue* is not to be thought of as what is revealed by a single slice through the evolutionary development of a language at a particular point in time. An *état de langue*, rather, is itself a phase in that development. It occupies 'a period of time of varying length, during which the sum total of changes occurring is minimal. It may be ten years, a generation, a century, or even longer' ([142]).

This second major revision of the opposition between synchrony and diachrony – for that is what it amounts to – is introduced almost casually, and accompanied by only the sparsest of explanations. The reader is simply referred to the historian's distinction between 'epochs' and 'periods', the former conceptualized as points in time, and the latter as lengths of time. 'None the less, a historian speaks of the "Antonine epoch" or the "Crusading epoch" when he is taking into consideration a set of features which remained constant over the period in question. One could likewise say that static linguistics is also in this sense concerned with epochs; but the term *state* is preferable' ([142]).

The implications of this revised concept of an *état de langue* are far-reaching. It should be noted first of all that herewith Saussure reverts again to time as the relevant dimension for defining a linguistic distinction, but now uses that dimension in a different defining role. In Part I, time had been treated (i) as the 'abstract' dimension validating the opposition between two different sets of relations (along the axes of simultaneity and succession), and (ii) as the 'real world' dimension providing the empirical basis for the action of social forces upon *la langue*. Now we have something different. The new viewpoint combines the two earlier treatments of time and supersedes them. In this third conceptualization of synchronic and diachronic relations, the sub-ordination of diachrony to synchrony is definitive. For now an *état de langue* is identified by its invariance over time: 'an absolute state is defined by lack of change' ([142]). Since diachronic studies by definition do not embrace the analysis of *états de langue*, this apparently excludes from the purview of diachronic linguistics any period in the history of a language during which no change occurs. Diachronic studies, conse-quently, are restricted to dealing with such periods of linguistic history as intervene between periods of stability. The text of the *Cours* seems to leave little room for doubt about this. 'Of two contemporary languages, one may evolve considerably and the other hardly at all over the same period. In the latter case, any study will necessarily be synchronic, but in the former case diachronic' ([142]). So now we have time itself, as the linguistic axis of succession, divided into successions of stability and change; while 'synchronic' and 'diachronic' become opposed modalities of investigation relative to the successive segmentations of this axis. Given the new concept of an *état de langue*, there will apparently be a simple one-one correspondence between period and modality of investigation; for each progressive transition along the temporal axis must be either a transition from stability to change or else a transition from change to stability.

The difference between this new temporal framework and the old one corresponds to the difference between the simple diagram of the two intersecting axes on p.[115] of the *Cours* and something more like the diagram shown opposite (p.105).

The new framework, it will be apparent, represents an elaboration of the chess analogy at the expense of the plant analogy. Intersection between horizontal and vertical axes is no longer a single momentary 'time-slice' revealing two exactly matching surfaces on the cross-cut, but a sectional excision laying bare non-identical patterns at either end. This corresponds exactly to the sequence of events in the game of chess. Any state of the board will remain unchanged for a variable length of time – as long as it may take between one move and the next. Once a move is

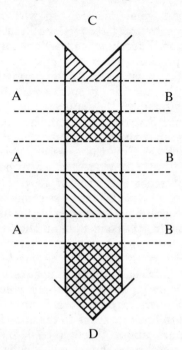

made, that puts an end to the preceding static period: the pattern on the board will no longer be the same as before. Each state of the board in turn is separated from the next by an interval, which may also be of greater or less duration, during which a change in the pattern of pieces is effected. Thus the game proceeds by regular alternations between states and changes. This is the model of linguistic development to be explored throughout Parts II and III of the *Cours*.

At this point in the text, one or two problems arising from the new framework are briefly mentioned. One is that of 'demarcation in time' ([143]). That is to say, there will be a problem in defining the chronological limits of a given *état de langue*. This problem is temporarily dismissed, however, by pointing out that since an exactly similar geographical problem arises over demarcation in space, the notion of an *état de langue* 'can only be an approximation' ([143]).

Ill prepared as the reader may have been for the first surprise about synchrony which the chapter held in store, this second one comes as an even greater shock. For now it appears that an *état de langue* is not only a period, but something much more enigmatic: a period with a geographical area. Saussurean commentators on the whole have displayed quite remarkable phlegm in dealing with this *prima facie* evidence of conceptual confusion. One would have expected it at least to provoke a footnote or two. Perhaps the explanation is that the coupling of the problem of chronological demarcation with that of geographical demarcation was taken by most readers simply as an elliptical way of saying that the question 'Exactly *when* was language X spoken?' can no more be answered precisely than 'Exactly *where* was language X spoken?' If so, this bears witness to a very superficial reading of the *Cours*. The text is quite specific. It speaks in both cases of 'the same problem', and of the difficulty it presents for 'the definition of an *état de langue*' ([143]). It is the first recognition in the *Cours* that a dimension *other than* time is relevant to linguistic theory.

The *Cours* does not take up the question again until Part IV on 'Geographical Linguistics'. However, it is worth pointing out briefly at this juncture in what sense the issue of geographical demarcation is relevant. The notion of an *état de langue* as something which has both a chronological and a geographical extension begins to make sense if we see it as the result of projecting the concept of an idiosynchronic system on to the plane of *la parole*. Here we encounter another of the hidden premises of Saussurean linguistics. It is: that the mechanism of diachronic continuity is contact between individual speakers. Already the reader was forewarned of this on p.[138]: 'everything which is diachronic in *la langue* is only so through *la parole*'. But there the context of the observation appeared to limit its scope to the question of explaining how linguistic change comes about through trial and error initiated by individuals. In fact, the remark has a much wider significance, which now emerges. Since each individual act of *parole* occurs in a spatio-temporally situated context, it follows that diachrony has spatial as well as temporal implications. Specifically, contact between individuals is what ensures diachronic succession: and this contact must take place *somewhere*. The world of Saussurean linguistics is a world of face-to-face interaction. Writing is overtly excluded by definition, and the possibility of transmitting the spoken word by telephone, radio or tape-recording is tacitly excluded as 'unnatural'. It is essentially a world which antedates the most recent of the technological revolutions in human communication, and the ensuing theoretical problems which arise concerning the location of communicative acts can consequently be ignored. Thus for Saussure there is no question of diachronic continuity without a chain of contact through *la parole* which is spatially identifiable. If two phylogenetically and geographically remote language-families were somehow to evolve identical dialects, that would be for Saussure a remarkable coincidence: but nothing which called for any kind of explanation in terms of linguistic theory.

Thus the problem of the geographical demarcation of the use of an idiosynchronic system and the problem of its temporal demarcation are quite literally, from a Saussurean point of view, *the same problem*. Why is this? The answer is that it must necessarily be so once the concept of an idiosynchronic system is mapped on to the facts of Saussurean *parole*, which is just what the new model of an *état de langue* accomplishes. More important for what follows is that this dual problem is now to be treated as of a merely practical rather than of a theoretical order. This is evident from the description of a linguistic state as a period 'during which the sum total of changes occurring is minimal' ([142]); from the recommendation that 'unimportant changes' be ignored, just as mathematicians 'ignore very small fractions for certain purposes, such as logarithmic calculation' ([142]); and from the appeal to a general scientific practice of 'conventional simplification of the data' ([143]). Whether this relegation of demarcational problems to the domain of the practical can ultimately be sustained is a quite different matter. Saussure's account of synchronic theory throughout the rest of Part II simply assumes that 'for all practical purposes' the linguist has managed to identify an epoch of linguistic history amenable to synchronic analysis, even if the exact demarcation of the relevant *état de langue* is still uncertain. The demarcation, indeed, is bound to remain uncertain until analysis has revealed the details of the idiosynchronic system on which that *état de langue* is based.

Also uncertain in the light of this new Saussurean interpretation of synchrony is what happens to the linguistic community in between periods of stability. Does it have no *langue*? By what means does communication continue, given that the previously established system has broken down and a new system has not yet replaced it? And if linguistic communication nevertheless does continue in the interim, what becomes of the original hypothesis that the sole linguistic reality for the speakers is an *état de langue*? Do they somehow carry on in the mistaken belief that they are still using the old system, without noticing that in fact its distinctions have collapsed? If so, are they already using a new system unwittingly, or using no system at all? Questions of this order inevitably arise once the concept of synchrony is no longer construed in terms of the very simple model provided by the two axes of simultaneity and succession. The conflicting demands of temporality and systematicity here, as elsewhere in the *Cours*, generate problems which are never satisfactorily resolved.

CHAPTER II

Concrete Entities of a Language

How is the linguist to identify the linguistic signs belonging to any idiosynchronic system? Saussure takes this question first for the obvious reason that unless an answer is available synchronic analysis cannot even begin. No system can be identified independently of its constituent signs, and to identify the constituent signs is *eo ipso* to engage in analysis of the system.

The reader is reminded in §1 of this chapter that in linguistics the 'concrete entity' is the linguistic sign, and that linguistic signs exist only in virtue of an association between *signifiant* and *signifié*. Consequently the linguist cannot proceed by trying to analyse sounds and meanings separately. The only viable method of procedure is to segment the continuous phonetic chain presented by each utterance into sections, each of which corresponds to a *signifié* in the spoken message. This method is represented schematically by the following diagram on p.[146]:

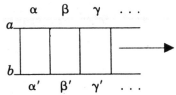

'Correct delimitation of signs requires that the divisions established in the sound sequence (α', β', γ' ...) match the divisions in the sequence of concepts (α, β, γ ...)' ([146]).

Only one example of this method is given: *sižlaprã* may be analysed either as *si-ž-la-prã* (= *si je la prends*, 'if I take it/her') or as *si-ž-l-aprã* (= *si je l'apprends*, 'if I learn it'), but in no other way, since no other segmentation of the sound sequence makes sense of the meaning. 'To check the results of this analysis and make sure that one has picked out the units, it is necessary to compare series of phrases in which the same unit occurs, and be able in each case to separate the unit in question from its context in a way corroborated by the sense' ([146-7]). In the two phrases *laforsdüvā* (= *la force du vent*) and *abudfors* (= *à bout de force*), 'the same concept coincides with the same sound-segment *fors* in both cases: thus it is clearly a linguistic unit' ([147]). But in *ilməforsaparlę* (= *il me force à parler*), '*fors* has a quite different meaning: so it is a different unit' ([147]).

The implications of this method of analysis are examined in §3. The most obvious is that the Saussurean 'concrete entity' or 'concrete unit' does not correspond to the traditional unit 'word'. For instance, the singular *cheval* ('horse') and its plural *chevaux* ('horses') will count as two separate concrete units, although they are traditionally treated as forms of a single word. Similarly the two possible pronunciations of the French word for 'month' (*mwa* and, in liaison with a following vowel, *mwaz*) count for Saussure as the *signifiants* of two different signs. Suffixes, prefixes and stems with clearly identifiable meanings will also qualify as concrete units, although they are not recognized traditionally as separate words. On the other hand, there are certain concrete units (compounds, fixed phrases) which are larger than single words.

Saussure does not deny that in many cases it is quite difficult to analyse sound sequences in this way and to determine which units are present: 'delimiting them is such a tricky problem that one is led to ask whether they are really there' ([149]). But this is seen as one of the features which distinguishes languages from all other semiological institutions. 'A language thus has this curious and striking feature. It has no immediately perceptible entities' ([149]).

In this chapter, the hidden premiss that the 'invisible' articulation of *la langue* will turn out to correspond to the 'visible' articulation of writing again comes to the surface; and this time not merely at the level of phonology. It is significant, for instance, that Saussure fails to discuss whether his first segmentation of *sižlaprã* requires a further division between *l* and *a*. His analysis stops short, in other words, when it reaches a unit which answers to the usual orthographic form of the pronoun *la*. The assumption, evidently, is that this pronoun form corresponds to a single concept (although no attempt is made to state what this concept is). But since in French *la* stands in contrast to *le* (*si je la prends* vs. *si je le prends*), it is a perfectly reasonable question to ask whether these units cannot be broken down further. One possible analysis would be that *l* signals the pronominal person (third person, in traditional grammatical terms) while the vowel signals the gender (feminine in the case of *la*, masculine in the case of *le*). This analysis would be supported by Saussure's own second segmentation, where the consonant *l* alone represents a third person pronoun of indeterminate gender. The text of the *Cours* leaves the reader uncertain as to whether this possibility simply did not occur to Saussure, or whether he had reasons for rejecting it.

It seems fairly clear that there are a number of other hidden premises lying behind Saussure's treatment of examples in this chapter. They appear to relate on the one hand to the native speaker's knowledge of *la langue,* and on the other hand to the organization of units within *la langue.* However, it is no easy matter to determine exactly what the content and theoretical status of these premises is, for reasons which will emerge in the discussion below.

Basically, Saussure seems to assume that the native speaker is normally able to make a correct identification of features of linguistic structure, by some simple process of introspection and reflection. The theoretical significance of this assumption it would be difficult to exaggerate. Only its unquestioned acceptance will justify Saussure's lack of concern with providing any systematic 'discovery procedure' for the identification of linguistic signs. There may be difficulties over marginal cases but not, it would seem, over most. He is evidently confident that his treatment of *sižlaprã* will strike any French native speaker as totally uncontentious, and that there is no need to present evidence in support of the two analyses proposed. His denial that any other segmentations of the sequence make sense is quite categoric. Thus it would seem that the intelligent native speaker has only to reflect upon the matter for a moment in order to arrive at exactly the same conclusion as the linguistic theorist. Likewise, Saussure appears to take it for granted that it will be intuitively obvious to the native speaker, on reflection, that *mwaz* must be a quite separate linguistic sign from *mwa,* that *fɔrs* has a quite different meaning in *la force du vent* and *il me force à parler,* and so on.

Particularly revealing is the case of *mwaz* (as in *un mois après*) vs. *mwa* (as in *le mois de décembre*). Saussure does not discuss the possibility of treating *mwaz* and *mwa* as alternate forms of the same *signifiant*; nor the possibility of analysing *mwaz* into *mwa + z,* where *z* is simply a structural unit devoid of meaning. The implied rejection of the latter possibility raises a rather crucial question: for one can see two possible ways of rationalizing it.

The case might rest on the psychological claim that native speakers of French do not as a matter of fact recognize that *mwaz* segments into two elements, the first of which means 'month' and the second of which is meaningless; but, on the contrary, recognize *mwaz* as a single unit meaning 'month'. Alternatively, the case might rest on the methodological contention that the linguistic analyst cannot proceed on the assumption that there may be a 'residue' on the plane of expression which is semantically unaccounted for. The difference between these two positions is important. The former case rests on an alleged fact about a particular generation or generations of speakers of French, and will have no general consequences. The latter case amounts to postulating a linguistic universal. The hidden premiss would then be that in *la langue* there are no semantic zero-elements. (Whereas, by contrast, Saussure evidently sees nothing odd about *phonic* zero-elements, as has earlier been made clear on p.[124].) The premiss, in other words, is that there is an asymmetry in the composition of the linguistic sign, which allows a *signifié* to have a zero *signifiant*, but does not allow a *signifiant* to have a zero *signifié*.

Such a premiss in effect introduces an important but unannounced limitation on the principle of arbitrariness. This limitation will clearly have far-reaching consequences for the linguist's programme of analysis. For the assumption will be that linguistic structure does not permit the arbitrary introduction of meaningless elements in order to satisfy rules which pertain solely to the plane of expression. On the other hand, if semantic zero-elements are theoretically permissible, then it becomes a merely contingent fact that there is no such element in *mwaz*. This is not merely a puzzle about the linguistic status of liaison consonants in French: on the contrary, it has quite general implications for linguistic analysis, and in particular the relevance of native speakers' awareness of linguistic structure.

In one case, the analyst must presumably try to devise a reliable way of discovering whether native speakers recognize certain sounds as independent structural units, albeit meaningless ones. In the other case, it makes no difference whether they do or not. Saussure never suggests any test that linguists might carry out to determine whether a sequence like *mwaz* is analysable into *mwa + z*, even though he admits that the delimitation of linguistic units may pose problems ([148-9]). The only check he proposes on analyses flowing from the immediate deliverances of intuition is quite clearly regressive ([146-7]): it consists of finding further examples of the 'same linguistic unit' in other contexts. The problem with this method of verification is that exactly the same uncertainty then arises at one remove. It will not solve the analyst's query to switch attention from *mwaz* in *un mois après* to *mwaz* in *deux mois après*. The question, precisely, is how to recognize the presence of the 'same linguistic unit' in either. (The most lucid discussion of this and related problems in Saussurean analysis is that of Love 1984.)

Further hidden premisses appear to lie behind the diagram on p.[146] and the requirement for 'correct analysis' that divisions in the sound sequence (α', β', γ' ...) match divisions in the sequence of concepts (α, β, γ ...). One such premiss is what might be called the premiss of 'linear cohesion': the assumption that the *signifiant* is a linear unit which is 'uninterruptable'. In other words, there will be no cases in which a single *signifié* is represented on the plane of expression by *two* discrete segments of the speech chain. This premiss of linear cohesion in effect rules out any possibility of the following schema of analysis:

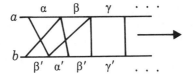

Why this should be impossible Saussure never explains. The lacuna may seem curious: for various examples given elsewhere in the *Cours* might suggest that recognizing the 'infixing' of one *signifiant* into another would be a plausible way of analysing the morphological structure of certain types of form. It is common in the Germanic languages, for example, to find morphological patterns in which vocalic variation with a fixed consonantal frame indicates a difference of tense, number, etc. (Saussure cites cases such as German *geben* vs. *gibt, schelten* vs. *schilt*, etc. in discussing the phenomenon of 'alternation' on pp.[217-20].) Similar patterning is even more prominent and regular in the Semitic system of consonantal roots (mentioned by Saussure on p.[256]).

The upshot of adopting the premiss of linear cohesion may be illustrated by reference to a simple English example: the plural forms *cats* and *mice*. On the basis of the premiss of linear cohesion, Saussurean analysis would treat *cats* as a combination of two *signifiants* but refuse to treat *mice* likewise. It will reject the possibility of treating the vowel of *mice* as a linguistic sign marking the plural, even though that is clearly what distinguishes *mice* from the corresponding singular *mouse* (just as the final *s* of *cats* is what distinguishes that from the corresponding singular *cat*). For this analysis of *mice* would entail treating the *signifié* 'mouse' as in this case having a *signifiant* split into the two linearly discrete elements [m] and [s]. The same example will also serve to illustrate a third possible hidden premiss, the premiss of 'representational discreteness'. This premiss would rule out the possibility of analytic schemata such as:

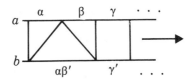

In other words, it rejects the possibility of treating a single *signifiant* as simultaneously functioning as the *signifiant* for two separate *signifiés*. The English plural *mice*, therefore, is not to be analysed as a form which simultaneously functions as the *signifiant* for both the *signifié* 'mouse' and the *signifié* 'plural'. The *signifié* of the form *mice*, accordingly, will be a single concept which in some way (not further elucidated) uniquely combines just the notions of plurality and mousehood. We have to treat it as unparadoxical, therefore, that *mice* means just 'mice', whereas *cats* does not mean 'cats' (but rather 'cat' plus 'more than one').

Between them, the premisses of linear cohesion and discrete representation yield a picture of linguistic structure which is clearly atomistic. That is to say, the *entités concrètes* of a language will emerge as units which never fuse or merge with one another, and cannot be split. These atomic units do not change their form or their behaviour when combined together, but retain their individual identities under all circumstances. The attractions of such a picture are not to be underestimated. It is precisely their atomistic invariance which will make the identification of such linguistic units possible; and this can hardly be a negligible consideration if the central task of linguistic analysis is indeed to identify them.

It will by now be clear what the problem is about the theoretical status of the hidden premisses on which this chapter of the *Cours* seems to be based. Saussure never says whether we are dealing here with psycholinguistic universals or just with methodological postulates. If the latter, he fails to explain whether these are the *only* postulates on which linguistic analysis might proceed, or merely one possible set. (He neither argues the case that no other postulates will do, nor justifies them as preferable to possible alternatives.) If the former, what the *Cours* conspicuously lacks is any rationale for treating these premisses as deriving from general 'laws' of the kind mentioned in Chapter II of the Introduction, or from higher-order principles of semiology either. The only glimmers of light which the text of the *Cours* sheds on this problem come much later – and almost incidentally – in the section devoted to Diachronic Linguistics: even then, they are no more than glimmers.

Whatever the answer, Saussure is clearly committed to an analytic methodology which poses at least two major questions concerning the analytic criteria for dealing with idiosynchronic systems. (1) By what criteria are *signifiés* to be identified? (2) By what criteria are *signifiés* to be located? The latter question is a question of 'location' by reference to the speech chain: for this is what the analyst's segmentation of examples such as *sižlaprã* involves. (Which segments of the sound sequence are the segments to which the *signifiés* α, β and γ correspond? The former question in practice resolves into two complementary questions: (1a) What are the meanings of the segments α', β', γ' (if they have any)? (1b) Are the meanings of α', β', γ' in this example the same as the meanings of the same phonic segments occurring elsewhere? These are the questions which have to be answerable if the atomic structure of discourse is to yield its secrets to the Saussurean analyst.

CHAPTER III

Identities, Realities, Values

Already in Chapter II the reader has been given various hints that matching up *signifiants* with their corresponding *signifiés* may be no straightforward matter. In Chapter III the nature of the difficulty is examined in greater depth. Saussure first emphasizes the point that in synchronic linguistics everything depends on the identification of linguistic units. This is not just a minor methodological issue: 'the fundamental concepts of static linguistics are directly based upon, or even merge with, the concept of a linguistic unit' ([150]). The whole of Chapter III is devoted to the demonstration of this proposition. The problem of linguistic units is broken down into three questions: A. What is a synchronic *identity*? B. What is a synchronic *reality*? C. What is a synchronic *value*?

The problem of synchronic identities is presented by Saussure as arising because occurrences of the same linguistic unit do not necessarily preclude either phonetic or semantic differences between one instantiation and the next. 'For example, we may hear in the course of a lecture several repetitions of the word *Messieurs!* We feel that in each case it is the same expression: and yet there are variations of delivery and intonation which give rise in the several instances to very noticeable phonic differences – differences as marked as those which in other cases serve to differentiate one word from another ... Furthermore, this feeling of identity persists in spite of the fact that from a semantic point of view too there is no absolute reduplication from one *Messieurs!* to the next' ([150-1]). The problem of identifying this 'sameness' is the same problem as that of defining the linguistic unit *messieurs*. A second example Saussure gives is that of the difference between the use of the verb *adopter* in *adopter une mode* ('to adopt a fashion') and *adopter un enfant* ('to adopt a child'), and between the use of the noun *fleur* in *la fleur du pommier* ('the flower of the apple-tree') and *la fleur de la noblesse* ('the flower of the nobility'). 'A word can express quite different ideas without seriously compromising its own identity' ([151]).

What kind of identity, then, is synchronic identity? Saussure proceeds to draw a distinction between formal or functional identity on the one hand, and material identity on the other. An example of formal or functional identity is the identity of the 8.45 train from Geneva to Paris ([151]), which is 'the same train' on different days in spite of the fact that locomotive, carriages and staff may be different. Another is the identity of a street, which survives demolition and reconstruction of its buildings ([151]). An example of material identity is that of a man's suit ([151]), which belongs to a particular individual, and will still be 'his' suit even if stolen. Linguistic identity, says Saussure, 'is not the kind of identity the suit has, but the kind of identity the train and the street have' ([152]). It is the task of the linguist to discover, in the case of linguistic units, on what factors this formal or functional identity is based.

Saussure's linguistic and non-linguistic examples here both call for comment. The linguistic examples cover two very different types of question. In the case of *Messieurs!* it is a question of the criteria for counting different utterances as utterances of the same word. In the case of *adopter* and *fleur* it is a question of the criteria for counting different usages as usages of the same word. The former problem is one nowadays commonly described in the terminology coined by C.S. Peirce (1931-58: 4.537, 2.245) as the problem of 'type-token' relations (Lyons 1977: 13ff; Hutton 1986). The latter problem is one of distinguishing between polysemy and homonymy (Ullmann 1962: 178ff.).

The distinction between linguistic types and linguistic tokens is classically exemplified by pointing out that a sentence such as *The cat sat on the mat* comprises in one sense six words, but in another sense only five, since the definite article occurs twice. In the sense in which only five words occur (which is the sense in which a dictionary lists words) the words are types. But in the sense in which six words occur (which is the sense a printer is interested in when calculating the length of a text) the words are tokens. Thus Saussure's lecturer will have uttered various non-identical tokens of the linguistic type *Messieurs!* The distinction between polysemy and homonymy, on the other hand, is usually construed as a matter of distinguishing between cases (i) in which the same word ('type') may be used in different senses, and cases (ii) in which two different words ('types') happen to be identically pronounced (or spelled). Thus the various related senses of the English noun *board* ('thin plank', 'tablet', 'table', 'food served at the table', etc.) would exemplify a typical case of polysemy; whereas the fact that the English word for an aquatic mammal of the Phocidae family and the English word for a piece of wax affixed to a letter are both pronounced and written identically (*seal*) would provide a typical case of homonymy (Ullmann 1962: 159). The difference between (i) and (ii) is problematic because, as Ullmann puts it, 'it is difficult to say in particular cases where polysemy ends and where homonymy begins' (Ullmann 1962: 178).

A preliminary query which therefore arises for the reader of the *Cours* is: does Saussure fail to see the difference between the type-token question and the polysemy-homonymy question? If we assume the answer to this to be 'yes', our estimate of Saussure's perspicacity as a linguistic theorist must be very low. But if we assume the answer to be 'no', then it presumably follows that Saussure here *deliberately* assimilates the two questions. The implications of this assimilation are worth thinking about. In the case of polysemy and homonymy it is notorious that individuals may differ as to whether they recognize 'the same word' in two divergent usages, even though they do not disagree as to the usages in question. Thus one important difference between the two problems of word-identity is that an appeal to speakers' intentions will not automatically yield comparable results. The lecturer who produces various pronunciations of *Messieurs!* presumably does intend to utter 'the same word' each time; whereas this will not necessarily be the case with different occurrences of *adopter* in the same lecture. By bringing together the type-token problem and the polysemy-homonymy problem, Saussure makes it clear that the criteria of synchronic identity which the linguist needs must simultaneously supply solutions to *both* problems, and that these criteria are *not* to be sought by reference to intentions or interpretations relating to particular speech acts on particular occasions. (These, for Saussure, would be factors belonging to the domain of *parole*, not of *langue*.)

This interpretation is borne out by the non-linguistic examples which follow. The 8.45 from Geneva to Paris corresponds to the word *messieurs*, which remains 'the same' in spite of the lecturer's variations of delivery. The passengers who travel regularly on the 8.45 doubtless intend to catch 'the same train' each time. But it is neither the invariance of the passengers' intentions, nor their possible failure to realize that the locomotive and coaches are different on different journeys, which either constitute or guarantee the identity of the train.

The case of the street demolished and rebuilt is a less happily chosen analogy. It runs the risk of suggesting that the 'sameness' here is one of diachronic continuity; but that would hardly be apposite as a Saussurean illustration of synchronic identity. The point here must be that, as in linguistic instances of polysemy and homonymy, recognizing or failing to recognize the buildings (because in fact they have changed) is irrelevant to the question of whether or not it is 'the same street'. Both 'the train' and 'the street' are, significantly, examples of social constructs. The identity of social constructs, for Saussure, remains unaffected both by material differences and by individuals' perception of – or failure to perceive – such differences.

The chapter next asks: 'What is a synchronic reality?' The question itself is significant: for it recognizes that systematic analysis alone is no guarantee that the realities of linguistic structure will be revealed. For

Saussure it remains an open question to what extent a systematic classification such as the traditional 'parts of speech' yields an inventory of the units of *la langue*: 'its division of words into nouns, verbs, adjectives, etc. does not correspond to any undeniable linguistic reality' ([152]). An even more telling example which Saussure might have chosen to make his point would have been the presentation adopted in the conventional dictionary. What the lexicographer provides, in effect, is an exhaustive inventory of lexemes, based on the principle of alphabetical order. Insofar as alphabetic spelling corresponds to the phonological structure of the words inventoried, this classification might claim to have a scientific basis. However, the principle of alphabetical order itself is completely extraneous to *la langue*; and, in any case, the relationships between words which derive from the order of constituent sounds are relationships of no linguistic significance whatever. In other words, systematic classifications, even when based on features of the linguistic units themselves, do not necessarily bring to light structural synchronic realities.

Finally comes the question: 'What is a synchronic value?' This will be discussed at greater length in Chapter IV. By way of giving a preliminary answer, Saussure reverts to the favourite analogy of chess, and compares the linguistic unit to a chess piece. The material properties of the individual chess piece do not matter: it can be replaced on the board by any other object, provided the substitute object is assigned the same value as the piece it replaces. *Mutatis mutandis*, the same applies to linguistic units. 'That is why in the final analysis the notion of value covers units, concrete entities and realities' ([154]).

CHAPTER IV

Linguistic Value

In the chapter on *La valeur linguistique* the question 'What is *la langue*?' returns once again to the centre of the discussion. It is without doubt the most important of the chapters on synchronic linguistics; and hence, arguably, the most important single chapter in the whole of the *Cours*. It attempts to resolve, although admittedly at a very general level and in a figurative rather than a practical way, the basic problem concerning *what* it is that synchronic analysis should be trying to analyse. It also includes some of the most celebrated of Saussure's analogies, and two of the most frequently cited of Saussure's epigrams: *dans la langue il n'y a que des différences* ([166]) and *la langue est une forme et non une substance* ([169]). These two dicta are often regarded, and not unreasonably, as summarizing the essentials of Saussure's linguistic teaching.

The notion of *valeur* is presented as the conceptual key to Saussure's solution of the problems of synchronic linguistics. But what exactly are linguistic *valeurs*? The chapter offers two remarkably contrasted approaches to defining the notion. One takes as its starting point the distinction between 'form' and 'substance', and attempts to explain *valeurs* as configurations of form. This approach relies for its exposition principally upon various versions of a geometrical metaphor; that of a 'plane' or 'surface'. The other approach attempts to explain *valeurs* in quasi-economic terms and relies principally on the metaphor of 'currency' or 'coinage'. To what extent these quite different approaches are successful will be discussed below.

The dichotomy between 'form' and 'substance' has a long history in European philosophy, of which the reader of the *Cours* is presumably expected to be aware. (Otherwise it would be baffling to know why those terms were chosen in order to express the ultimate linguistic truth that *la langue est une forme et non une substance*, neglect of which is responsible, according to Saussure, for 'all our mistakes of terminology, all our incorrect ways of designating things belonging to *la langue*'

([169]).) To be aware of that history, moreover, is to realize that Saussure's way of expressing that truth is itself an academic figure of speech. His version of the distinction between form and substance is not any of the classic philosophical versions; but there are parallels which are not fortuitous. It is a philosophical commonplace that form does not inhere in substance, even though it is embodied in substance. A chair does not exist apart from the wood, leather, etc. of which it is made; but those substantial components have to exist in a certain form in order to constitute a chair. It is the form which makes the chair a chair, and thereby distinguishes it from pieces of furniture which are not chairs. Analogously for Saussure, it is not the sound we articulate or the thought in our mind, or both, which make our utterance an utterance of the word *chaise*; but the way our utterance has a form determined by the synchronic system of values which we call 'the French language'.

Saussure's doctrine of form and substance is in certain respects quite unmysterious. At an elementary level, it can be read simply as a warning against confusing linguistic analysis (as formal analysis of *la langue*) with the study of 'substantially' related matters. Among these is phonetics. On this issue, §3 of the chapter is quite emphatic. 'It is impossible that sound, as a material element, should in itself be part of *la langue*' ([164]). Even more explicitly, the *signifiant* is 'not in essence phonetic'. It is not constituted by its *substance matérielle* but solely by the differences which distinguish it from other *signifiants* ([164]). Again, 'speech sounds are first and foremost entities which are contrastive, relative and negative' ([164]). A parallel caution is issued against confusing the *signifié* with an idea in the mind. Thus although the French word *mouton* and the English word *sheep* may 'have the same meaning' (by which Saussure presumably means that both may on appropriate occasions be used to express the same idea), their *valeurs* do not coincide, since in English *sheep* stands in contrast to *mutton*, whereas in French *mouton* covers both the animal (cf. *sheep*) and the meat of the animal (cf. *mutton*) ([160]). Thus far, Saussure is saying no more, *mutatis mutandis*, than many a philosopher might have said to the effect that a study of forms is not to be confused with a study of their material manifestations.

Where Saussure's distinction between linguistic form and substance takes on a metaphysics every bit as enigmatic as Plato's or Aristotle's is in the account Saussure gives of the dimension in which formal configurations are articulated. This dimension is described as a surface or, more exactly, an interface between the two substances of sound and thought. The meeting of these two substances is described as being like the contact between air and water: 'changes in atmospheric pressure break up the surface of the water into a series of divisions, i.e. waves. The correlation between thought and sound, and the union of the two, is like that' ([156]). Prior to this contact, Saussure claims, both planes are featureless and unstructured. The structure which results from their contact is *la langue*. The contact automatically gives rise to two 'planes' whose smooth expanses and corrugations match exactly: the atmospheric plane and the aquatic plane in the case of air and water, the conceptual plane and the phonetic plane in the case of language.

Puzzling as this metaphysics of 'contact' between thought and sound is, its evident purpose is to stress two ideas. One is that *la langue* does not belong to a third layer of substance. The other idea is that of the absolute interdependence and complementarity of the two 'faces' of the linguistic sign, *signifiant* and *signifié*. The relationship between them, in fact, is such that it makes no sense to think of separating the two. This idea is reinforced by a second 'surface' analogy: that of the recto and verso of a sheet of paper. 'Thought is one side of the sheet and sound the reverse side. Just as it is impossible to take a pair of scissors and cut one side of paper without at the same time cutting the other, so it is impossible in a language to isolate sound from thought or thought from sound' ([157]). Any attempt to separate the two will lead to 'pure psychology' or 'pure phonetics', not linguistics. In this version of the metaphor, the paper is 'substance' and the shape cut out is 'form'.

Valeurs, then, in terms of the 'surface' metaphor, are the formal thought-sound configurations which constitute *la langue*. They are the linguistic counterparts of the 'waves' at the interface where air makes contact with water, and the 'shapes' cut out by scissors in the sheet of paper. Saussure's dichotomy of form and substance has by this stage lost all connexion with its parent philosophical model (where it makes no sense at all to envisage form as the product of contact between different substances). As if to rescue the notion of *valeur* from this bleak metaphysical limbo, §2 proceeds to give a much more down-to-earth account, based on comparison with the more familiar notion of economic value.

Saussure's economic analogy assimilates the act of speech to a commercial transaction, and words to coins. For Saussure the *valeur* of a linguistic unit is like the value of a coin. The reader is told that in order to determine what a five-franc coin is worth, it is necessary to know two things: '(1) that the coin can be exchanged for a certain quantity of something different, e.g. bread, and (2) that its value can be compared with another value in the same system, e.g. that of a one-franc coin, or of a coin belonging to another system (e.g. a dollar).' Two such requirements are then identified in the linguistic case also. 'Similarly, a word can be substituted for something dissimilar: an idea. At the same time it can be compared to something of like nature: another word.' From this the reader is invited to draw the conclusion that the *valeur* of a word is 'not determined merely by that concept or meaning for which it is a token. It must also be assessed against comparable values, by contrasts with other words' ([160]). As in the case of the coin, then, the value is nothing concrete or tangible, but something determined by functional equivalences and differences within a system of exchange.

Whatever problems the reader may have with this account, they are at least of a different order from those encountered along the hypothetical interface between shapeless masses of sound and thought. In their own way, however, they are no less intractable. In the first place, Saussure's economic comparison simply does not work unless we are prepared to ignore the difference between coins as the objects actually exchanged in commercial transactions and coins as units in a system of currency: in other words, precisely the distinction which corresponds in the linguistic case to that between items of *parole* and items of *langue*. For whereas a five-franc coin in the former sense can be exchanged in a shop for five one-franc coins, or else for a certain quantity of – for example – bread, there is no sense at all in which 'the French five-franc coin' can be exchanged for either, whether in a baker's shop or anywhere else. This disanalogy is disastrous for Saussure's case, since what needs explication is the linguistic counterpart of the value of 'the French five-franc coin' (in other words, the unit of currency), and *not* the value of the coin in the shop. The value of the latter is simply whatever it will buy in that particular shop; or, alternatively, its various cash equivalents in small change from the till.

Worse still, there is no sense in which the Frenchman who utters the word *chaise* gets in exchange the idea of a chair (or an actual chair either). Linguistic transactions are in this respect not at all like commercial transactions. On the contrary the Frenchman who utters the word *chaise* is thereby not *receiving* anything, but *giving* his interlocutor certain information (which the interlocutor may or may not have asked for, and may or may not respond to by giving certain information in turn). If shops operated on this principle, it would revolutionize the world of commerce. However, even if we set these difficulties on one side, there remains a more important respect in which Saussure's analogy is contentious.

As Aarsleff notes (Aarsleff 1967: 233-4 fn.; 1982: 307-8), the application of the currency metaphor to language has a long history in the Western tradition, going back at least as far as Quintilian. Less remotely, where Saussure is concerned, the notion of linguistic value and its link with the economic concept of exchange is to be found in the work of Saussure's predecessor at the Ecole des Hautes Etudes, Michel Bréal. Bréal said that we treat words as bankers do securities, 'as if they were the coin itself, because they know that at a given moment they could exchange them for the coin' (Aarsleff 1982: 307-8). Saussure's use of the metaphor, however, differs from Bréal's, and in one crucial respect. The currency metaphor lends itself to two interpretations. For Saussure's purposes, it is quite essential to exclude the notion that the substance of which the coin is made is itself of value. A striking example of the alternative interpretation, which treats the coin itself as a piece of valuable metal, is provided earlier in the nineteenth century by its use in Bonald's *Législation primitive* (Bonald 1802: I, 99; Aarsleff 1967: 233-4 fn.). Bonald said of speech that it was 'to the commerce of thoughts what money is to the commerce of goods, a real expression of values, because it is of value itself.' What Bonald was attacking was the idea that speech is based upon conventional signs. That, he argued, would equate speech merely with the use of 'paper money': words would then be signs 'without value'. Bonald, who believed in the divine origin of language, goes on to say that paper can be made to designate anything we like, 'but it expresses nothing, except inasmuch as it can be cashed at will for money, which is the real expression of all values'. In other words, for Bonald we are confusing designation with expression if we think that words are just exchange counters. For Saussure, on the other hand, that is exactly what they are and no more.

Here we see, then, a conflict between two versions of the currency metaphor. In Bonald's terms, Saussure would be a theorist who believes that all money is paper money: or rather, a theorist who denies that there is any difference between paper money and gold coins. Precisely what a Saussurean economist could not accept would be the idea that a gold coin has an intrinsic value whereas a note has not, because it is 'only paper'. For it is of the essence of Saussurean structuralism that *valeur* derives not from the sign itself, but from the place which the sign occupies in the total system. It is indeed the system of values which determines the signs, and not the signs which come together to form a system.

Why does Saussure offer these two quite different analogical approaches to the definition of *valeur*? Readers interested in this question will not have failed to note that the dual approach is no unnecessary reduplication of labour. The two analogies do not cover exactly the same ground. In particular, the 'surface' analogy sits more comfortably with the Saussurean principle of arbitrariness, and to this the text of the *Cours* draws our attention. ('These observations clarify our earlier remarks about the arbitrary nature of the linguistic sign. Not only are the two areas which are linguistically linked vague and amorphous in themselves, but the process which selects one particular sound-sequence to correspond to one particular idea is entirely arbitrary' [157].) What this leaves unelucidated, however, is the sense in which values constitute a *system*; and it is here that the 'commercial' analogy offers a more attractive and readily understandable model.

This brings us back again, via a somewhat different route, to the dichotomy between 'form' and 'substance'. For Saussure, evidently, to suppose that the linguist is concerned with the analysis of linguistic signs as 'substance' would be like supposing that the economist is concerned with the study of coins. But granted that *valeurs* belong to the domain of form, we have now been given two rather different accounts of what 'form' is. The 'interface' analogy presupposes a state of affairs in which two intrinsically unstructured media (thought and sound) are brought into contact, and from this contact a system of values (*la langue*) somehow emerges. The 'commercial' analogy, on the contrary, presupposes a state of affairs in which two independently structured systems (commodities on the one hand and currency on the other) are brought into correlation, and the system of values (*la langue*) emerges from this correlation. Now either of these conceptualizations of a system of values may be independently comprehensible. What is quite incomprehensible, on the other hand, is how both could be combined. Is this simply an unfortunate clash of metaphors? That is one possibility. However, as will be argued below, there are also reasons for thinking that this clash of metaphors represents an unresolved contradiction in the Saussurean view of language.

CHAPTER V

Syntagmatic Relations and Associative Relations

Chapter V now distinguishes between two different orders of values. One order of values derives from relations into which signs enter as items linearly concatenated in discourse. Such concatenations are termed *syntagmas* by Saussure, and the corresponding relationships are 'syntagmatic' relationships. By occupying a linear place in a syntagma, 'any unit acquires its value simply in opposition to what precedes, or to what follows, or to both' ([171]). The other order of values is derived from the way signs are associated with one another in the memory, independently of the arrangements in which they occur in discourse. These connexions are 'associative relations'. The distinction between the two types of relation is assumed by Saussure to be absolute. 'Syntagmatic relations hold *in praesentia*. They hold between two or more terms co-present in a sequence. Associative relations, on the contrary, hold *in absentia*. They hold between terms constituting a mnemonic group' ([171]).

The first question which may arise in the reader's mind is whether the distinction between these two orders of values is as clear as the *Cours* seems to assume. For one obvious connexion which would lead to signs being associated in the memory is the connexion which derives from frequent occurrence in the same or similar syntagmas. In other words, Saussure seems to leave out of account the kind of relationship between words which Firth later christened 'collocation' (Firth 1951: 194ff.). Saussure's notion of associative relations does not cover this, for although according to §3 of this chapter the mind 'creates as many associative series as there are different relations' ([173]), the relations mentioned break down into similarities between *signifiants* and similarities between *signifiés* (or both). The kind of diagram provided on p.[175] for the associative series which contribute to the value of the word *enseignement* will hardly accommodate the kind of association which Firth identifies as linking the English word *time* with *saved, spent, wasted, frittered away, presses, flies* and *no.*

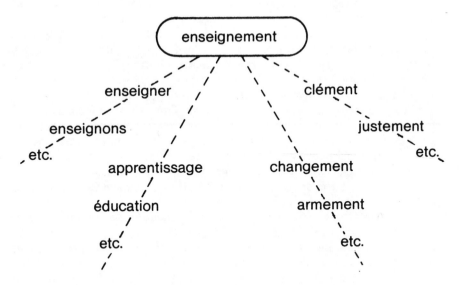

This flaw in Saussure's account is all the more glaring in that the *Cours* makes the point specifically on p.[173] that the establishment of linguistic 'types' depends on whether or not the relevant 'tokens' are to be found in sufficient abundance. In the discussion of syntagmas, the reader is told: 'Since there is nothing abstract in *la langue*, such types will not exist unless sufficiently numerous examples do indeed occur' ([173]). The 'occurrence' here referred to must be occurrence in *parole*: for in Saussurean terms there is no other domain of occurrence available. Once we accept this, however, there seems no reason to exclude the possibility that, say, the single word *fleece* may, in virtue of its occurrence in a well-known nursery rhyme, bring to mind the syntagma *Mary had a little lamb.*

Leaving on one side for the moment the issue of distinguishing Saussure's two orders of values, let us first consider the order of values deriving from syntagmatic relations. The disappointingly sparse remarks about syntagmatic relations in §§1-2, and the few examples given, leave a number of questions unanswered. First and foremost among these is: what exactly *is* a syntagmatic relation? In particular, is a syntagmatic relation defined solely and simply in terms of linearity? What the *Cours* says is that these relations are 'based on the linear character' of *la langue* ([170]); but what exactly that means is not altogether perspicuous. If syntagmatic relations are simply linear relations under another name, it seems doubtful whether they can be regarded as linguistic relations at all. If, for example, we take a syntagma consisting of 'noun + verb + adverb' occurring in that order, the *linear* relation between noun and verb will be exactly the same as the *linear* relation between verb and adverb: namely, a relation of immediate consecution in the chain. However, it is difficult to think of an example where the linguistic relation between noun and verb could plausibly be regarded as on a par, in the same syntagma, with the linguistic relation between verb and adverb. By contrast, it is very easy to think of examples in which such linguistic relations appear to be quite independent of linearity: *He arrived yesterday* vs. *Yesterday he arrived*. That is *prima facie* awkward for Saussure, since if the syntagmatic relationship is simply the *grammatical* relationship under another name, then syntagmatics *per se* has no basis in linearity. The linear order of units is only one possible means a language may utilize in order to signal grammatical relations.

A second question concerning syntagmatic relations is the question of exactly what is syntagmatically related to what. Given any syntagma (for example, the English syntagma *some unusually tall trees*), we may ask which of the constituent linguistic units is syntagmatically related to any of the others. Let us suppose, for purposes of this particular example, that a Saussurean analysis would recognize the following segmentations: (i) *unusually* = *un + usual + ly*, and (ii) *trees* = *tree + s*. The units *some* and *tall*, we will assume, are indivisible. On the basis of these assumptions, we may now ask such questions as the following. To which units is *some* syntagmatically related? Is *un* syntagmatically related to *tree*? Is *ly* syntagmatically related to *s*? Do any of the syntagmatic relations hold between a single unit and a combination of units, or are they all relations between single units?

On the last question the *Cours* gives some guidance. The reader is informed on p.[172] that 'it is not sufficient to consider merely the relation between the parts of a syntagma'. Thus in *contre tous* ('against all') and in *contremaître* ('overseer') account must be taken of the relation between the whole and the parts. The trouble is that this precept is easy enough to follow when a syntagma is clearly bi-partite, as in Saussure's two examples. It is more obscure in cases where a syntagma is complex; because the question which then arises is the question of how exactly the 'whole' in question divides into 'parts'. In the example *some unusually tall trees*, for instance, it is unclear whether the word *unusually* divides into *un + usually*, or into *unusual + ly*, or into *un + usual + ly*, or into all of these but in separate stages; and the question then focuses on which sequence the stages are to be taken in. Problems of this order Saussure never discusses, but they were extensively discussed by his transatlantic successors under the head of 'immediate constituency' (Bloomfield 1935:209f.). That discussion, however, did little to resolve the original question about syntagmatic relations. For problems of 'immediate constituent analysis' were discussed by

Bloomfield and others on the assumption that grammatical relations were in principle independent of linearity.

Comparable questions arise in respect of associative relations. If associative relations are simply, as the term suggests, relations of psychological association, it is legitimate to ask whether they are *eo ipso* linguistic relations at all. For presumably many terms may be associated in the mind for reasons other than linguistic reasons. But if this is so, then the need arises for a linguistic analyst to be able to distinguish between mnemonic groupings which have a linguistic basis and mnemonic groupings which do not. How to draw such a distinction is by no means obvious. Is the group *president-White House-Reagan* a group which generates values in the Saussurean sense? If not, how does one recognize the mnemonic groups which do?

Nowhere is the linguist who has already managed to analyse *sižlaprã* into constituent segments told explicitly how to proceed with the task of determining the *valeur* of each segment. This, nevertheless, is presumably the major part of the descriptive enterprise. If the analysis involves, as Saussure seems to imply, identifying all the relevant associative and syntagmatic relations, the task of describing even the single syntagma *sižlaprã* immediately assumes monumental proportions. One cannot, as Saussure has already made clear, 'suppose that a start could be made with individual signs, and a system constructed by putting them together' ([158]). On the contrary, in order to identify which sign in the system *prã* represents in *sižlaprã* it is presumably necessary to consider all those relationships *in absentia* and *in praesentia* which determine it. That will involve specifying which potentially available French forms *prã* displaces in this syntagma; and the number will clearly be very large indeed. It must be noted that there is no Saussurean short-cut via the use of traditional grammatical classifications ('verb', 'first person', 'present tense', 'singular', 'transitive', etc.), since from a Saussurean point of view the meaning of classificatory terms has first to be established by reference to the particular system of *valeurs* obtaining in the language in question. Nor, for the same reason, is there a ready-made system of semantic classifications available to specify the meaning of *prã*. Specifying that meaning will presumably involve considering how it alters if the syntagmatic context alters. For instance, by adding *avec moi* ('with me') or *demain* ('tomorrow') the range of interpretations is narrowed considerably from those available for *sižlaprã* in isolation. In short, the apparently simple task of giving an analysis of *sižlaprã* will turn out to be ultimately coextensive with the task of analysing very large areas of the grammatical structure of French. This must necessarily be so if, as Saussure consistently maintains, *la langue* is a system in which the parts do not exist independently of the whole.

CHAPTER VI

The Language Mechanism

The misgivings which the reader may have felt in Chapter V will no doubt surface again in Chapter VI. Here we are told straight away (as if it had been already established) that 'the whole set of phonetic and conceptual differences which constitute *la langue* are thus the product of two kinds of comparison, associative and syntagmatic' ([176]). (But are there, one asks, just *two* kinds of comparison involved? And if so, are the comparisons rightly contrasted as 'linear' vs. 'mnemonic'?) Misgivings of this order will not merely recur but be reinforced, and the concomitant analytic problems rendered even more acute. For it is not sufficient, apparently, to analyse *désireux* into two independent segments: stem *désir* + affix *eux*. The *valeur* of *désireux* is not a mere 'addition' of the *valeurs* of these two component units. It is a 'product' (*désir* × *eux*). 'The whole depends on the parts, and the parts depend on the whole. That is why the syntagmatic relation between part and whole is just as important as the syntagmatic relation between one part and another' ([177]).

If this is true of *désireux*, one supposes that it must also be true of any syntagma in which *désireux* itself occurs as a unit. For *désireux* cannot be the only combination in which the two units *désir* and *eux* occur. (If it were, it would not be recognized as a syntagma.) This expectation is corroborated explicitly on p.[177]. We are dealing here, the *Cours* tells us, with a 'general principle'. 'There are always larger units, composed of smaller units, with a relation of interdependence holding between both.'

Taken at face value, this must mean that Saussurean syntagmatics recognizes no maximum unit. This, again, is a theoretical position which appears to have quite alarming consequences for any Saussurean linguist attempting an enterprise of structural description. If, for example, the first line of Vergil's *Aeneid* stands in a relation of syntagmatic interdependence with all the following lines, that itself is problematic enough; for it means that a linguistic analysis of the first line will have to wait upon an analysis of the whole poem. But if there is no guarantee of being able to treat the whole poem as a maximum syntagmatic unit either (it being a mere accident of *parole* that Vergil did not incorporate it into an even longer Latin epic), then a syntagmatic analysis of *Arma virumque cano* becomes a research project which will require the services either of an endless supply of linguists, or at least of one or two blessed with indefinite longevity.

The only way Saussurean syntagmatics could have extricated its would-be practitioners from this predicament would have been by proposing – as a minimum – criteria by which *sižlaprã*, or any other sequence, might be recognized as incorporating consecutive signs or groups of signs between which there is *no* syntagmatic connexion. (Then it would be a purely contingent question as to whether in the *Aeneid*, as a matter of fact, it is possible to detect such internal syntagmatic boundaries or not.) However, as Martinet points out (Martinet 1974: 225-6), one thing the *Cours* fails to offer – and presumably deliberately – is any test for delimiting the syntagma by reference to linear succession, *even though* syntagmatic relations are said to be based on linearity. The theoretical implications of this reticence will be discussed at greater length below (p.233ff.).

The 'mechanism' of *la langue* to which the title of this chapter alludes is described more fully in §2. It consists of the simultaneous functioning in *la parole* of the 'dual system' of values, syntagmatic and associative. 'Our memory holds in store all the various complex types of syntagma, of every kind and length ... When someone says *marchons!*, he thinks unconsciously of various associative groups, at whose common intersection appears the syntagma *marchons!* This syntagma belongs to one series which includes *marche!*, *marchez!*, and *marchons!* stands in opposition to both as a form selected from this group. At the same time, it belongs to another series which includes *montons!*, *mangeons!*, etc., and represents a selection from this group as well. If the forms *marche!* and *marchez!* were to disappear from the language, leaving *marchons!* in isolation, certain oppositions would automatically collapse and *ipso facto* the value of *marchons!* would be different' ([179]).

The same must presumably hold for the lexical contrast between *marchons!* and *montons!*. Thus if there were no French verb *monter*, the value of *marchons!* would be different in yet another respect. This reinforces the conclusion the reader will already have drawn from the preceding chapter that even to identify the values of elements in a single syntagma demands a Saussurean descriptive enterprise of considerable magnitude, since the *mécanisme de la langue* makes it impossible to specify values in any other way than contrastively. Once again we are brought to face the descriptive consequences of the fact that *dans la langue il n'y a que des différences*.

The *Cours* then goes on to announce an important generalization. The mechanism just described operates at *all* levels of analysis. It applies not only 'to syntagmas and sentences of all types, even the most complex' ([179]) but also to phonetic units in the speech chain. 'If we take a hypothetical sequence like *anma*, the sound *m* is in syntagmatic opposition with the preceding and following sounds, and also in associative opposition with all the sounds the mind can suggest, as shown:' ([180])

$$a\ n\ m\ a$$
$$v$$
$$d$$

This generalization about the way the 'mechanism' of *la langue* operates has extensive implications, both theoretical and psycholinguistic. The psycholinguistic implications seem to be that for Saussure any utterance is to be viewed as the product of a simultaneous series of (unconscious?) choices by the speaker on a hierarchy of different levels. Presumably these choices cannot be independent of one another since some will determine others, although exactly what relations of dependence obtain in the 'mechanism' Saussure does not venture to state. The lowest level in the hierarchy is presented as being that of the choice of individual phonetic segments *a, n, m,* etc. Since the selection of any given phonetic segment (say *m*) can itself be treated as involving a selection of phonetic features – nasality, bilabiality, etc. – one may ask why there is not an even lower level of choice. The reason is not explicitly stated in the *Cours*, but seems to be that the level of discrete segments in the speech chain is the lowest level at which the utterance can be regarded as the product of a series of *single* syntagmatic selections from a succession of associative series presenting other possibilities. In other words, analysed in terms of distinctive features, the selection of *m* would have to be regarded not as a single choice, but a simultaneous multiple selection of the features of nasality, bilabiality, etc. from a total set of features. Since the individual choices involved at this level have no separate *linear* representation, they cannot be regarded as involving the operation of the 'language mechanism' as such (i.e. the 'dual system' of values). To put the point another way, for Saussure a phonetic choice such as 'nasal vs. oral' has no syntagmatic status. It is merely an 'abstraction' from the comparison of members of an associative series available at a certain point in the speech chain. In short, this is where the teeth of Saussure's principle of linearity bite at the level of identification of *signifiants*. Variations in pronunciation will be non-linguistic variations (that is, belong to *parole* and not to *langue*) if they do not implement different syntagmatic choices. This is what explains (as the *Cours* has already pointed out on pp.[164-5]) the tolerance of wide variations in pronunciation, such as those characteristic of French *r*.

So far, so good. The rest of the course is not such plain sailing. For if

Saussure is to apply to syntagmatic choices of segments in the speech chain (*a, n, m* ... etc.) the same rationale as applied to *marchons!*, he must presumably argue that the value of *m* in *anma* would be different if the associative oppositions were different (say *f, t*, as distinct from *v, d*). In other words, a necessary condition of linguistic identity for two occurrences of 'the same' *m* is that the same associative oppositions obtain. An *m* which is syntagmatically selected from the series *m, v, d* will not be the same as an *m* selected from the series *m, f, t*. Phonetic identity, therefore, does not guarantee linguistic identity. This is perfectly consistent with Saussure's claim that the *signifiant* is 'not in essence phonetic' ([164]): consequently, there is no paradox for Saussure in admitting the possibility that a language might be structured in such a way that one phonetic segment (say *m*) represented a variety of different units in the identification of *signifiants*. Here we see the opening up of a gap which was later widened by Saussure's successors into an axiomatic separation of phonetic analyses from phonemic analyses.

What happens, however, if simultaneously we apply the parallel rationale to the syntagmatic order of values in the case of *anma*? Or, for that matter, to *marchons!*? It must still be the case, presumably, that mere phonetic identity is no guarantee of linguistic identity; so if we take at face value Saussure's pronouncements about 'syntagmatic interdependences' ([176]) and treat every unit as acquiring its syntagmatic *valeur* simply 'in opposition to what precedes, or to what follows, or to both' ([171]), then there is no way to avoid the conclusion that the *m* of *anma* cannot be linguistically 'the same' as the *m* of, say, *amna*; for the syntagmatic oppositions are different, irrespective of the associative oppositions. On precisely the same reasoning, the final vowel of *marchons!* cannot represent 'the same' linguistic sign as the final vowel of *montons!* or of *mangeons!*

Why, it may be asked, should this conclusion in any way be a theoretical embarrassment to Saussure? The answer is that it need not be, if Saussure were willing to accept the principle that the operation of the *mécanisme de la langue* ensures that different linguistic contexts automatically entail different linguistic units. But that, clearly, is *not* one of the propositions which feature on the Saussurean programme for linguistics. On the contrary, the whole thrust of the Saussurean endeavour in linguistic theory is to establish that there *are* linguistic invariants identifiable across variations of context, that knowledge of these invariants is what makes it possible for members of a linguistic community to communicate with one another, and, finally, that these invariants are objectively available for 'scientific' description by the impartial observer (that is, the linguistic analyst).

A shadow of this theoretical embarrassment falls athwart the next section of the chapter, devoted to the distinction between 'absolute' and 'relative' arbitrariness. The terminology suggests a belated admission that the linguistic sign is after all not as arbitrary as Saussure's 'first principle' of linguistics would have us believe. *La langue*, Saussure tells us, 'is founded upon the irrational principle that the sign is arbitrary' ([182]). However, if this principle were applied without restriction, it would result, in 'utter chaos' ([182]). The mechanism of *la langue*, therefore, has to be viewed as 'a way of imposing a limitation on what is arbitrary' ([183]). 'There exists no language in which nothing at all is motivated. Even to conceive of such a language is impossible by definition' ([183]). Here Saussurean synchronic theory lies agonizing on a bed of nails of its own manufacture. Having accepted arbitrariness as a 'first principle', Saussure is at a loss to explain why this principle apparently fails to capture the most significant and characteristic properties of linguistic structure.

Saussure's problem here is that he has confused questions of arbitrariness with questions of systematicity. The confusion is evident in his own discussion ([181]) of the difference between *dix-neuf* ('nineteen') and *vingt* ('twenty'). According to Saussure, *vingt* is an example of a word which is absolutely arbitrary or 'unmotivated', while *dix-neuf* is only relatively so. This is presumably because although the elements *dix* ('ten') and *neuf* ('nine') are themselves arbitrary, their combination in *dix-neuf* is seen as corresponding 'rationally' to the meaning 'nineteen' (nineteen being the sum of ten and nine). To contrast *vingt* with *dix-neuf* on these grounds, however, is simply a muddle. For while it is true that *dix-neuf* goes with *dix, neuf, dix-huit, soixante-dix*, etc., it is also true that *vingt* goes with *vingt-deux, vingt-trois, quatre vingts*, etc.; and, on the other hand, it is no less arbitrary that *dix-neuf* should mean 'nineteen' (rather than 'ninety' or 'one hundred and nine') than that *vingt* should mean 'twenty'. Someone learning French has to learn that the word for 'nineteen' is *dix-neuf* (not *neuf-dix* or *neuze*), and this is on all fours with having to learn that the word for 'twenty' is *vingt* (not *dix-dix* or *deuzante*).

The muddle may not be unconnected with the fact that Saussurean linguistics gives no recognition to the tendency for systematicity (which Saussure misleadingly calls the *arbitraire relatif*) increasingly to dominate linguistic structure as one proceeds from smaller to larger syntagmatic combinations. It is on the whole more likely that a regularity of sentence construction will have no exceptions than that a declensional or conjugational regularity will have none, or a pattern of word formation. It may come as a surprise to the learner of French to find that the future tense of *voir* is *verrai*, but nothing like as much of a shock as it would be to find that although *Pierre voit Jean* meant 'Pierre sees Jean' and *Pierre voit André* meant 'Pierre sees André' the French for 'André sees Jean' was *Jean voit André*. Why this should be so Saussure never explains, and possibly his failure to do so arises from his confusion of systematicity with reduced arbitrariness. (The order 'subject-verb-object' is – in Saussure's sense – no less arbitrary than the order 'object-verb-subject'.)

To put the point in terms of one of Saussure's favourite analogies, it is important to see that the identity of shape between all pawns in a chess set belongs to a quite different order of facts from the fact that the particular shape in question is what it is. The systematicity in the design of the chess set has nothing at all to do with whether or not the shape of the pawn is arbitrary. These are not two 'degrees' of the same relationship, as the terms *arbitraire absolu* and *arbitraire relatif* unfortunately imply. Or, to switch to another of Saussure's analogies, the fact that the price of a loaf of bread is arbitrarily fixed at five francs does not mean that charging two and a half francs for half a loaf is only relatively arbitrary. This is simply a gross *non sequitur*. Both prices are equally arbitrary, and that arbitrariness has nothing to do with the systematicity which relates them. To concede as much in the case of language, however, would be tantamount to calling in question whether it makes sense to treat arbitrariness as the 'first principle' of linguistics. Saussure's distinction between *arbitraire absolu* and *arbitraire relatif* is a fudge, which serves the primary purpose of maintaining the 'first principle' at all costs.

CHAPTER VII

Grammar and its Subdivisions

Chapter VII embarks on a brief but trenchant criticism of misconceptions associated with the traditional notion of grammar. The first of these is a failure to see that grammatical relations cannot link items across linguistic systems. In other words, 'there is no such thing as "historical grammar" ' ([185]). What is commonly called thus is, for Saussure, simply diachronic linguistics. This conclusion is, clearly enough, simply a corollary of the Saussurean concept of a system of *valeurs*. Since French sentences and Latin sentences derive from different systems of *valeurs*, there is no way a grammatical relation could obtain between any item or feature of a French sentence and any item or feature of a Latin sentence.

Granted, however, that grammar is a matter of synchronic relations, the traditional subdivisions into morphology and syntax, together with the traditional exclusion of matters pertaining to vocabulary, are all highly questionable from a Saussurean point of view. The distinction between morphology and syntax is 'illusory' ([186]), since 'forms and functions are interdependent' ([186]). Similarly, the distinction between grammar and lexicology draws a distinction where none may exist: Latin *fio* ('I become') contrasts with *facio* ('I make') in just the same way as the passive form *dicor* ('I am said') with its active *dico* ('I say'). Thus it is clear that in a given language lexicological and syntactic devices may overlap. Grammar, Saussure concludes, 'needs a different basis, and a better one' ([187]).

It will come as no surprise to the reader that the better basis which Saussure proposes is a systematization based on the distinction between syntagmatic relations and associative relations. 'Everything in a given linguistic state should be explicable by reference to a theory of syntagmas and a theory of associations' ([188]). This will 'organize the whole subject-matter of grammar on its two natural axes' ([188]).

Brief as this chapter is, it sums up what for Saussure was one of the basic mistakes of nineteenth-century linguistics: that putting the adjective 'historical' in front of the traditional metalinguistic terms would automatically transpose a set of distinctions which had been originally drawn for pedagogic purposes into a valid, 'scientific' conceptual framework for the study of language.

CHAPTER VIII

Abstract Entities in Grammar

It is not until this final chapter in the section on Synchronic Linguistics that Saussure first makes explicit the proposal that synchronic linguistic analysis is ultimately to be judged by its correspondence with a psychological reality. 'One may say that the sum total of deliberate, systematic classifications set up by a grammarian studying a given state a-historically must coincide with the sum total of associations, conscious or unconscious, operative in speech' ([189]). Earlier Saussure had expressed misgivings about the correspondence between grammarians' classifications and linguistic realities ([153]), and here these misgivings are repeated. Saussure does not deny the reality of grammatical categories, parts of speech, etc. Such things 'exist in the language, but as abstract entities. It is difficult to study them, because one can never be sure whether the awareness of speakers of the language always goes as far as the grammarians' analyses' ([190]).

Worse still, the only detailed example which the *Cours* gives of the correspondence between an *entité abstraite* and a traditional grammatical classification, that of the Latin genitive, is not merely in itself a particularly awkward example from Saussure's point of view, but calls in question the whole rationale of including abstract entities in synchronic analysis. The case is badly argued to boot. What the *Cours* says is that although the three Latin genitive endings -*ī*, -*is* and -*ārum* afford no phonetic basis for constituting an associative series, they are nevertheless linked in the mind in virtue of an 'awareness of their common value'. Unfortunately, just the thing which -*ī*, -*is* and -*ārum* do *not* have is the same *valeur* in the Saussurean sense; for they stand in opposition in their respective paradigms to quite different sets of endings. So Saussure's claim that their 'common value' is 'sufficient to set up an association, in the absence of any material support' – and thus account for how 'the notion of "genitive", as such, takes its place in the language' as an abstract entity – is quite unfounded. Furthermore, the endings -*ī*, -*is* and -*ārum* do not even share a *signifié* in common (two of them being singular endings and one a plural). So it is actually far from clear on the basis of these considerations that Saussurean synchronic analysis offers any support for the recognition of the Latin genitive as an *entité abstraite*. On the contrary, the reader might have expected Saussure to cite this as an example where a traditional grammatical classification did *not* correspond to any real associative series in *la langue*.

However, even if the example were allowed to stand as valid, it would be quite unclear what purpose is served by recognizing 'Genitive' as a separate *entité abstraite* in Latin. For the various individual facts about the endings -*ī*, -*is*, -*ārum*, etc. will need to be stated separately in any case, each of these presumably being an independent *entité concrète* of the Latin language. What *else* there is to state over and above all this in a synchronic description is something of a mystery. In other words, we come face to face with a descriptive dilemma: *either* there is nothing more to say about the entity 'Genitive' other than what will already have been said about the entities -*ī*, -*is*, -*ārum*, etc., in which case the entity 'Genitive' is redundant, *or* there is more to say, in which case 'Genitive' cannot be an abstract entity after all (that is, it must be present in the *mécanisme de la langue* in some form which is not exhausted by its manifestations in the endings -*ī*, -*is*, -*ārum*.) Traditional grammar encounters no such dilemma, since for traditional purposes the classification 'Genitive' simply enables the grammarian to make generalizations about a whole class of Latin endings. Saussure, on the other hand, has specifically raised the question of how to determine when such classifications as this do and do not correspond to realities in *la langue*. So the one simple justification which synchronic analysis cannot accept is the straightforward grammarian's justification of descriptive utility.

Mutatis mutandis, what applies to the Latin 'Genitive' will apply to any putative candidate for recognition as an *entité abstraite*. Saussure is quite adamant that 'it would be a mistake to believe in the existence of an incorporeal syntax' ([191]). So it might be. But if we reject the notion of an incorporeal syntax, the role for abstract entities to play in *la langue* becomes immediately problematic, appearing to resolve itself always into a mere duplication of the role already played by particular concrete entities in particular cases. It is difficult to avoid the conclusion that Chapter VIII constitutes a major error of theoretical strategy on Saussure's part. The 'upper limit' for synchronic analysis of *la langue* would have been more satisfactorily drawn at a point corresponding symmetrically to its 'lower limit', which for Saussure, as has been made clear in Chapter VI, is the point determined by the limitations on single choices in the speech chain imposed by the phonological structure of the language. At the level of signs and sign combinations, the corresponding point has already been defined – even though evasively – by Saussure; it is the syntagma 'constructed on a regular pattern' ([173]). In other words, it is the point at which the sequence of syntagmatic combinations is not a choice freely determined by the individual speaker, but a choice imposed upon the speaker by *la langue*. However difficult a precise determination of that boundary might prove, it would supply a theoretically more elegant solution for Saussure than belatedly opening up the Pandora's box of *entités abstraites*. A wiser Saussure – or perhaps wiser editors – would have kept that lid firmly closed.

PART THREE
Diachronic Linguistics

CHAPTER I

General Observations

Saussure's discussion of diachronic linguistics begins by reiterating the conclusion already stated at the end of Part One concerning the scope of the subject. Unlike synchronic linguistics, it will study relations between 'successive terms substituted one for another over a period of time'. The formulation given on p.[193] makes an interesting comparison with that presented on p.[140]. The later statement drops the reference to 'systems' and to the 'collective consciousness'. It retains, however, the notion of 'substitution'.

This notion is clearly the keystone of diachronic linguistics. It raises a number of theoretical questions which are not at all obvious as long as attention remains focussed upon specific examples of linguistic change. The reader might perhaps have expected that the heading *Généralités* would have provided just the peg on which to hang a theoretical discussion of diachronic substitution in general. But neither here nor anywhere else in the *Cours* is a definition of the relation given. The lacuna is significant: just how significant will not emerge until later. Saussure initially appears to take for granted (i) that there exists a relationship of diachronic substitution, and (ii) that instances of this relationship are recognizable from the observational vantage point of historical linguistics.

Instead of plunging straight away into an examination of these assumptions, Chapter I offers a few rather banal Heracleitean maxims (to the effect that languages are constantly in a process of change, in spite of the appearance of stability which may be conveyed by a literary language ([193-4])), and a brief typological prospectus which predictably includes sound changes, changes of meaning and changes of grammar. However, the prospectus is accompanied by warnings against confusing the study of a change with the study of its consequences ([195]), and even vaguer warnings about the problems which arise because the evolution of one particular item 'splits up into a number of separate things' ([196]). This is as near as the chapter comes to acknowledging that there may be any general theoretical problem about the notion of diachronic substitution lying in wait.

CHAPTER II

Sound Changes

Without further ado, the *Cours* embarks on the topic of sound change. The examples it cites hold no surprises for a student of Indo-European comparative philology: that is part of the expository strategy. Where Saussure scores points is by showing that these familiar examples are misunderstood unless recast in terms of the Saussurean dichotomy between synchrony and diachrony. Thus Verner's law, for instance, is mis-stated in the form 'in Germanic *þ* in non-initial position became *đ* if followed by the stress' because that formulation obscures (i) the fact that *þ* tended to voice in medial position, and (ii) that the cases in which this tendency was checked are cases in which the stress fell on the preceding vowel. So, as Saussure says, diachronically 'everything is the other way round' ([200-1]). This is the classic case of a misrepresentation which results from confusing the synchronic and diachronic perspectives. The condemned formulation of Verner's law conflates a synchronic result (the eventual voiced-voiceless distribution) with a diachronic process (the voicing).

More contentious is Saussure's general proposal to replace the traditional distinction between 'absolute' and 'conditioned' sound changes by a distinction between 'spontaneous' and 'combinative' changes. It is difficult to see that this is more than a terminological quibble. 'If a sound change is combinative', argues Saussure, 'it is always conditioned. But if it is spontaneous, it is not necessarily unconditioned' ([200]). The reason given for saying this is that a sound change may be conditioned negatively by the *absence* of certain factors relevant to change. But this is logic which simply amounts to defining all change as conditioned, including cases of 'zero change'. No more convincing is Saussure's account of 'spontaneous' phonetic developments. These, which include cases of zero change, are assumed to be produced by some 'internal cause' in the sound itself. What that internal cause was in any particular case we may have no means of knowing. So, for example, the development of Latin *qu* from Indo-European k_2, except when followed by *o* or *u*, Saussure claims was spontaneous, i.e. due to some internal cause in k_2; but this internal cause was presumably prevented from operating by the presence of following *o* or *u*. Since the internal cause remains unidentified, the mechanism of its alleged inhibition by certain following vowels must likewise remain unidentified. But then one wonders what has been explained by postulating an 'internal cause' in the first place.

Some aspects of what must nowadays strike the reader as gaps or deficiencies in Saussure's historical phonetics are not so much due to Saussure's own shortcomings as to the 'state of the art' in his day. Saussure's generation had never seen a sound spectrogram, and the sociolinguistic study of speech variation was in its infancy. The entire approach to sound change in the *Cours* reflects the preoccupations of an era in which the principal evidence on which such discussions were based was the orthographic evidence supplied by changes in spelling over time, attested in the documentary legacy of earlier centuries. That having been said, however, it is none the less true that Saussure's treatment of sound change seems conservative, and marked by the kind of rigidity often associated with the Neogrammarians. He evinces no inclination to challenge the doctrine that sound changes are 'exceptionless'. He insists again, as earlier in the *Cours* ([132]), that sound changes are particular, isolated events: they affect sounds as such, not words ([198]). He never suggests that the unit of change in some cases might be the cluster or the syllable, rather than the individual consonant or vowel. To this extent, his historical phonetics is entirely 'alphabetic'. (That does not preclude, however, a carpet-pulling suggestion later in Part III that perhaps we do not understand what the units of diachronic development are.)

Saussure does not even consider here the possibility that the historical fate of a particular sound might depend in part on its morphological function, even though this is just the kind of point a structuralist might perhaps be expected to make. But the reason for Saussure's reluctance to admit this is not difficult to see. To concede that a sound might be treated differently over time in different words, depending on whether it had a morphological function or not, would be tantamount to granting in some sense the reality of 'historical grammar'; and this Saussure is at pains to deny. His position is that grammatical units and relations have no history, in the sense that they cannot be passed on intact from one synchronic system to its successor. To allow morphological function as a possible conditioning factor in historical phonetics would for Saussure be a denial of the basic dichotomy between synchrony and diachrony.

Similarly, when the discussion moves on to general reasons ([202-8]) for the phenomenon of sound change (as distinct from particular types of change), Saussure goes through all the factors commonly adduced (race, climate, the 'law of least effort', conditions of learning, political circumstances, substratum influences, fashion), but conspicuously fails to add to this traditional list the one contribution which might have been expected from the founder of linguistic structuralism. He does not, in other words, argue that the structure of the linguistic system itself may promote or inhibit sound change. (This contribution to the subject was posthumously made on his behalf by others.)

The point of interest here is that the Saussure of the *Cours* is clearly willing to admit that the structure of the system may affect certain features of pronunciation (as is evident from the explanation ([165]) of the latitude of articulation allowed for French *r*). But features of pronunciation in this sense are features of *parole*. The step Saussure never takes is the step the Prague school phonologists later took, which involves extending the same way of thinking to sound change itself.

Again, there is for Saussure a major theoretical obstacle. Structural explanations of change have to assume that 'the system' as such evolves. The reason why this is unacceptable is that it automatically bridges the basic dichotomy between synchronic and diachronic. Hence the Saussurean preference for siding on this issue with the Neogrammarians and upholding the doctrine that sound changes operate 'blindly'. (The word *aveugle* is used on p.[209] in a context which leaves no doubt about its theoretical implications.) This is another example of the way in which the Saussurean demands of theoretical consistency to some extent block the explanatory potential of the theory itself.

The 'blindness' of sound change is in turn explained by reference to the arbitrary nature of the linguistic sign ([208]). That is why the effect of a sound change is 'unrestricted and incalculable' ([209]). If it were otherwise, then again 'sound change would merge with synchronic fact, and that is intrinsically impossible' ([209]). The reader will note that by this point in the *Cours* theoretical difficulties have become intrinsic impossibilities.

CHAPTER III

Grammatical Consequences of Phonetic Evolution

Chapter III occupies a particularly important place in the Saussurean argument, since it is by now apparent that a dichotomy between synchronic and diachronic has as one of its major corollaries the necessity of a clear differentiation between (i) a sound change and (ii) its grammatical (i.e. synchronic) consequences. If this differentiation should prove difficult or problematic in many cases, then much of the support for the basic dichotomy would be lost, and the whole edifice of Saussurean theory immeasurably weakened. A great deal therefore depends on the examples which this chapter supplies. There are several dozen of them, and the great majority are taken from French and German. This is no coincidence, since everything here assumes that the reader will accept the examples as intuitively plausible. The *Cours* simply presents them, offering virtually no evidence to show that they actually corroborate Saussure's case.

The main consequences of sound change, according to this chapter, are the disruption of grammatical links between signs ([211-12]), the obliteration of word-composition ([212-13]) and the establishment of alternations ([215] ff.). The case is flawed, unfortunately, by pervasive equivocation over the notion of 'consequence' itself, which is never clarified. The reader is treated like someone willing to suppose that if an earthquake occasioning widespread damage is followed by the implementation of an extensive rebuilding programme, that shows the rebuilding to be a consequence of the earthquake. There is no awareness that the establishment of a consequential relation might involve rather more than comparing a prior state of affairs with a subsequent state of affairs and then, in effect, inviting everyone to infer a consequential relation between them. Rather, the assumption seems to be that a consequential relation can be simply *exhibited* by juxtaposing the two states of affairs thus allegedly connected. What this amounts to is a licence to use the notion 'consequence' in virtually any instance where there is a diachronic connexion.

The difficulty here is that a theorist in Saussure's position cannot afford the luxury of using the notion 'consequence' in quite this generous way, since the account of associative relations already offered in Part Two makes it clear that in *la langue* there are no necessary phonetic conditions for the establishment of an associative series. The only phonetic conditions are sufficient conditions ([174]). In other words, the *Cours* has already supplied the reason for concluding that associative series are in principle immune from disruption by phonetic change unless phonetic change actually obliterates the distinctions between the *signifiants* in question. But this is certainly not the case in the examples cited here in §§1-2.

Thus, for example, it is question-begging to claim ([212]) that the Latin contrast between a Nominative *comes* and an Accusative *comitem* 'becomes' (*devient*) in Old French, as the result of sound change, a contrast between *cuens* (Nominative) and *comte* (Oblique), and thus *le rapport normal qui existait entre deux formes fléchies d'un même mot* ([212]) was broken. Had any comparative philologist said this, Saussure would have been the first to complain about the conflation of synchronic and diachronic perspectives. For according to Saussure ([134]f.) there is no 'panchronic' point of view from which it would be possible to identify a *rapport normal* between inflected forms of 'the same word'. Furthermore, to compare the Latin case system (of six possible oppositions) to the Old French case system (of only two) is an exercise which students convinced by Parts One and Two of the *Cours* ought by now to reject out of hand; for the *valeurs* are clearly not comparable. Nor does the *Cours* offer any evidence that in the twelfth century those who spoke, wrote or read Old French had any difficulty at all in recognizing *cuens* as the 'Nominative Singular' of *comte* (whatever in psycholinguistic terms that might involve). In short, what the example tacitly appeals to is the fact that 'we' (i.e. twentieth-century students of Old French) find *cuens* an 'unpredictable' Nominative Singular form, given 'our' expectations about relationships between Nominatives, Obliques, etc.

It is likewise question-begging to cite the French example *brebis* vs. *berger* as an instance of the obliteration of word-composition, by comparing it with Latin *vervex* vs. *vervecarius*. 'This separation,' says Saussure, 'naturally has an effect upon the value of the terms: hence in some local patois *berger* becomes specialized to mean "oxherd" ' ([211]). Here at least there is an attempt to back up the claim that a connexion between *brebis* and *berger* is lacking, by citing a semantic development in French patois. The trouble is that it assumes in advance what needed to be demonstrated; namely, that the semantic specialization is a consequence of the failure to connect *berger* and *brebis*. The fact that no such specialization has occurred in other French dialects, or in the literary language, evidently does not count for Saussure as significant. What damages Saussure's case in this and similar instances is that the *Cours* dodges the question of whether associative relations are relations of which the speakers are aware or not. It avoids discussing whether it might be possible for some members of a linguistic community consciously to recognize relationships which other members failed to recognize, and whether this would make any difference to their respective systems of *valeurs*. As a result, it is never quite clear what statements about the consequences of sound change mean in psycholinguistic terms. If the assumption is that speakers can operate grammatical systems of which they are not consciously aware *at all*, then it becomes difficult to see how it would be possible to prove that *brebis* and *berger* are *not* treated as derivationally connected. For at some inaccessible level of 'mental representation' they might be. So there is the possibility that the claim that sound change disrupted the grammatical relations might be quite simply wrong. If, on the other hand, the claim is that speakers of French do not consciously recognize in the relationship between *brebis* and *berger* the same relationship which obtains between *vervex* and *vervecarius*, the reply to that is presumably – as Saussure has given ample reason for maintaining – that this would be by definition out of the question. Even if speakers of French know Latin, the two grammatical systems are not linguistically comparable. This leaves the problem of establishing consequential relations between sound change and grammatical system in a theoretical deadlock. Saussure can hardly afford to accept the proposition that *any* sound change, since it must affect *some* associative series, thereby automatically disrupts *some* grammatical relation to *some* extent. For then indeed his attempt to drive a wedge between diachronic and synchronic facts would be on a hiding to nothing. The terms 'sound change' and 'grammatical change' would become interdefinable and it would be possible in theory to have a synchronic system which could be defined by reference to its immediate predecessor plus one sound change. Diachronic description would thus become simply an alternative way of stating facts about a succession of synchronic states.

A section of particular interest in this chapter is the one devoted to arguing that there are no phonetic doublets ([214-15]). Why, the reader may ask, does Saussure bother to argue that? Again, the answer is that otherwise (i.e. if there *are* phonetic doublets) the separation of synchrony from diachrony is palpably threatened. For if an *état de langue* includes phonetic doublets, this amounts to conceding that it may be impossible to determine whether a sound change has taken place or not. (That is to say, the 'earlier' form and the 'later' form coexist.) So again the diachronic fact merges with the synchronic fact. A way of dealing with all conceivable counterexamples is here proposed: namely, to dismiss them as 'borrowings' from a different system. Thus even if speakers manifestly alternate between two different pronunciations of a given word, this can always be explained by treating one of the pronunciations as a borrowing from a neighbouring dialect. Here emerges the theoretical significance of the proviso laid down much earlier in the *Cours* ([128]) that the distinction between idiosynchronic systems must be applied not only to languages but to dialects and subdialects. (Otherwise the 'borrowing' explanation would not hold water.)

CHAPTER IV

Analogy

Analogy for Saussure is the force which 'counterbalances' ([221]) the disruptive effects of sound change in the linguistic system. An analogical form is one 'made in the image of one or more other forms in accordance with a fixed rule' ([221]). Analogy 'works in favour of regularity and tends to unify formational and flexional processes' ([222]), but does not always succeed in eliminating irregularities. Thus it is sometimes 'capricious'; since 'it is impossible to say in advance how far imitation of a model would extend, or which patterns are destined to provoke it' ([222]). By emphasizing the 'capricious' nature of analogy, Saussure makes it clear that both the major forces operative in linguistic evolution (sound change and analogy) produce unpredictable results.

§2 of the chapter is devoted to the proposition that 'analogies are not changes'. According to Saussure, the 'illusion of analogical change' ([226]) is created simply by the fact that over a period of time a new form ousts an old form. Thus the old Latin nominative *honōs* was eventually replaced by *honor*, analogically formed on the basis of *honōrem, orator, oratōrem*, etc. Consequently, claims Saussure, it is a mistake to say that in Latin *honōs* 'changed' to *honor*: *honōs* did not change (it simply disappeared), while *honor* was not a changed form of anything but a new creation. What is the reader to make of this curiously strained reasoning?

The argument depends, clearly, on another terminological manoeuvre: in effect, the term 'change' is tacitly equated with 'phonetic change'. Once that is accepted, then it follows that any development which is not a phonetic change is not a change *tout court*. Hence there are no analogical changes. But why go to the trouble of such terminological contortion at all? The explanation is once again to be sought in the theoretical rigidity of the way the *Cours* applies the separation of synchronic from diachronic facts. It appears to take for granted that to admit the possibility of 'analogical change' would be tantamount to conceding that the morphological system itself evolves. This is Saussurean heresy, since it would mean that systematicity extends over time from one synchronic state to the next. Such 'changes', therefore, have to be dismissed as illusory (unlike phonetic changes, which can be allowed to count as 'real' because they merely disrupt existing systems).

In §3, it becomes even more evident that Saussure will simply refuse to admit that analogy could in any way be a diachronic phenomenon, even if this means redefining the concept 'change'. For analogy is needed as the mainspring of the Saussurean mechanism of grammar. It is what holds the parts of the system together. Analogy involves 'awareness and grasp of relations between forms' ([226]). By insisting on the exclusion of analogy from diachronic processes, Saussure is now in a position to tie up in a theoretically elegant way one loose end which has so far been left dangling in his account of linguistic evolution: how does the dichotomy between synchronic and diachronic relate to the no less important dichotomy between *langue* and *parole*? The answer has already been hinted at much earlier: *tout ce qui est diachronique dans la langue ne l'est que par la parole* ([138]). But only now does it become clear exactly how that interconnexion works. Analogy, which involves 'awareness and grasp of relations between forms', is a psychological function of the individual. Hence it is the individual who alone can create new forms ([227]). Whether the individual's analogical innovations will gain eventual acceptance in *la langue* is a separate matter: some may but others may not. Thus *parole* provides, as it were, a pool of individual analogical creations from which *la langue* may then choose.

Here the *Cours* is meticulously careful to distinguish two factors in the process of analogical creation: '(1) grasping the relation which connects the sponsoring forms, and (2) the result suggested by this comparison, i.e. the form improvised by the speaker to express his thought' ([227]). The latter alone, we are told, belongs to *parole*. Why insist on this? The reason is doubtless that without this distinction the explanation of the role of the individual runs the risk of suggesting that the grammatical system itself is a psychological creation of the individual. In other words, it cannot be admitted that the individual is free to imagine grammatical relations which just do not exist. *La langue* has to be a supra-individual reality. Hence stage (1) in the analogical process has to be removed from the domain of *parole*.

What this leaves unexplained is the sense in which, according to the definition given earlier in the chapter, analogical forms are made 'in accordance with a fixed rule' ([221]). Individual speakers, presumably, do not have the authority to invent fixed rules. But if the fixed rules are already part of *la langue*, that appears to make the individual's role in analogical creation superfluous. (For then all individuals will follow the fixed rule, and the analogical form will be automatically part of *la langue*.) Furthermore, a corollary of the fixed rule will presumably be that different individuals are not free to create different analogical innovations (given the same set of sponsoring forms). But if that is the case, then the reader begins to wonder in what sense the individual was ever free to create the analogical form in the first place. The chapter see-saws, as if the author feared that his explanation of analogy might perhaps be read as attributing *too much* freedom of linguistic action to the individual, and felt it necessary to reassert the restrictions imposed on that freedom by the collective institution.

This impression may be reinforced by Saussure's observations about the extent to which analogical possibilities are already inherent in *la langue* before the 'appearance' ([227]) of any new form. 'The continual activity of language (*langage*) in analysing the units already provided contains in itself not only all possibilities of speaking in conformity with usage, but also all possibilities of analogical formation' ([227]). This statement, which has attracted little attention from commentators, is one of the most theoretically crucial in the whole of the *Cours*. It explicitly assimilates the language-user's capacity for analogical innovation to the capacity for producing the ordinary syntagmatic structures of discourse. In other words, both are seen as creative procedures, which go beyond mere repetition or imitation, even though the patterns on which the creativity is based are already laid down in the language. The source of both is described as being *l'activité continuelle du langage*, a phrase not previously encountered in the text of the *Cours*. What does it mean? The activity envisaged is an analytic activity, since it involves the decomposition of linguistic units. It is evidently the activity of that *faculté de constituer une langue* ([26]) which Saussure claims to be one of the natural human faculties.

The chapter goes on to suggest ([228]) that in every language there is a distinction to be drawn between analogically 'productive' forms and analogically 'sterile' forms. The 'sterile' forms turn out to be those which are unanalysable (e.g. *magasin* 'shop', *arbre* 'tree', *racine* 'root'). This distinction between sterile and productive forms is explicitly linked to the distinction previously drawn between 'lexicological' and 'grammatical' languages ([183]). Chinese, on this scale, turns out to be an archetypically lexicological language, since most of its words are monosyllabic and (therefore?) unsegmentable ([228]). Esperanto, on the other hand, turns out to be maximally grammatical ([228]). Saussure is here revamping a well-known nineteenth-century typology of languages. This typology (Robins 1980: 250ff.) recognized a classification of languages into (i) isolating (or 'analytic'), (ii) agglutinative, and (iii) fusional (or 'inflecting'). What Saussure proposes, in effect, is a reinterpretation of this tripartite classification by collapsing the latter two categories, on the ground that in both of them the *arbitraire relatif* is favoured over the *arbitraire absolu*. However, to distinguish between 'sterile' and 'productive' forms is a particularly unhappy distinction to draw for a theorist who takes Saussure's view of linguistic structure. Sterility or productivity, for a Saussurean, can hardly reside in individual forms. What matters, as the preceding discussion of analogy in the *Cours* has made abundantly clear, is not the individual forms but the patterns of relationship between them. Why, then, is analogical potential or lack of potential attributed to the forms themselves? In the context of this chapter of the *Cours*, the answer seems to be that this is another way of emphasizing the point that the role of the individual in analogical creation is limited to actualizing a potential already present and embodied in the material supplied by *la langue*.

Finally, taking up the explanation of analogy in terms of proportions of the form $a : b = c : x$, Saussure suggests that this can be interpreted in two different ways, each of which reflects the 'predominant tendency' in different languages. One interpretation is typical of the descriptive methods of the Hindu grammarians, and the other of European grammarians. The former involves analysis and recombination of the elements present in the forms a, b and c of the proportion. The latter takes recognition of the proportionality itself to be a sufficient explanation for the generation of the missing x. 'In that way,' Saussure says, 'there is no need to credit the speaker with a complicated operation too much like the conscious analysis of the grammarian' ([229]). The observation is revealing. It shows that Saussure, who favours the 'analytic' interpretation of the proportion, evidently does not see attributing complicated analyses to individual language-users as something to be avoided. This ties in with the remarks on p.[189], where an equation is posited between the conscious classifications of the grammarian and the 'conscious or unconscious' associative series in the mind of the language-user. It appears, then, that a speaker is normally able, according to Saussure, to produce analogical forms without recognizing, understanding or reflecting upon the operations involved. Unfortunately, if this is so it leaves Saussure vulnerable to the objection that he has failed to show – and indeed cannot show, by his own account – that the proportional explanation provides the correct explanation of analogy in the first place; and still less can he show that the 'analytic' interpretation of the proportion is the correct one. Nevertheless, making the work of producing analogical forms in *parole* unconscious is another way of diminishing the contribution which the individual makes and of reaffirming the importance of the contribution made by *la langue*.

This chapter on analogy, therefore, shows Saussure grappling with the problem of attributing too much or too little to the individual. Both extremes are uncongenial to Saussurean theory. If the individual is allowed too much analogical freedom, this threatens the whole concept of *la langue* 'as a collective institution. On the other hand, if individual freedom is too narrowly circumscribed, this not only makes it appear (as on p.[227]) that individuals can only choose to initiate historical innovations which have already been determined in advance by *la langue*, but even calls in question whether a language ever changes at all (as distinct from implementing at various times various possible – but already inbuilt – potentialities). Why are these extremes uncongenial from a Saussurean point of view? Because in one case *langue* merges with *parole*, and in the other case synchrony merges with diachrony.

CHAPTER V

Analogy and Evolution

The beginning of Chapter V clears up one point which might have been left in doubt in the reader's mind from the discussion of analogy which the *Cours* has presented in the immediately preceding pages. This concerns the difference between the first appearance of an analogical form and its subsequent generalization. The two phenomena, for Saussure, evidently have quite different explanations. The former is due to the operations of a mental process involving proportionality (as described on p. [225]ff.). The latter, however, is due simply to imitation. An initial improvisation by one individual is imitated by others until it becomes accepted usage ([231]).

This throws a certain amount of light on the earlier definition of analogy ([221]) which referred to formation 'according to a fixed rule'. It now becomes apparent that this was *not* intended to suggest spontaneous implementation of some existing rule of analogical formation throughout the membership of a given linguistic community. In other words, the generalization of a successful analogy and its establishment in *la langue* here emerges clearly as a contingent – i.e. historical – process, and furthermore one in which 'external' linguistic factors (in the sense defined on p.[40]ff.) must play a key role. For the chances of the successful spread of an analogical form will presumably depend on the communicational contacts between its original improviser and its potential imitators, together with the sociolinguistic implications of these contacts. What might determine the diffusion of an analogical innovation, however, Saussure discusses only later, and then in very general terms, in Part IV of the *Cours*. The fate of an analogical innovation is not distinguished in any special way from the fate of other innovations. To this extent, there might appear to be a sizeable gap in the Saussurean account of analogy as it affects linguistic evolution.

In spite of this lacuna, Chapter V represents a theoretical triumph for Saussurean linguistics. For it exposes one of the major deficiencies of nineteenth-century historical linguistics and offers a solution. The deficiency in question resides in the fact that nineteenth-century historical linguistics had tacitly equated the study of linguistic evolution with the study of linguistic *change*. Linguistic *stability* was in practice ignored, and no explanation offered other than in terms of 'external' factors (political conditions, geographical isolation, the influence of education, etc.). Saussure, on the other hand, emerges from the *Cours* as a theorist who is fully aware that absence of change stands in as much need of theoretical explanation as change. It is all the more incumbent upon him to provide such an explanation as a theorist who proclaims that the linguistic sign is arbitrary (and hence intrinsically open to change, as already conceded on pp. [110-11]).

The brilliance of the Saussurean solution is that it is able to explain *both* change *and* absence of change by appeal to the same factor. Analogy, which is responsible for the appearance of new forms, is at the same time responsible for the conservation of old ones. 'Forms are kept because they are ceaselessly remade analogically' ([236]). This is the other – and less obvious – result of the same *activité continuelle du langage* which the human linguistic faculty sponsors.

CHAPTER VI

Popular Etymology

In spite of its title, this chapter offers no detailed account of popular etymology. Its sole purpose is to argue that popular etymology is not the same thing as analogy. The interesting question, again, is why there is any need to argue this: for in practice, as the *Cours* admits ([283]), the results are often similar. Commentators have pointed out that Saussure's editors subsequently toned down the dismissal of popular etymology by removing the description of it as a 'pathological phenomenon' from the text of the second (1922) edition (Ullman 1962: 103; de Mauro 1972: 473 n.286). It has been suggested that the great interest shown by linguists in the study of popular etymology made its condemnation as 'pathological' unacceptable: but the possible reasons for the editors' belated censorship of the term are not what is at issue here.

Popular etymology is an awkward nut for Saussurean linguistics to crack for two reasons. One is that it appears to be, as Vendryes later put it, *une réaction contre l'arbitraire du signe* (Vendryes 1952: 6); and since examples are widespread and well attested, their existence might be taken as undermining Saussure's 'first principle' of linguistics. When the *Cours* dealt with possible objections to that principle ([101-23]), however, popular etymology was not among them. Nor in this chapter is popular etymology defended as another manifestation of the effort to replace *l'arbitraire absolu* by *l'arbitraire relatif*. The problem is that although popular etymologies, as Saussure concedes, look like attempts to 'make sense' of words which are unfamiliar or poorly understood, the resultant innovations sometimes make just as little sense as the original forms, or even less. Seen as rationalizations of the arbitrary, popular etymologies in many cases appear to be either incomplete or misguided rationalizations. So it is difficult in such cases for a theorist who takes Saussure's position to explain (i) why the original arbitrary sign gave rise to any problem in the first place, (ii) why manifest failures to rationalize it satisfactorily should ever gain acceptance into *la langue*, (iii) what prevented 'better' attempts at rationalization (given that, in view of the arbitrary nature of the linguistic sign, nothing circumscribes in advance the extent to which parts of the original *signifiant* may be altered), and (iv) why popular etymology is not even more widespread (that is, why no attempts have been made to re-interpret many comparable forms which strike one as obvious candidates for rationalization). These difficulties suggest that there may be analytic and associative processes at work in language which Saussurean linguistics is in principle unable to account for. Somehow, therefore, Saussure needs a way of playing down the significance of popular etymology as a linguistic phenomenon.

The second reason why popular etymology is particularly irksome for Saussure is that on the surface it appears to involve exactly the same associative operations as analogy; and analogy, as the preceding chapters have made clear, occupies a very important position in Saussurean explanations of how language works. It is difficult, consequently, to dismiss or simply to ignore popular etymology. That would call in question the adequacy of his basic account of analogy. Therefore he chooses to argue instead that, in spite of certain similarities, analogy and popular etymology are fundamentally different. His analysis of the difference, however, relies heavily on dubious psychologizing. (The subsequently suppressed term 'pathological' suggests a hint of desperation in the attempt.) Saussure tries to claim that, unlike analogy, popular etymology does not involve creative analysis. It is a kind of mistake or 'distortion' ([240]), due to ignorance. Unlike analogy, it does not belong to 'the normal functioning of a language' ([241]). It always involves dimly 'remembering' the old form, whereas analogy involves 'forgetting' it. Given Saussure's earlier hesitations about the conscious or unconscious nature of associative relations, none of this carries much argumentative weight.

Why not, then, opt for admitting that popular etymology and analogy are basically the same, and treating popular etymologies as simply one type of result produced by the working of analogy? Because that would lead straight away to a paradox about *la langue*; namely, that part of the normal functioning of the *mécanisme de la langue* is to produce, in addition to regular, complete and symmetrical patterns, other re-analyses of linguistic structure which are irregular, fragmentary and poorly motivated. This would immediately make Saussure's triumph of the previous chapter hollow: for then analogy could no longer be given as the simultaneous explanation for the introduction of new regularities and the maintenance of old regularities. Even less could it be adduced to explain in addition the production of syntagmatically regular combinations in ordinary discourse. (For it might equally well produce irregular ones.) Come what may, therefore, popular etymology has to be banished as some kind of freak or deviation not belonging to the normal 'healthy' functioning of the *activité continuelle du langage*.

Unfortunately, the attempt to avoid one paradox leads straight into another. For if popular etymologies are indeed 'mistakes' perpetrated by ignorant language-users who are unfamiliar with certain forms in *la langue*, it becomes extremely difficult to explain how these mistakes ever gain acceptance in *la langue*, except on the assumption that most of its users are just as ignorant as the individual who perpetrated the original 'mistake'. The reader is then left with a theoretically puzzling picture of linguistic communities whose members do not know their own native language. The gap in Saussurean theory which begins to show here will be considered in detail later: it concerns Saussure's failure to reconcile Durkheimian and non-Durkheimian concepts of the collectivity.

CHAPTER VII

Agglutination

Agglutination presents another problem which is no less fraught for Saussurean linguistics than that of popular etymology. For agglutination, looked at from the point of view of its diachronic results, appears to be the antithesis of analogy. In other words, it innovates by obliterating existing distinctions, whereas analogy preserves and reinforces them. How can these two contradictory tendencies both be explained as due to the working of the same *mécanisme de la langue*? One is self-preserving but the other self-destructive.

It would doubtless have been possible for Saussure to argue that, as in the case of popular etymologies, agglutinations are simply the product of ignorance on the part of language-users who fail to grasp the structure of the forms they are using. But, given that he has just been forced to use that explanation to deal with popular etymology, perhaps a second appeal to the incompetence of native speakers would have sounded like one appeal too many. Instead, the *Cours* puts a bold face on things and claims that agglutination is a 'mechanical' syntagmatic process which amalgamates the meanings of the forms involved.

The explanation limps both on its semantic leg and on its phonetic leg. It limps on its semantic leg because in the examples of agglutination which are offered for the reader's consideration it is often quite unclear in what sense the meaning of the agglutinated form could possibly be the result of applying 'the concept as a whole to the sequence of signs as a whole' ([243]). Thus, for instance, the agglutination which produced French *encore* ([243]) from Latin *hanc horam* ('this hour') results in a unit with a new meaning which can hardly be explained just as a failure to distinguish the two separate elements in the original combination of *signifiés*. Furthermore, Saussure's suggestion that this is due to the fact that when a compound concept is expressed by a very familiar sequence of significant units 'the mind takes a short cut' ([243]) is a metaphor that scarcely makes sense in the context. (It is reminiscent of crude attempts to explain linguistic change as due to 'laziness' on the part of language-users.) There is no 'short-cut' for the mind to take in these cases if the intention is indeed to express the compound concept. And in any case it is difficult to see what 'short-cutting' the analysis of a compound concept like 'this hour' could mean.

The explanation limps no less badly on its phonetic leg. Saussure claims it would be a mistake to suppose that phonetic merging precedes and causes semantic merging. On the contrary, he argues, it is the other way round: it is the perception of a 'single idea' in two sequential elements which leads to their phonetic coalescence into a single word ([243]). But this is quite unconvincing in view of the frequency of agglutinations where phonetic merging still leaves two quite distinguishable elements and no accompanying 'amalgamation' of the concepts. The form *I'm* is no less analysable than *I am*, and *don't* no less analysable than *do not*, in spite of the phonetic consequences for the morphological units involved. Perhaps it might be argued that Saussure would have to reject these as examples of agglutination, on the ground that two elements are still recognizable, regardless of the phonetic coalescence uniting them into a syntagmatically inseparable combination. If so, it is hard to see how standard cases like *possum* from *potis + sum* ([244]), or *ferai* from *facere + habeo* ([245]fn.) could be allowed to count as examples of agglutination either. Since we are not told how the analyst is to recognize the difference between a single idea and a combination of two ideas, just as we are not told what the criteria are for distinguishing between an agglutinated syntagma and a non-agglutinated syntagma, it is difficult to pursue the question much further.

Even if this omission leaves the Saussurean concept of agglutination somewhat obscure in certain respects, what emerges clearly enough is a reluctance to accept the view that agglutination is determined or even triggered by changes in the pronunciation of two forms when they become syntagmatically linked. It is interesting to ask what the reason is for this reluctance. The answer is bound up with another enigmatic feature of this chapter: its insistence that agglutination is 'mechanical'. The mechanical nature of agglutination, we are told, sets it apart from analogy, which is now – for the first time – described as a linguistic 'procedure', as distinct from a linguistic 'process'. The difference between the two is that a procedure 'implies will and intention' ([242]). Thus whereas agglutination is 'totally involuntary', analogy on the contrary 'presupposes analyses and combinations', and is 'an activity of the intelligence' ([244]).

Now at first sight the notion that agglutination is mechanical appears to favour the explanation that the phenomenon results from purely phonetic factors which operate when two *significants* are habitually linked in syntagmatic combination. But, as noted above, this is evidently *not* the explanation Saussure proposes. The distinction now drawn between procedures and processes has a quite different theoretical objective. It is to deal with a problem which is consequential upon the new role assigned to analogy in the last chapter but one. This is the problem of explaining why it is that the conservative force of analogy, to which the *Cours* has just given the major theoretical role of guaranteeing the maintenance of regular forms, is apparently powerless to prevent agglutination from obliterating distinctions between signs already established in *la langue*. In short, we are dealing here with a possible objection to the idea that analogy is capable of fulfilling the conservational function allotted to it.

The objection is potentially a serious one, and it is important to see how the distinction between procedures and processes is designed to take care of it. Unfortunately, the *Cours* draws this distinction in terms which could easily give rise to misunderstandings. Three chapters previously the reader has been offered an account of analogy which fairly clearly implies that in many cases its workings do not take place at the level of conscious awareness on the part of the individual speakers. Yet now we are told that analogy is 'procedural' in nature, and linguistic procedures are defined as involving the intervention of the will and the intelligence. From that it might seem that the operations of analogy must fall under *parole*, which was early on in the *Cours* characterized as the domain of acts of 'the will and the intelligence' ([30]). And it might seem even more difficult to reconcile that assignment with having been told specifically on p.[227] that the initial improvisation of a new form is the only part of analogy which belongs to *parole*. In short, the reader may well feel that in the text of the *Cours* there is by now an internally generated muddle over whether analogy belongs to *langue* or to *parole*, and, specifically, to what extent it involves intentionality on the part of the language users.

It is difficult to exonerate Saussure or his editors entirely from blame on this score. What the *Cours* tells us could hardly be more vague. However, the reading which seems to make best theoretical sense of the distinction between linguistic processes and linguistic procedures is as follows. Processes and procedures do not belong to *parole* at all or to diachrony, even though it is in *parole* and in diachrony that their joint results become manifest. Process and procedure are two basic types of operation in the *activité continuelle du langage* which ceaselessly shapes *la langue* in the minds of its speakers (or perhaps in the collective mind of the community, if we construe Saussurean metaphysics in that way). Procedures are the creative analytic operations. Processes are merely mental handling operations. Procedures are responsible for the systematicity of *la langue*. Processes simply arrange the items and implement the patterns systematically created by procedures. (Hence the claim that agglutination is exclusively a syntagmatic phenomenon, and involves no associative relations ([244]).) However, processes may sometimes have marginal repercussions on the organization of *la langue*, for reasons which are purely internal to the handling operations required by the *activité continuelle*. Such a case is agglutination, in which the relevant factor is simply that it is operationally easier to amalgamate two units which are constantly being syntagmatically combined and treat them as if they were a single unit of *la langue*. Thus it is not that analogy is powerless to prevent agglutination, but that agglutination results from the constant processual implementation of those very syntagmatic relations which analogic procedures have established. In short, the appearance that agglutination counteracts or overrules analogy is another diachronic illusion (on a par with the diachronic illusion that there are analogical changes).

The above interpretation of the Saussurean distinction between processes and procedures, although speculative, has two merits. One is that what the *Cours* says about analogy can at least be construed as internally consistent. (Whether it is convincing is another matter.) The other is that in this particular chapter it ties in with the rejection of the view that agglutination, although a mechanical phenomenon, is not explicable by reference to phonetic factors.

To summarize, the underlying rationale seems to be this. If phonetic coalescence were a cause rather than a consequence of agglutination, and if no distinction were drawn between processes and procedures, this would leave Saussurean linguistics lacking an available explanation not only for (i) why a new sign should be 'spontaneously' generated simply as the result of the syntagmatic proximity of two *signifiants*, but also for (ii) why, given that the linguistic sign is arbitrary, phonetic merging should in any case lead to semantic merging, and (iii) how it is possible for agglutination to obliterate boundaries between signs, given that these boundaries reflect already established associative series in *la langue*.

Again, a chapter on a purportedly diachronic phenomenon turns out to be devoted principally to defending the implications of Saussurean synchronic theory.

CHAPTER VIII

Diachronic Units, Identities and Realities

The final chapter of Part III at last turns to the question which, arguably, ought to have been discussed at the outset. By now, the reason for the delay is apparent. Without the important synchronic caveats which have just been announced, it would be impossible to give a complete Saussurean analysis of the problems of diachronic substitution. Without these caveats, moreover, it would be legitimate to read into the second paragraph on p.[248] a complete retraction of almost everything that the *Cours* has hitherto argued about the irreducible difference between synchronic and diachronic facts. (It is one of the besetting sins of Saussurean exegesis to juxtapose quotations cited out of context, and from different sources. Doubtless the whole botched textual history of the *Cours* made that in one sense inevitable. But inevitability is never a substitute for justification.)

What the reader is told on p.[248] is that an alteration in the linguistic sign is a shift in the relation between *signifiant* and *signifié*. 'This definition applies not only to changes in individual items, but to the evolution of the whole system. Diachronic development in its entirety is just that.' *Eppur si muove*? Is historical grammar a reality after all? Not so. It would be a mistake to look here for any last-minute recantation of the Saussurean faith that the linguistic system itself is *immuable* ([121]). As a conclusion to this section of the *Cours* devoted to Diachronic Linguistics, such a recantation would certainly be the most seat-raising second-act curtain of all. Nor would one wish to deny that whoever drafted those particular lines of the script on p.[248] had a keen sense of academic drama. (Otherwise they would fall flat.) The dramatic point, however, is precisely that now at last the reader is in a position to see how the apparent evolution of the *system* is a diachronic illusion. That illusion is all of a piece with the illusion that analogical innovations are changes. The truth is that the system does not evolve over time, and cannot evolve. The illusion is created by a succession of relations between *signifiants* and *signifiés* which retrospectively look as if the whole language were moving in a certain direction. Time plays a role, in brief: but its role is in the eye of the beholder. Here we eventually come to the full interpretation of that Sibylline diagram on p.[113], which represented the language and the community as static units, linked nevertheless by a chronological arrow. Simultaneously, we come to yet another application of the Saussurean dictum that the point of view creates the linguistic object.

Saussure's editors have been criticized for their strategic decision to postpone until this point the presentation of the connexion which Saussurean theory postulates between synchronic and diachronic identities (de Mauro 1972: 473,n.288), although it was announced as early as p.[150]. Any impartial academic inquiry into the alternatives must no doubt rule in favour of the editors. They saw that it would be merely confusing to incorporate into the section on Synchronic Linguistics a general discussion of problems of identity, before the reader had even been introduced to the full implications of the Saussurean dichotomy between synchrony and diachrony. That having been said, the fuss would be over nothing if it now emerged that the connexion was in any case uncontroversial.

Far from being uncontroversial, it raises the dire question of the extent to which diachronic linguistics is possible at all. This is the unexpected sting in the tail of Chapter VIII. 'Only the solution of the problem of the diachronic unit will enable us to penetrate beyond the superficial appearance of linguistic evolution and grasp its essence. Here, as in synchrony, understanding what the units are is indispensable in order to distinguish illusion from reality' ([248-9]). Do we, then, understand what the diachronic units are? Saussure, evidently, does not claim to. If we do, then we are cleverer than the author of the *Cours*. But he warns us against imagining that we have discovered the diachronic units merely by extrapolating from our identification of synchronic units. There are doubtless many kinds of diachronic change. 'The units identified for these purposes will not necessarily correspond to the units recognized in the synchronic domain' ([248]). On the contrary, one thing we can be fairly sure of is that 'the notion of a unit cannot be the same for both synchronic and diachronic studies' ([248]).

The same doubts are immediately confirmed by the dismissal on p.[249] of the facile claim of the historical philologist to be able to recognize diachronic identities simply by tracing the development of the individual sound changes from Latin *calidum* to French *chaud*, Latin *mare* to French *mer*, etc. This, argues Saussure, is to stand the problem on its head: for the basis for determining the historical continuity of individual sounds is precisely the assumption that the pairs *calidum* and *chaud, mare* and *mer*, etc. are indeed in diachronic correspondence.

How then can we break out of the circle? Saussure's enigmatic reply is stated with tantalising brevity on the very last page. Diachronic identities are extrapolations from series of synchronic identities 'without the link between them ever being broken by successive sound changes'. Hence the question of identifying diachronically Latin *calidum* with French *chaud* is directly related to the problem of identifying repetitions of the word *Messieurs!* in the same speech. The diachronic problem is simply 'an extension and complication' ([250]) of the synchronic problem. Unfortunately, the synchronic problem has itself been left unresolved on p.[152].

It is small wonder that historical linguists of Saussure's day preferred not to pursue the final implications of Chapter VIII. They might have found themselves inescapably cut off from a whole tradition of linguistic studies. Nowadays, however, considerations of that order are hardly relevant for a reader who is simply trying to make sense of the theoretical position which the *Cours* presents. For such a reader the question is what is meant by the claim that the problem of diachronic identity is simply an 'extension and complication' of the problem of synchronic identity.

It is difficult to shrug off the nagging suspicion that the very way in which the connexion between these two problems is raised betrays a deep Saussurean conflation between questions of *identity* and questions of *identification*. If we go back to the examples the *Cours* provides when discussing synchronic identity ([151-2]), it might appear that initially Saussure distinguishes between the *objective* question of whether a suit on a market stall is (or is not) my suit which had been stolen, and the *subjective* question of whether I identify the suit in question as mine. These appear to be two quite different issues: success or failure in identification does not, in principle, affect identity. Perhaps, after all, the suit I now claim as mine is not the one which was stolen: in which case I have confused two *non-identical* objects. (When the confusion is between one person and another person, such mistakes are commonly called cases of 'mistaken identity', but perhaps it would be less misleading if they were called cases of 'mistaken identification'.) Identity, in brief, is here not a matter of opinion or mere mortal judgment (unlike identification): either the suit is in fact mine or it isn't. Identity does not depend on how convinced I am that the suit is mine; nor on how good the evidence is for my identification. Questions of identification are quite different. How we identify things belongs to that area of psychology which deals with recognition, memory, attention, etc. Such questions, unlike questions of identity, are essentially *subjective*.

In the chapter on synchronic identities the reader was told that linguistic identity is *not* like the identity of the suit ([152]), but like the identity of the 8.45 train from Geneva to Paris, or the identity of the street demolished and rebuilt. In these latter examples, clearly, identity does *not* depend on the same material continuity: it is a formal or functional identity. But what exactly constitutes a formal or functional identity was left hanging in the air: metaphors were supplied in place of a definition. It is the chapter discussing diachronic identities which now brings the reader's attention back to those previously uninterpreted metaphors. For here we seem to be told that diachronic identity *is* indeed a matter of continuity (of the Latin word *calidum* with the French word *chaud*, etc.), but not of *phonetic* continuity. This is the point of the insistence on p.[249] that the identity '*chaud = calidum*' cannot be explicated purely and simply in terms of regular sound changes (even though they hold, as it happens).

All this is certainly puzzling, to say the least. For if the laws of sound change do not guarantee diachronic identity, what does? One possible answer is already dismissed when we recall that for Saussure there is no such thing as *panchronic* identity ([134-5]). The puzzle deepens further with the remarks on pp.[249-50] to the effect that the French dialect differences between *se fâcher* and *se fôcher* are simply divergent developments of a single form. But at the same time, if the two French dialects represent different idiosynchronic systems, there is no way *se fâcher* and *se fôcher* can be synchronically identical. Furthermore, in the same breath ([250]) the *Cours* tells its readers that the French negative *pas* is identical with the French noun *pas* (but without distinguishing between synchronic identity and diachronic identity).

Culler (1976: 39) interprets Saussure as saying that in the passage from Latin *calidum* to French *chaud* the succession of phonetic changes (*calidum* to *calidu, calidu* to *caldu, caldu* to *cald*, etc.) is linked by the synchronic identity, at some stage, of each of the successive pairs of different phonetic forms. However, as Love has pointed out, this leaves unresolved the problem of how to justify the identification of 'the *calidu* that occurs as a *messieurs*-type variant of *calidum* at stage one with the *calidu* that occurs as a *messieurs*-type variant of *caldu* at stage two'. Love concludes: 'The logic of the concept of an idiosynchronic language-state leaves one with just two ways to jump: either all the historical variants of a given form belong theoretically to the same *état de langue*, or there are uncountably many *états de langue* and no such thing as a diachronic identity. Culler's attempt to occupy a halfway house between these positions only serves to reveal the conceptual discontinuity between the notions of synchrony and diachrony, as expounded by Saussure'. (Love 1984: 228).

Is there any reading of Chapter VIII that can unscramble this tangle of confusions? It would take both a bold and an ingenious reader to maintain that there is. On the face of it, the reasons why a hearer might *identify* two utterances in a speech as utterances of the 'same word' (*messieurs*) have little to do with (a) whether the first utterance is auditorily or meaningfully indistinguishable from the second, or (b) whether a historian might claim that the French word *messieurs* is identical with some Latin word or expression (e.g. *meos seniores*). What might seem to bridge the gap is that an etymologist might identify a certain Latin form as the etymon of a certain French form (by saying 'It's the same word'), and two speakers of French might also (by saying 'It's the same word') identify one occurrence of *Messieurs!* with another occurrence. But all that shows – sceptics will doubtless claim – is that Saussure plays fast and loose (for his own purposes) with the concepts of linguistic identity and linguistic identification, or juggles with different metalinguistic interpretations of the term *same*.

Committed defenders of Saussure will doubtless reply that when it comes to questions of language, the distinction between identity and identification immediately becomes less clear cut and more contentious. This is because linguistic units do not, like garments or people or buildings, have an identity which can be defined in terms of spatio-temporal continuity. On the contrary, whether we are dealing with the same linguistic unit or two different linguistic units seems to be far more dependent on identification. This is due to the nature of language. What matters ultimately for linguistic comprehension is that the hearer correctly *identify* what the speaker has said. Hence the temptation to treat the identity of a linguistic unit as residing purely and simply in its identifiability across all the many instances of its occurrence in discourse. Provided that identifiability is guaranteed, it seems superfluous – and even nonsensical – to look for any *further* criteria of linguistic identity. So any contrast between the objectivity of identity and the subjectivity of identification, which holds good generally for our dealings with the physical world, immediately becomes blurred in the case of language.

Appendices to
Parts Two and Three

[NB. The erroneous title of this section survives from an earlier plan of the
Cours, in which Part I was to have comprised material on writing and on
phonetics, eventually incorporated into the Introduction. The editors
evidently failed to notice that in consequence *Appendices aux troisième et
quatrième parties* should have been altered to read *Appendices aux
seconde et troisième parties*.]

Saussure's new distinction between 'subjective' and 'objective' analysis
(Appendix A) raises two points of interest. Its connexion with *la
distinction radicale du diachronique et du synchronique* ([252]) is not
disguised. As earlier discussion in the *Cours* has already made clear, the
distinction between synchrony and diachrony would have no basis were it
not that the native speakers' view of their language and the historian's
view of it will in certain respects inevitably and fundamentally differ.
Nevertheless, to introduce the terms 'subjective' and 'objective' implies a
relationship between these contrasting viewpoints for which no
theoretical foundation has so far been laid in the *Cours*. For while it is
clear in what sense the synchronic point of view may be called *subjectif*
(namely, that it derives from the *sujet parlant* ([251])), that does not
automatically validate the historian's point of view as an 'objective' one.

The reader is presumably expected to recall that on p.[189] an (ideal)
equation was posited between the classifications proposed by the
synchronic descriptive grammarian and the 'conscious or unconscious'
associative series operative in *parole*. Now that equation already yields a
sense in which the (ideal) synchronic description is or may be judged
'objective' (depending on whether or not its classifications do or do not
correspond to the associative series of the native speaker). But nothing
similar has so far been proposed to yield a sense in which the (ideal)
diachronic description would be comparably 'objective'. History, in
short, has so far been left to the eye of the historian (which is notoriously
liable to take a view as 'subjective' as any).

It is only if we bear this in mind that the full significance of the ensuing
attack on the Neogrammarians on p.[253] can be appreciated. At first

sight, it looks like a case of pot calling the kettle black. For the *Cours* has already conceded on p.[153] that the linguist is condemned to working with concepts originally introduced by grammarians. So why should the Neogrammarian school in particular come under fire for 'remaining encumbered with a scientific apparatus which it could not dispense with after all' ([253])? Is not this precisely the charge which might be levelled at the author of the *Cours*? For does he not too speak constantly of 'words', 'roots', 'suffixes', 'nouns', 'verbs', and so on, even while proclaiming in the same breath that the validity of these terms is dubious?

The interesting point is that the Neogrammarians are *not* condemned just for retaining an inadequate descriptive terminology (or who should escape whipping?); *nor* for failing to acknowledge its descriptive inadequacies; but for attempting to justify it nevertheless on the grounds of 'convenience of exposition' ([253]). In short, they threw out the historical baby with the analytic bathwater.

This is an accusation which discloses more about the assumptions underpinning Saussurean diachrony than anything that has been explicitly admitted thus far in Part III. For the position here attributed to the Neogrammarians (whether justifiably so or not makes no difference) is that they simply wash their hands of the terminological question by making no claims for their descriptive framework *other than* convenience of exposition. Saussure, it will be noted, does not deny them that advantage. Nor are the Neogrammarians here attacked on the more general intellectual ground that to claim that a descriptive framework is justified on grounds of convenience of exposition alone must be either incoherent or disingenuous. The sins of the Neogrammarians on this score are, for Saussure, of a different order.

The first sin is that their terminological handwashing sets a bad academic example. In other words, linguistics could not possibly be a science ever if all its practitioners adopted this attitude. Specifically, synchronic linguistics could claim no analytic superiority over the practical pedagogic linguistics of the traditional grammarian. (For whatever is 'convenient' in terms of exposition is then automatically justified, and linguistics becomes one of the systematic sophistries of education.) The Saussurean inquiry into setting the study of language on a scientific basis is by implication condemned to futility if all the justification its conceptual frameworks ever need is 'convenience of exposition', and any 'pure abstraction of the mind' ([253]) which serves this purpose is *eo ipso* validated. So the Neogrammarians have to be punished on this count *pour encourager les autres*, if for no other reason.

The second Neogrammarian sin is different. It is the sin of historical agnosticism. By renouncing the task of devising an appropriate diachronic terminology, the Neogrammarians have in effect renounced the task of discovering the operative units of diachronic change. They rest content with being able to state the resultant diachronic correspondences in conveniently simple terms. For Saussure this will not do, *even if* the summarizing statements are unobjectionable. In other words, the hidden premiss underlying Saussurean diachrony is that history is 'real'; and this historical realism is what informs the choice of the term 'objective' to describe the kind of analysis which the linguistic historian *should be* engaged in. This is the other reason why the Neogrammarians cannot be allowed to get away with saying that their descriptive units are 'pure abstractions'.

The path to theoretical salvation which the *Cours* offers Neogrammarian heretics is a straight and narrow one. It is to embrace the belief that 'objective analysis, being linked internally to subjective analysis of the living language, has a legitimate and clearly defined place in linguistic method' ([253]). A more aggressive way of pronouncing the same punitive sentence would have been to say that *unless* objective analysis can be shown to be internally linked to subjective analysis, it has no legitimate place in linguistics. What exactly the nature of this crucial 'internal link' is the *Cours* never explains. All we can infer is that it does *not* validate an automatic correspondence between synchronic and diachronic units, since there is none ([248]): and that seems to leave internal linkage as a simple but fundamental article of Saussurean faith.

Faith, in this particular instance, is hardly fortified by the discussion of Greek stems and affixes which immediately follows (Appendix B), and purports to demonstrate that 'one cannot establish a method or formulate definitions except by approaching the task synchronically' ([253]). What in fact it bears witness to is a failure to distinguish between certain synchronic relationships which were subsequently recognized by Saussure's successors. Thus, for instance, on p.[254] Greek *zeug-* is held to have been an 'irreducible', 'second-grade' stem. Its irreducibility is unquestionable because 'by comparing related forms it is impossible to take its segmentation any further' ([255]). What this means in practical terms is that it is the twentieth-century linguist who is unable to take the process of segmentation any further. What it proves about the subjective analysis of those who spoke ancient Greek, however,is another matter. The discussion on pp.[254-5] concedes that this 'irreducible' Greek stem *zeug-* had what are called 'variants' (*zeuk-*, *zug-*), but does not allow the existence of these variants to cast doubt on the basic assumption that segmentation is the only valid procedure by which we can establish 'subjective' units for Plato, Aristotle and their contemporaries. In other words, Saussure here attributes to native speakers of ancient Greek a grammatical mentality corresponding to what post-Saussurean linguists later called the 'item-and-arrangement' model (Hockett 1954). It must be debatable whether that gratuitous historical attribution is preferable to a historical agnosticism which would make no bolder claim about Greek than that it is 'descriptively convenient' to treat *zeug-* as an unanalysable stem. The more modest claim at least does not suggest any diachronic *ivresse des grandes profondeurs*.

The reader's confidence in the method of analysis advocated here does not increase as the discussion proceeds. By p.[257], a *suffix* is defined as 'the element added to the root in order to form a stem (e.g. *zeug-mat-*), or to one stem in order to form a second-grade stem (e.g. *zeugmat-io*)'. But on p.[254], *zeug-* itself was already described as a 'second-grade' stem. Evidently, we have a conflation between (i) the relationship which links a root to the word forms based on that root, and (ii) the relationship which links the stem of any given word form to its ending. The trouble is the difficulty of treating both types of relationship as *linear* relationships. In short, this is just the kind of example which ought to have led to a rethink about the wisdom of adopting linearity as a 'second principle' of Saussurean linguistics. But evidently it did not.

Finally, etymology (Appendix C) is brought into the methodological picture. This is the unkindest cut of all to the Neogrammarians, whose achievements stand or fall by the reliability of their etymological evidence. But etymology, for Saussure, is a linguistic jack-of-all-trades. 'To achieve its aims, etymology makes use of all the means which linguistics makes available, but does not scrutinize the nature of the processes it is obliged to engage in' ([260]). In other words, it is endemically tainted with the failure to distinguish between synchronic and diachronic relations. This polemic completes the case against etymology already foreshadowed on p.[249], where it was argued that diachronic identity of forms could not be established on the basis of sound change, under pain of circularity: for the establishment of valid etymologies is itself a prerequisite for the recognition of any sound change.

PART FOUR
Geographical Linguistics

CHAPTER I

On the Diversity of Languages

Part IV is the only section of the *Cours* devoted to 'external linguistics' ([262]), apart from general comments on the subject in Chapter V of the Introduction, and a brief discussion of a rather random selection of topics in Part V. Why does linguistic geography command the lion's share of attention when other aspects of external linguistics find no mention in the *Cours* at all? (No mention is ever made for instance, of social diversity, which is no less conspicuous than geographical diversity.) Two reasons might be suggested. The first is that the latter part of the nineteenth century and the early years of the twentieth had seen the growth of European dialectology and the compilation of dialect atlases emerging as one of the major fields of empirical research in linguistics. To have ignored linguistic geography, therefore, would have run the risk of suggesting that the *Cours* represented a brand of armchair theorizing quite out of touch with contemporary developments in language studies. The second reason is that linguistic geography happens to be a field in which the relevance of certain Saussurean principles can be easily demonstrated. Indeed, it is conspicuous that this chapter of the *Cours* selects only those topics which afford this possibility of demonstration. Other less tractable problems of dialectology are simply ignored.

At the same time, in Part IV no opportunity is lost of emphasizing that linguistic geography is 'external' and the nature of its subject matter precludes it from any systematic scientific treatment within the linguistics of *la langue*. Throughout, Saussure points out the haphazard character of the phenomena which linguistic geography studies: the unpredictability of direction of change ([272]), of areas of diffusion ([274]), of dialect boundaries ([277-8]), of language boundaries

([278-80]), and in general of the interaction between the forces of parochialism and intercourse ([284]). The cumulative effect of this is to suggest that the methods of linguistic geography, far from throwing much light on *la langue* or on the structure of linguistic communities, on the contrary bring to light much which stands in need of explanation.

The only reference to the possibility that 'external' linguistics might be able to make some positive contribution to 'internal' linguistics occurs on p.[263], and there it is not linguistic geography as such but comparison between languages and their histories which holds out the prospect of revealing 'certain constant phonetic and psychological facts which circumscribe the establishment of any language'. According to Saussure, 'it is the discovery of these constant factors which is the main aim of any comparison between languages unrelated to one another' ([263]). Evidently these purely linguistic universals are of less importance for Saussure than the more general semiological universals referred to earlier in the *Cours*. That may be why there is no attempt to pursue the difficulty of establishing whether two languages are ultimately related or not. Saussure speaks simply of cases where 'no relationship is recognizable or demonstrable'. Since he concedes that even if all languages were phylogenetically related, the relationship 'would not be provable, because too many changes have taken place' ([263]), it presumably remains in doubt what value to attach to the eventual evidence of comparative studies on this score.

Comparison in general raises a theoretical problem about which the *Cours* is noticeably reticent, although it recurs at various points throughout Part IV. On p.[263] the reader is told that comparison 'is always possible and useful', that it can be made 'of grammatical systems and of general ways of expressing ideas, as well as of sound systems' and also of diachronic as well as synchronic facts. However, whether linguistic comparison is possible on a systematic or scientific basis Saussure does not say. Nor, if it *is* possible, is the appropriate scientific methodology described here. Whether, therefore, comparison requires a different linguistic 'point of view', neither that of subjective nor that of objective analysis, is a question apparently left open. The implication seems to be that comparison itself belongs to 'external' linguistics, and consequently its basis may vary according to the particular external factors involved. (It is far from clear, nevertheless, that this move lets 'internal' linguistics off the hook altogether, since the question of diachronic substitution, left unresolved at the end of Part III, presumably presupposes the possibility of comparison between diachronically connected *états de langue*. Without that possibility it is difficult to see that any statement to the effect that certain forms replace others over a period of time would be admissible in linguistics.)

CHAPTER II

Geographical Diversity: Its Complexity

The reader might be forgiven for supposing that the title of this chapter was chosen with tongue in cheek. Not only are the 'complications' discussed remarkably uncomplicated, but they are also dismissed with lightning speed. Chapter II in fact provides an unwitting demonstration of how narrowly ethnocentric the Saussurean approach to problems of external linguistics can be. The hidden premiss – only half-hidden, or in places barely concealed – underlying Saussure's whole treatment of linguistic geography is that the kind of linguistic distribution shown by the large-scale linguistic atlases of modern Europe represents a universal norm. The 'ideal' form of geographical diversity, we are told, is that in which 'different areas correspond to different languages' ([265]). Clearly, that happens to be the form to which the European linguistic situation closely approximates; but why it should be 'ideal' and other situations treated as deviations from it the *Cours* does not explain.

The first major consequence of this premiss is that bilingual situations are by implication counted as abnormal or marginal (even though on a world scale bilingualism predominates over monolingualism), while linguistic phenomena such as pidginization and creolization are not even mentioned at all in connexion with linguistic variation. The only kind of bilingualism in which any interest is shown here is the bilingualism which results from the superimposition of a literary language on a local dialect of the same language (which, again, happens to be a typical phenomenon of post-Renaissance European culture). Otherwise, the type of contact between linguistic communities envisaged is simply their separate coexistence within a given country or area.

In a quite breathtaking dismissal of 'non-ideal' linguistic facts, Saussure concedes that although certain types of departure from the monoglot situation occur so frequently 'that they might seem to be normal in the history of languages', it is necessary to set them aside because they 'obscure a clear view of natural geographical diversity' ([269]). 'This schematic simplification may seem to distort reality; but the natural state of affairs must first be studied in its own right' ([269]). The short answer to Saussure on this is that the schematic simplification proposed does not merely 'seem to distort' but actually does distort reality. What Saussurean linguistics here unaccountably takes to be 'the natural state of affairs' is simply a theoretical abstraction which isolates just those factors which it is convenient for the theorist to deal with by means of the techniques of linguistic geography.

CHAPTER III

Causes of Geographical Diversity

Having invented an 'ideal' type of geographical diversity, the *Cours* immediately proceeds to offer its ideal explanation, or rather to highlight one feature of an ideal explanation. The essential feature turns out to be that, contrary to appearances, geographical diversity has little to do with space, but everything to do with time. 'Geographical diversity has to be translated into temporal diversity' ([271]). Furthermore, 'the instability of the language depends on time alone. Geographical diversity is thus a secondary aspect of the general phenomenon' ([272]).

At first sight it is by no means clear exactly what Saussure is driving at here. Earlier in the *Cours* we have already been told that 'time changes everything', that 'there is no reason why *la langue* should be exempt from this universal law' ([112]), and that 'languages are always changing, however minimally' ([142]). These considerations hardly establish time as a *cause* of change. It would be naive to treat the statement that 'time changes everything' on a par with, say, 'compression changes density'. Time is not an external force causing changes but a dimension in which changes occur. Likewise, space is a dimension. But we all knew that anyway, a reader may reasonably object. So why is Saussure apparently so keen to make the point that it is time not space which changes languages? And exactly what point is it?

As so often in the *Cours*, in order to understand the line Saussure takes on a particular issue, it is essential to identify the theoretical error which is implicitly under attack. Here the clue is given by cryptic warning at the end of §1. 'The unity of related languages is to be traced only through time. Unless the student of comparative linguistics realizes this, all kinds of misconceptions lie in wait for him' ([272]). In short, the reader needs here to refer back to the temporal arrow in the diagram on p.[113], and even further back to the remarks about the failure of Bopp to found a 'true science of linguistics' ([16]). What Saussure is saying, with the indirectness which passes for academic *politesse*, is that the currently fashionable study of linguistic geography can no more offer a scientific basis for linguistics than Bopp could: *and for the same reason.* The reason is that it divorces the comparison of linguistic data from chronology.

This in turn throws light on Saussure's reticence about the theory of comparisons, already noted above. For Saussure, a linguistic atlas of the kind Gilliéron produced was simply the product of comparing the results obtained by sending round investigators with questionnaires at an arbitrarily chosen point in time. What is in principle inadequate about this has already been spelled out in the *Cours* on p.[128]; 'The object of synchronic study does not comprise everything which is simultaneous'. In other words, sending out a linguistic questionnaire to many speakers on January 1st 1900 in no way guarantees that the replies will somehow dovetail to present a picture of a synchronic system. Thus Gilliéron's approach exemplifies for Saussure an antipodean inversion of Bopp's mistake (Bopp having supposed that linguistic data could be compared *irrespective of* their coming from widely different chronological periods). The target of Saussure's attack is in both cases the same: it is a misconception of the temporality of languages.

Comparison cannot, for Saussure, be valid if it is based on this kind of misconception. The linguistic geographer's mistake here is perhaps even worse than Bopp's. For when Bopp compared a Latin form with a Sanskrit form, he did not suppose that their comparability was assured by their historical contemporaneity. On the other hand, when the linguistic geographer compares a form recorded at one locality in his survey with a form recorded at another locality he may well make precisely that assumption. (Here Saussure raises a problem for which twentieth-century sociolinguistics has yet to provide a convincing solution.)

Furthermore, it appears that geographical comparison of the type Gilliéron undertook must rely to some extent on the kind of nomenclaturism already roundly condemned in the opening pages of Part I ([97-8]). For example, a typical item of geographical linguistic comparative data ([275]) is that whereas at Douvaine the word for 'two' is *daue*, a few kilometres away it is *due*. This comparison, however, presupposes that there is a given numerical concept ('two'), and that both dialects independently have a word for it. The comparison leaves itself open to precisely the same order of objections as were earlier levelled against equating a French plural with a Sanskrit plural ([161]). For it remains to be demonstrated whether the numerical system at Douvaine is 'the same as' the numerical system at a village a few kilometres away. The fact that it is only a few kilometres away does not warrant dismissing the question as unimportant: this is the other cutting edge of Saussure's claim that in linguistic geography the distances involved are irrelevant ([271]). Exactly the same question would arise if the dialect with the form *due* happened to be spoken in Cambodia instead of at the foot of the Salève.

So there is for Saussure a sense in which all geographical developments are secondary and merely circumstantial, whereas historical change is primary. Once this underlying train of thought in Chapter III is grasped, it leads on to the otherwise startling conclusions that naturally there are no dialect boundaries (§3) and no language boundaries either (§4). How could there be? For geography plays no role whatever in the determination of an idiosynchronic system. Thus when geographical comparison appears to reveal a sharp territorial division between one language or dialect and its neighbour, what in fact it brings to light is simply the result of the obliteration in that locality of any intermediate varieties which would bridge the gap. Such 'boundaries' are 'the outcome of circumstances which have militated against the survival of gradual, imperceptible transitions' ([279]).

CHAPTER IV

Propagation of Linguistic Waves

Chapter IV shows the *Cours* at its most inscrutable. Its tone is blandly pedagogic and its examples very simple; but the lesson it presents can easily be read in the light of what has been said in previous sections of the *Cours* as a demonstration of the explanatory poverty of linguistic geography. Straight away, the linguistic geographer is presented as treating the propagation of linguistic features as if they were 'subject to the same laws as any other habit, such as fashion' ([281]). But presumably we are expected to read this in the light of the earlier highly critical remarks on p.[208] concerning the inadequacy of attempts to explain sound change as analogous to changes in fashion. In fact the general point made on p.[208] is exemplified quite specifically in this chapter in connexion with the change of *t* to *ts*. Saussure here emphasizes the importance of distinguishing 'carefully between areas of innovation, where a sound evolves solely along a temporal axis, and areas of propagation ... When a *ts* originating elsewhere is substituted for a *t*, that is not modification of a traditional prototype but imitation of a neighbouring dialect, regardless of the prototype' ([283]). Now it is clear that the linguistic atlas not only fails to indicate that distinction, but actually obscures it. Not unless we can compare a succession of linguistic maps for successive periods does it become possible to detect the likely area of innovation. In other words, diachronic information is necessary in order to interpret geographical information; and this connects up with the thesis of the preceding chapter that 'geographical diversity has to be translated into temporal diversity' ([271]).

The whole discussion of intercourse and parochialism as the forces responsible for geographical differentiation implicitly echoes the question left unanswered earlier; that of 'identifying the starting point of the imitative process' ([208]). The problem is rendered more rather than less crucial by §2, which argues that in any case intercourse and parochialism are simply positive and negative aspects of the same force. Nowhere, it appears, does linguistic geography bring to light specifically linguistic factors which explain the imitative process: on the contrary, only appeal to the vagaries of this unknown process and its mysterious mode of operation will explain the unpredictable peculiarities of geographical variation.

Furthermore, inasmuch as this is simply a general call to psychology for help (as in the case of changes in fashion), it would seem that linguistic geography even fails to bring to light any respects in which the diffusion of linguistic innovations differs from the diffusion of any other kind of 'habit' ([281]). Nor are distinctions drawn between the diffusion, say, of phonetic innovations and the diffusion of morphological features. All this highlights the extent to which linguistic geography is concerned with matters of an 'external' nature. Once again, the kind of point one might have expected the founder of linguistic structuralism to make about the spread of linguistic innovations is conspicuous by its absence. There is no suggestion, for instance, that the diffusion of feature a might facilitate the diffusion of feature b if the two were structurally related in some way; or that the motivation for 'imitation' by Dialect X of a feature in Dialect Y might have something to do with the internal structure of Dialect X at the time of borrowing.

Why are there no hints in this direction? The answer takes us back again to the Saussurean reluctance to supply structural explanations for sound change. The two cases, in fact, are exactly parallel. The *Cours* treats the geographical transmission of linguistic features in just the same way as the diachronic transmission of sound changes: that is, treats them as isolated one-off 'intrusions' into an otherwise static system. In both cases, the reason is the same: to admit any connexion between two or more such transmissional events would be tantamount to admitting that systems (or parts of systems) are themselves mobile. That in turn would mean denying, in one case, the independence of synchrony from diachrony, and in the other case the independence of co-existing *états de langue*. In terms of Saussurean theory, there is in principle no difference between the separateness of two systems in time and the separateness of two systems in space. So there can be no difference either in how features manage to be 'transferred' from one system to another. Just as Saussure denies the possibility of 'historical grammar', so he must also, for consistency's sake, deny the possibility of 'geographical grammar'.

This in turn explains the emphasis on the fact that linguistic geography falls into the domain of external linguistics. Otherwise the geographically 'visible' transitional gradations from one area to the next would call in question the very notion of a Saussurean *état de langue* as a homogeneous system. At the same time, as in the diachronic case, any *prima facie* evidence of grammar extending across *états* can be dismissed as another (this time 'geographical') illusion.

This ties in with the obvious parallel which there is for Saussure between the unpredictability of sound change and the unpredictability of geographical diffusion. Both are potentially disruptive for already established linguistic structures in the same way that meteorites from outer space are potentially disruptive for physical structures. The damage caused may necessitate extensive reconstruction. But that need cannot be assessed until the damage has actually occurred. That is why for Saussure it would make no sense to devote one chapter of the *Cours* to disruptions typically caused by geographical contact and a separate chapter to disruptions typically caused by evolution over time. These, within the Saussurean framework, are inseparable: for geographical variation simply *is* variation over time projected on to a map.

PART FIVE

Questions of Retrospective Linguistics Conclusion

CHAPTER I

The Two Perspectives of Diachronic Linguistics

Part V of the *Cours* is by any standards a disappointing conclusion to a boldly innovative book. It neither pursues the theoretical implications of what has gone before, nor even recapitulates the main Saussurean themes. The editors seem to have treated it as a ragbag into which they could put any material not, for one reason or another, incorporated into the main body of the text. The decision to treat this residue as constituting Part V, rather than as a simple Appendix (in the same way as pp.[251-60]) is puzzling; but no less puzzling than why the material in question had not already been incorporated into earlier chapters.

The discussion of the two perspectives of diachronic linguistics rightly belongs in Part III, and it is difficult to see any reason for not having included it at that point, particularly since the topic was broached as early as p.[128], and the terms 'prospective' and 'retrospective' already introduced there. Perhaps it might be argued on behalf of the editors that the choice which a linguist has to make between 'setting out the history of a language in detail following the chronological sequence' and the alternative of 'proceeding retrospectively against the chronological sequence of events' ([292]) is merely a second-order question of convenience and practicality, and is therefore rightly kept separate from the basic problems of diachronic linguistics treated in Part III. Nevertheless, the chapter also has theoretical implications, in view of Saussure's claim that in linguistics 'it is the viewpoint adopted which creates the object' ([23]).

The prospective and retrospective viewpoints in diachronic linguistics do not converge to create a single object. They create two different objects. This is clearly shown by the examples given on p.[294]. A prospective set of statements about what happened to Latin vowels in French cannot automatically be converted by a 'reversal' of viewpoint into an equivalent retrospective set of statements about the sources of French vowels in Latin. 'A study of sound changes will present a very different picture depending on which perspective is adopted' ([293-4]). A 'very different' picture is not just the same picture seen from the diametrically opposite point of view. This emerges even more clearly from Saussure's morphological examples. The fact that such disparate French forms as *aimé, fini, clos*, etc. have in common that they represent the ultimate development of descendants of forms originally containing the Proto-Indo-European suffix *-to-* has no place in the retrospective history of French at all. The 'development of *-to-* in French' is a 'fact' or set of 'facts' created solely by taking Proto-Indo-European as a point of departure and adopting a prospective viewpoint (which in this case includes deciding to treat the history of *-to-* as prolonged indefinitely into the future by means of any forms which continue forms themselves continuing forms which originally contained *-to-*). Thus *-to-* continues to have a prospective history long after it has disappeared, and will continue to do so long into the future. This history corresponds to no linguistic reality *either* for speakers of French themselves *or* for someone writing a retrospective history of the French language (which does not go back beyond Latin, when *-to-* had already ceased to exist).

This is also the lesson to be drawn from the comparison with geology ([293]), the point of which the editors seem to have missed entirely. In geology, the adoption of a prospective or retrospective viewpoint makes no difference, because either yields an account of the history of the earth's crust with the same factual content. In linguistics this is not the case, because where languages are concerned the facts are not, like the facts of geology, given in advance.

CHAPTER II

Earliest Languages and Prototypes

Chapter II returns to the theme of comparison. The first paragraph takes up again the criticism of Bopp and the comparativists. The objection is that linguistic comparison is not only worthless but potentially misleading when divorced from history. Thus quite different pictures emerge from comparing the Indo-European languages (i) on the assumption that all are descended from an unattested common ancestor, and (ii) on the (mistaken) assumption that Sanskrit was the parent of the others. This spells out in greater detail an objection voiced as early as the first chapter of the *Cours*, where the comparativists were taxed with not having grasped the fact that comparison alone offers no basis for drawing conclusions ([16-17]).

The chapter goes on to attack the 'muddled notion of antiquity' which results from conflating the question of the date of the earliest written records of a language with the question of the archaism of the forms it preserves. The connexion between this and the first paragraph of the chapter, apart from the fact that both errors were committed by the same scholars studying Sanskrit, is presumably that both can be seen as variants of the same basic failure in linguistics to ask what can legitimately be compared with what.

CHAPTER III

Reconstructions

Although the title of Chapter III and its position in the text suggest that it should be read simply as a further amplification of points relating to the methodology of retrospective linguistics, the points in question turn out to be not merely of some theoretical significance, but theoretically controversial into the bargain.

The question at issue in §1 is the theoretical status of the items which result from those comparisons which are not merely the 'sterile' ([299]) comparisons of comparative philology previously condemned. In other words, by placing comparison in an appropriate 'chronological perspective' ([299]), is it possible to arrive at reconstructed forms which have some degree of scientific value; and if so, what exactly is it? These pages, among the most fascinating in the *Cours*, show Saussure grappling once again with the problem of historical 'reality'.

Now the vacillations are more agonized and protracted than before. Already committed to the thesis that in linguistics the viewpoint creates the object, Saussure is desperately reluctant nevertheless to concede that the objects reconstructed are merely 'abstractions' which reflect the methods and assumptions of the linguist. For that is precisely the objection to the 'sterile' linguistic comparison already dismissed as worthless. On the other hand, how can the linguist *qua* scientist reasonably claim that hypotheses about the forms of languages long since extinct and never recorded at all have exactly the same status as descriptions of *états de langue* manifested in the observable *parole* of living speakers?

In this chapter, Saussure hops uncomfortably from one foot to the other. In §1 it is conceded that to say that, for instance, the Proto-Indo-European word for 'horse' was *akvas* is simply a summation of a certain set of hypotheses. 'The aim of reconstruction is thus not to restore a form for its own sake, which would be in any case rather ridiculous, but to crystallize and condense a series of conclusions which are held to be correct in the light of the evidence currently available. In a word, it records the progress made to date in our science' ([301]). On this 'nominalist' view, *akvas* designates nothing at all: it merely expresses in an abstract form certain opinions held by modern scholars. So the statement that the Proto-Indo-European word for 'horse' was *akvas* has, apart from a certain formal symmetry, virtually nothing in common with the statement that the French word for 'horse' is *cheval*. For the latter, presumably, is not a hypothesis of any kind, but an observational statement of fact.

Saussure's dilemma is that as a theorist he cannot afford to admit that, in spite of its form, the statement that the Proto-Indo-European word for 'horse' was *akvas* – whether accurate or not – is not a synchronic statement, but merely a disguised reformulation of several separate diachronic statements. For that would be tantamount to saying that no synchronic analysis of dead languages is possible; or, at the very least, to blurring in those cases the very distinction between synchronic and diachronic studies which he is committed to maintaining as absolute.

Blatant nominalism will in any case not satisfy the historical realist whom the reader has already recognized as the author of the earlier chapters on diachronic linguistics. It comes as no surprise, therefore, to find that in §2 a rather different tune is being sung. In this section, the question is presented as being to what extent a 'degree of certainty' can be attached to the reconstructed forms which summarize sets of hypotheses. Presumably a reconstruction of which the elements are only 50 per cent certain ranks lower than a reconstruction of which the elements are 75 per cent certain. In other words, the degree of certainty to be assigned to *akvas* is a total arrived at by adding up the certainty attached to the separate hypotheses underlying the five phonetic units involved. Even if each hypothesis were wrong, Saussure appears to take the view that it would at least be certain that there were only five units to be right or wrong about ([303]). So even if *akvas* as a set of individual hypotheses incorporated mistakes on every single count (i.e. even if the Proto-Indo-Europeans actually called a horse *igfoz*) nevertheless the reconstruction *akvas* itself could still be awarded a degree of certainty *qua* synchronic statement.

As an attempt to have the best of both worlds, this is brave but bungled. In the first place, introducing the notion of 'degree of certainty' fudges the issue, inasmuch as certainty can be ambiguously construed as (i) a matter of being objectively correct, and (ii) a matter of being subjectively confident. Only if the two are conflated does §2 of this chapter offer any possibility of a solution to the problem posed in §1. For certainty of the order of 100 per cent of type (ii) affords no guarantee at all of certainty of type (i).

Second, if a comparable criterion of certainty were adopted throughout synchronic linguistics, the notion of describing an *état de langue* would be reduced to absurdity. The statement that the French for 'horse' is *chufor* would be accorded a certain degree of descriptive validity (i.e. insofar as *chufor* has the same number of consonants and vowels as the French word for 'horse'). The fact that there is no French word *chufor* could not be held to invalidate it.

Third, it is this attempt to rescue some semblance of synchronic 'reality' for historical hypotheses which forces Saussure to opt for claiming that the task of Proto-Indo-European reconstruction is not to identify the words actually used (in the sense that *cheval* identifies a word actually used in French) but merely to identify the abstract units which enter into their composition. Thus 'one could designate the phonetic elements of a reconstructed language simply by figures or symbols of any kind' ([303]). The figures or symbols in question would be defined simply in terms of contrast and recurrence. Thus a sound could, 'without specifying its phonetic character, be classified and designated by a number in a table of Proto-Indo-European sounds' ([303]).

If this proposal is to be taken at face value, then it might seem that according to Saussure the statement that the Proto-Indo-European word for 'horse' was *akvas* actually goes too far. All that the linguist needs is some such statement as that the Proto-Indo-European word for 'horse' was '15819' (where '1' is defined as 'the same sound, however pronounced, which occurs in both first and fourth positions in the following words ...') Thus we are led to a treatment of sound systems (retrospectively attributed to Saussure by some of his successors) in which the sound system is simply an abstract matrix of contrasts, about the phonetic implementation of which nothing – in theory – need be known at all. But to go this far is to go further than the *Cours* itself takes us.

It is important to see that for Saussure hypotheses about Proto-Indo-European sounds are not 'pure abstractions' because of the realist position he adopts in phonetics. He is committed to the general proposition that the *signifiants* of all languages used a fixed inventory of sounds ([303]) and furthermore to the proposition that 'given any word, one can distinguish clearly its constituent sounds, how many of them there are, and where they begin and end' ([302]). The basic set of sound types, for Saussure, is determined by elementary physiological possibilities of the vocal apparatus, as described in detail in the Appendix to the Introduction of the *Cours*. Therefore, when a Proto-Indo-European sound is identified as being 'the sound which occurs in the following positions in the following words', this is a description which can ultimately, at least in principle, be given a concrete interpretation by reference to the chart of physiologically possible sounds. The statement is to the effect that one of these sounds recurs time and again in the positions stated. The 'sameness' is ultimately a physiological sameness of a known type, even if the precise details are debatable (but within known parameters). In other words, the ultimate justification for such reconstructions is that we know (or assume we know) what sounds the Proto-Indo-European vocal apparatus could produce. If we had any reason for thinking that in fact Proto-Indo-European had been a language of Martian invaders, producing sounds by means of vocal organs with unknown properties, that justification would automatically fall. To claim to identify a Martian word as '15819', in the absence of any chart of Martian phonetics, would, in Saussure's terms, be quite meaningless. There would not even be any guarantee that Martian vocal signs were linear. But if we assume that Proto-Indo-European *signifiants* were linear and that the elements linearly concatenated were drawn from a physiological inventory of known types, we rescue even inaccurate synchronic statements about the word for 'horse' from the limbo of 'pure abstraction'.

CHAPTER IV

Linguistic Evidence in Anthropology and Prehistory

This chapter may be looked upon as taking up the remarks which conclude Chapter II of the Introduction, referring to the 'prejudices, illusions and fantasies' of all kinds which the study of language has fostered, and laying it down as the linguist's task to denounce them. The scepticism Saussure expresses here concerning the extent to which linguistic evidence can throw light on questions of anthropology, ethnography and prehistory clearly relates to his own theoretical position on the relevant linguistic issues. Thus his denial of any inherent connexion between language and race (§1), coupled with his acceptance that language is an important constituent factor in cultural unity (§2), reflects his theoretical commitment to the two propositions that languages are social institutions, not biological legacies, and that they are social institutions based on arbitrary signs. The section on linguistic paleontology (§3), with its warnings against leaping too hastily to conclusions about specific cultural practices, is a disguised sermon about the reliability of historical reconstructions. Most characteristic of all is the refusal in §4 to accept that particular features of linguistic structure may be considered reflections of the 'group mentality' of the language users. Here the reasons offered reflect quite openly Saussure's adherence to the view that sound changes act 'blindly', and that every linguistic system is constructed on the basis of the materials fortuitously bequeathed by random historical processes. Thus he points out, for example, that the Old French construction *le cor Roland* emerged 'purely by chance', and argues that the parallel construction in Semitic may well have done likewise. 'The psychological characteristics of the language community count for little as against facts like the fall of a final vowel or a modification of stress' ([311-12]).

Arguments of this kind throw an interesting if indirect light on the question of the relations between linguistics and other disciplines. Thus when Saussure, speaking *qua* linguist, denies there is any linguistic evidence to support the view that the psychological characteristics of the community determine certain features of linguistic structure, that denial is in fact a disguised assertion of a particular theoretical position within linguistics. It is not a question of what the 'linguistic evidence' shows at all. For the linguistic evidence is equally consonant with the opposite view. Indeed, there is no difficulty at all in principle in reconciling Saussure's claim that sound changes act 'blindly' with the theory that the 'group mentality' will nevertheless favour certain ways of constructing a new linguistic system out of the debris inherited from the past. Saussure, in short, never addresses the question of what counts as linguistic evidence on such matters: for to take that question seriously would be already to concede that there might be systematic factors at work other than those allowed for within the conceptual framework of Saussurean linguistic theory.

CHAPTER V

Language Families and Linguistic Types

The concluding argument of the preceding chapter is here reaffirmed and generalized. It applies, claims Saussure, to the whole question of language typology. 'A language, as we have seen, is not directly subject to the control of the minds of its speakers. Let us conclude by emphasizing one of the consequences of this principle: no family of languages rightly belongs once and for all to a particular linguistic type' ([313]). What 'we have seen', however, is something of a rather different order; namely, that Saussure cannot accept the idea that in different communities there might be different but permanent psychological factors at work which restrict in different ways the available options for combining *signifiants* with *signifiés*. The reason for this reluctance is not difficult to see. To admit the possible existence of such factors would mean acknowledging restrictions on the basic principle of *l'arbitraire du signe*; and Saussurean linguistic theory makes no provision for such restrictions.

Again Saussure's attitude towards 'linguistic evidence' on a point like this speaks for itself. Given a case like the Semitic languages where, as he admits, over a very long period of time the 'persistence of certain characteristics' of linguistic structure is very striking ([315]), Saussure produces two weak counterarguments: (i) that particular characteristics analogous to those which look as if they are 'permanent' in Semitic may appear as relatively transitory features in other languages or language families, and (ii) that even in the Semitic languages one finds occasional exceptions to these supposedly 'permanent' features. By implication, this presumably means that the only features which Saussure would accept as *prima facie* evidence of permanent characteristics inherent in a language family would be: (i) features admitting no exceptions whatever, and (ii) features not found in any other language. In other words, the evidential demands are placed at a level where there is no prospect of meeting them. The question as to why the Semitic languages have preserved these particular characteristics is dismissed with the quasi-tautological remark that this simply means they have undergone less change than many other languages. 'There are no unchangeable features: permanence is due to chance' ([316]). This the reader will recognize as a reiteration of the thesis earlier advanced on pp.[129-34] that languages are not governed by diachronic laws.

* * *

The famous concluding sentence of the *Cours*

> *la linguistique a pour unique et véritable objet la langue envisagée en elle-même et pour elle-même*

has been rejected as not authentically Saussurean. Since there appears to be no textual basis for it in the manuscript sources, Saussure's editors have been held responsible, and, by implication, responsible too for the fact that it was subsequently quoted as evidence in support of attributing to Saussure a somewhat narrow and 'exclusive' concept of linguistics (de Mauro 1972: 476-7, n.305). Seen in this light, then, it appears as a final and ineradicable blot on the editorial copybook. Bally and Sechehaye not merely exceeded their brief, but in the end proved incompetent to formulate a clear, unmisleading statement of Saussure's teaching.

'Nothing in the manuscript sources indicates that Saussure uttered this famous pronouncement or, even less, clearly, that it represents the "fundamental idea" of his teaching' (de Mauro 1972: 476). The 'even less' (*encore moins*) epitomizes a philological obsession which has dominated readings of Saussure for the past quarter of a century. Nothing can possibly be authentically Saussurean unless textual evidence other than the *Cours* can be cited in support (however second-hand, implausible or manifestly dubious it may be). The philologists would be fouling their own Saussurean nest, however, to attribute to the editors totally unmotivated fantasies or inventions. It has to be conceded that Bally and Sechehaye did not make the conclusion up '*e nihilo*' (de Mauro 1972: 476). Hence the hypothesis that perhaps 'they thought they were writing something in line with the principle stated on p.[25]: *il faut se placer de prime abord sur le terrain de la langue et la prendre pour norme de toutes les autres manifestations du langage*' (de Mauro 1972: 476).

A simple philological point which this philological reading overlooks is that the phrase *unique et véritable objet* of this last sentence in the *Cours* ([317]) clearly echoes the phrase *véritable et unique objet* ([13]) in the opening sentence of the same text three hundred pages earlier. Whether the two are syntagmatically related may be open to dispute. That they are associatively related can hardly be a subject of contention. Could this be a 'mere coincidence' in a text like the *Cours*? (This particular conjunction of adjectives and nouns occurs nowhere else in the intervening chapters.) The reader will recall that the opening chapter identified various stages through which linguistics had passed *before* identifying its *véritable et unique objet*. That implicitly opens up a question-and-answer format for the *Cours*. Question: 'What is this *objet*?' The question, raised on the first page and then pursued in all its ramifications throughout the following chapters, is eventually answered on the final page. Not only did subsequent Saussurean exegesis object to the eventual answer, but patently failed to recognize the pertinent question.

What might the shades of the editors reply to this ultimate vote of no confidence by posterity? That an attempt to answer the main question raised by someone's teaching is not to be confused with giving a synopsis of that teaching, much less with passing a verdict on it? Or that the full complexity of Saussure's teaching had already been amply reflected in preceding chapters? Perhaps all the reply needed to posterity would be to point out that posterity itself had for decades failed to see anything unSaussurean in that *explicit*. The controversial concluding sentence doubtless has its ambiguities: but they match, with masterly exactness, the ambiguities of the *Cours* itself.

PART TWO
Saussurean Linguistics

… the chauvinism of science is a much greater problem than the problem of intellectual pollution.

P. Feyerabend

CHAPTER I

Strategy and Programme

Many people must have come to the end of reading the *Cours de linguistique générale* with the uncomfortable feeling that they did not quite know whether they had understood the message or not, in spite of having grasped various general principles and particular arguments along the way. General linguistics, as presented by the *Cours*, seems to emerge as a form of inquiry which is simultaneously possible and impossible. Can the reader even go on to ask: 'But which is it?'

Part of the difficulty is that in spite of its title what Saussure's *Cours de linguistique générale* offers is not a course but a charter. The programme itself is fixed only in broad outline. What is astonishing about the genesis of the text is not that the editors subsequently took material from three sets of university lectures and turned it into a manifesto for an as yet untried approach to language, but, on the contrary, that the manifesto was formulated as lectures for students in the first place. That academic context alone, nevertheless, tells us a great deal.

It is hardly surprising that what emerge as predominant questions in the *Cours* are precisely the questions which would be foremost in the mind of someone who had spent a lifetime teaching the kind of syllabus accepted as constituting Indo-European linguistic studies in the latter half of the nineteenth century, and was not only worried by its inadequacies, but foresaw the possibility that disciplines such as psychology, physiology, sociology and anthropology might well sponsor forms of linguistic inquiry which would be potential rivals for recognition as the modern science of language. This determined in advance that any eventual Saussurean programme would need to reconcile (i) the need to carve out a defensible scientific territory for linguistics, and (ii) the need to partition that territory internally in such a way as to accommodate within it certain traditional vested interests. These joint interdisciplinary and intradisciplinary requirements circumscribed any answer to what we may call Saussure's 'primary theoretical problems'. Nowhere is there any indication that Saussure had the visionary breadth to found general linguistics *de novo*, in the sense of asking himself where and how the human sciences of the twentieth century would need inquiry into language to be directed. In the *Cours* there is not even a breath of academic ecumenicalism. To the extent that Saussurean linguistics is radical, it is radically conservative.

That would at the same time explain one of the most striking omissions in the whole of the *Cours*: that a work devoted to laying the foundations of general linguistic theory never once addresses the question 'What do we need general linguistic theory for?' The omission tells us a great deal about the Saussurean concept of science. The hidden premiss seems to be that sciences simply are endeavours to bring together and interrelate under a few general laws or principles as many disparate facts as possible pertaining to one subject. The idea that perhaps such an endeavour makes better sense in some subjects than in others, and therefore might need a rather different kind of justification in linguistics than, say, in physics is totally lacking in the *Cours*. Saussure appears to assume, simply, that as all-embracing a systematization as possible is automatically desirable and of value for its own sake. Be that as it may, he was certainly right in thinking that no such systematization had been produced in the nineteenth century.

Although the point of departure for Saussurean theorizing is dissatisfaction with the inheritance of nineteenth-century language studies, and the realization that 'the fundamental problems of general linguistics ... still await a solution' ([19]), the *Cours* at no point claims to provide that solution. But at least, as a first step, it seeks to provide an analysis of what the problems are, and to propose some general principles on the basis of which they might be tackled. That, clearly, is as far as Bally and Sechehaye saw their colleague's thinking as having progressed by the time of his death ([10]); and nothing in the subsequently published manuscript material suggests that judgment was wrong. Consequently it would have been a misrepresentation to attempt in the *Cours* a definitive systematization which removed all doubts and precluded certain possibilities of development. Over a period of years, the possibilities of development and the consequent balance of emphasis in the Saussurean conceptual schema for general linguistics doubtless varied in Saussure's own mind. This, again, the editors were fully aware of: as they say in their Preface, Saussure was someone for whom thinking was a constant process of intellectual renewal ([8-9]), and the variations between the three courses of lectures which he gave over the years 1907-11 bear them out. What they were too modest to mention was a possibility that must certainly have occurred to them as they drafted the *Cours*: that such a draft as theirs might well have helped Saussure, had he lived, to see more clearly just how far his own thinking had progressed, and exactly what there was 'still awaiting a solution'. On the other hand, what they are not likely to have foreseen is that the very incompleteness – even vagueness – of that state of Saussure's thought which the *Cours* represents would subsequently prove one of its major interdisciplinary attractions, and enhance its potential as a stimulus for other disciplines than linguistics.

Saussure had certainly progressed as far as seeing how the two basic needs of his programme could be reconciled. The 'territorial' need in any case could not be satisfied by defining the boundaries of linguistics in terms of subject-matter; for, as subject-matter, language and linguistic phenomena were already shared with other disciplines. What was required here was to identify something essentially 'linguistic' which other disciplines could not plausibly claim to study, in spite of the overlap of subject-matter. At the same time, the 'internal' need was to accommodate within this territory topics of the kind which Indo-Europeanists and dialectologists had already established as focal points of scholarly attention. In short, the programme was one which would rescue the subject from the clutches of historians and philologists, but at the same time establish it in a scientific enclave where it was safe from the encroachments of physiologists, psychologists, sociologists and others.

The base-line of the programmatic answer which the *Cours* proposes is the fundamental distinction drawn between *la langue* and *la parole*. Linguistics is proclaimed to be first and foremost a science of *la langue*. This leads straight to the question *Qu'est-ce que la langue*? In one sense, it strikes the reader as a very odd question indeed; and inevitably so. For initially we have no guarantee, as Calvet observes (Calvet 1975: 139), that it is a question which is meaningful at all. The *Cours*, it should be noted, does not propose *langue* as a linguistic technical term (although in fact for Saussure it is) and then offer to define it. On the contrary, there is a strenuous denial that *la langue* is an illusory abstraction, conjured up by terminological sleight of hand ([31]). This is because for Saussure the claims of a subject to be a science depend essentially on whether or not what it studies really exists. (That is precisely the burden of his complaint against nineteenth-century linguistics. It presupposed belief in all kinds of linguistic entities which do not exist: languages which remain 'the same' in spite of splitting up into different dialects; words which remain 'the same' in spite of changing their pronunciation and meaning; grammatical paradigms which remain 'the same' in spite of losing their flexional distinctions; and so on.) For Saussure, it will not do to anchor linguistic reality to samenesses which exist merely retrospectively in the eye of the historian. Hence, 'What is *la langue*?' *has* to be presented as a factual question (on a par with 'What is electricity?' or 'What is the national debt?'). If there is no such thing as *la langue*, then it will not do as the basis for any kind of science at all.

So *la langue* has to be something real, something about which general truths can be discovered (despite the notorious diversity of actual languages), and something which is essentially involved in the social practices and psychological events normally reckoned to be linguistic in nature. Unfortunately, that conjunction of requirements still does not automatically pick out any one thing which can be identified as *la langue*, and Saussure is therefore obliged simply to postulate that *la langue* is somehow both a social institution in the community and at the same time a cognitive system in the mind of the individual. This awkward equation compels Saussure, in spite of his dislike of abstractions, to 'dematerialize' the linguistic sign and treat *la langue* merely as a structure constituted by a set of relations. For only at that level can it plausibly be claimed that the social institution and the individual cognitive system are 'really' one and the same thing.

It is this same equation which leads to what was later called the 'Saussurean paradox' (Labov 1972: 186) in descriptive linguistics. If *la langue* is stored inside every speaker's head, the testimony of a single individual in principle suffices as data for the linguist's description of *la langue* (even if – and perhaps ideally if – the witness and the linguist are one and the same person). By contrast, data for the description of *parole* can be obtained only by observing speech events as and when they occur in social interaction, because such events are not already stored in the heads of any individuals, even the participants themselves. This conclusion is said to be paradoxical because it reverses the basic Saussurean characterization of *langue* as social, as opposed to *parole* as individual ([30]): for it turns out that to study *la langue* it will suffice to study the individual, whereas to study *la parole* will require collecting evidence from the community.

Whether this so-called 'Saussurean paradox' detected by Labov is paradoxical at all has, however, been questioned. According to Pateman, the paradox is 'little more than an index of Labov's naive conceptions of scientific activity' (Pateman 1983: 113). But *ad hominem* rebuttals of this order merely obscure what is at issue, which is neither a verbal dispute about the use of the term *paradox*, nor a question of the validity of anyone's view of 'scientific activity'. The point is that, whether we call it a 'paradox' or not, the *Cours* appears to be committed to an account of how the individual acquires *la langue* which is at odds with a programme for linguistics which claims that '*la langue*, as distinct from *la parole*, is an object that may be studied independently' ([31]).

More precisely, the 'Saussurean paradox' arises from a conjunction of two separate incompatibilities: (i) between 'average' and 'aggregate' concepts of *la langue*, (ii) between either of these and the role assigned to *la langue* in the Saussurean speech circuit. The latter demands uniformity between speaker and hearer: otherwise communication breaks down. But the account given of *la langue* as a social product of *parole* does not yield uniformity. Saussure hesitates between saying that *la langue* is a communal average (*une sorte de moyenne* ([29])) established between individuals, and saying that it is a communal aggregate (*la somme des images verbales emmagasinées chez tous les individus* ([30])), without appearing to realize *either* that these two are quite different concepts of *la langue*, *or* that neither offers any guarantee that speaker and hearer operate with identical cognitive systems for the purposes of *parole*.

Furthermore, neither the 'average' concept of *la langue* nor the 'aggregate' concept supplies any theoretical warrant for a methodology which assumes that in order to study *la langue* it will suffice to study the individual. For it is impossible to identify a communal average without studying the evidence taken from a reasonable cross-section of the community, and it is impossible to identify a communal aggregate without studying all the evidence the community has to offer. These methodological principles hold regardless of whether we are studying language or any other social practice. But in the *Cours* all such difficulties are simply brushed under the broadest of theoretical carpets by a straight equation between social institution and cognitive system.

The 'Saussurean paradox' is one in a series of what we may term Saussure's 'secondary theoretical problems'. These are the problems internal to the Saussurean programme itself. How – and how satisfactorily – some of them are dealt with has already been queried at various points in the preceding commentary on the text of the *Cours*. For the moment it should be noted that in this instance, as in others, the 'internal' problem arises because of an attempt to deal with an 'external' difficulty: here it is the equation between cognitive system and social institution which is forced on Saussure by the need to present (Saussurean) linguistics as a single, unified science with its own autonomy. If *la langue* were not *both* cognitive system *and* social institution, its study would have to be split into at least two separate enterprises, each answerable to a different set of theoretical assumptions.

Having postulated this unified socio-cognitive entity called *la langue* as the primary focus of linguistic investigation, Saussure next has to map out the internal partition of linguistics and show how all aspects of linguistic study are catered for. For this purpose, the initial dichotomy between *langue* and *parole* has to be supplemented by a further dichotomy between synchrony and diachrony. Thus room can be allowed for the study of linguistic change and of dialectal variation, but without the danger of relapsing into the chaos of nineteenth-century failures to distinguish *faits de langue* from *faits de parole*. However, the necessity to integrate the two dichotomies itself generates more 'secondary theoretical problems'.

A certain preoccupation with this new set of secondary problems surfaces intermittently throughout the *Cours*. It gives rise to the impression that this is a text written by someone with a nagging obsession about time, and specifically about the relationship between temporality and systematicity. Ideally, one feels, Saussure would have liked to be able to adopt the extremely elegant solution of treating time as the common dimension which orders all the relevant sets of relations which linguistics has to deal with. But there are various reasons why this will not work. Chief among them is what we may call the 'real time' trap: sometimes temporal relations match linguistic relations, but sometimes they do not. Thus, for example, it is possible to have two languages, of which L1 is still in use centuries after L2 is defunct, even though L2 represents an *état de langue* which is the 'successor' of L1. Saussure is therefore obliged to construe linguistic time relatively to systems, and distinguish an *axe des successivités* from an *axe des simultanéités*. Even this will not quite work, because 'real time' simultaneity does not guarantee systematicity. So the notion of synchrony has to be replaced ultimately by that of idiosynchrony. Avoiding the 'real time' trap by resorting to linguistic time unfortunately means that the orthogonal axes no longer parallel those which plot the history of language communities: but fictionally they are deemed to. We end up with a *Cours* in which the debris of that ideally elegant treatment of time, uniting linguistic events with linguistic systems in perfect theoretical harmony, remains visibly scattered throughout the text (the failure to discard the terms *synchronique* and *diachronique* in spite of their inappropriateness; the attempt to show that geographical variation reduces to temporal variation; the survival of succession in real time as the principle of linearity, etc.).

It is another aspect of the 'real time' trap which obliges Saussure to adopt what Collingwood might have called a compromise view of linguistic history: a compromise, that is, between 'substantialism' and 'anti-substantialism' (Collingwood 1946: 42ff.). Substantialism is the view that the particular time-bound acts and events which constitute the material of history flow from something which itself remains changeless throughout (a city, a nation, an institution, etc.) The opposite view treats this hypothetically changeless entity which allegedly survives through the changes brought by time as a fiction, myth, category mistake, or something similar. Now for Saussure an *état de langue* does not change simply because over a period of time a great variety of acts of *parole* are performed by a great variety of speakers: on the contrary, it may remain unchanged for generations. To that extent, Saussure takes a substantialist view of the linguistic institution itself. However, there are for Saussure certain historical changes which it must be impossible for an *état de langue* to survive. Otherwise twentieth-century French would still represent the same *état de langue* as second-century Latin. So there is a limit to Saussurean substantialism on one level, even while on another level an unbroken continuity of *parole* between generations of speakers is hypothesized. What is it that can survive unchanged to establish that continuity across successive *états de langue*? Merely linguistic material or substance, according to Saussure; but not linguistic form. Thus it makes perfectly good (Saussurean) sense to say that the *t* of the Latin *terra* has survived in French *terre*, even though the French consonant system is quite different from the Latin consonant system. This is rather like saying that the material of a Roman wall can survive in a twentieth-century French building, even though its architectural context and function may have altered entirely. But any variety of substantialism which claims that elements of linguistic form survive from Latin to modern French Saussure will dismiss as based on historical illusion.

Saussure's compromise view of history is also dictated by the internal partitioning requirements of his programme. A theorist who took an uncompromising anti-substantialist position would have to maintain not only that the word *terra* does not survive from Latin into French (which is Saussure's claim) but that – *pace* Saussure – the initial sound *t* does not survive either. According to the anti-substantialist, the 'survival' of the *t* would be just as much a historian's illusion as the 'survival' of the Latin word in French *terre*: for since neither words nor speech sounds are at all like bricks, stones or other physical objects, it is absurd to claim that sounds can survive whereas words cannot. Thorough-going anti-substantialism of this order, theoretically legitimate though it might be, would leave no slot in the linguistic programme for any traditional form of historical linguistics. This is why Saussure cannot accept it. His compromise at least allows historical phonetics to continue as a 'non-illusory' form of inquiry, and this was bound to please all those linguists who regarded the working out of Indo-European 'sound laws' as one of the great intellectual triumphs of the nineteenth century. At the same time, the compromise allows Saussure to deny the validity of the other much-acclaimed achievement of nineteenth-century comparative and historical linguistics, 'historical grammar'. In this way, the Saussurean programme does not reject historical linguistics altogether, but teaches it a lesson and puts it firmly in its place within a new theoretical framework, based on the rigid separation of synchronic facts from diachronic facts.

Calvet's diagnosis (Calvet 1975: 61) hits the nail on the head when it describes structuralism in linguistics as being born of a rejection of *linguistique externe*, and a desire to abstract *la langue* from the social practice in which it is manifested. Well and good, *provided that we interpret this diagnosis in terms of the exigencies of an academic programme*, and not as reflecting some personal ideological stance on the part of Saussure. Otherwise we confuse the original rationale of a linguistic theory with the reasons for its runaway success in the subsequent intellectual history of the twentieth century. It would be unpardonably naive to suppose that the fortunes of Saussurean structuralism had anything to do with the world's sudden interest in the internal affairs of the academic conduct of language studies. That would be like attributing the success of the Beatles to a worldwide fascination with the local culture of Liverpool.

Perhaps as important as any of the factors which Calvet mentions is simply the extent to which Saussurean structuralism appealed to the profound anti-historicism of the twentieth century. Like the twentieth century's most influential theories in all fields (in art, architecture, politics, sociology, etc.) what Saussure urged could be read as legitimizing a rejection of the cultural past. The historical process as portrayed in the *Cours* is one of disruption of old linguistic systems and their replacement by totally new systems. These new systems are not just the old systems patched up, adapted or transformed: they are original whole creations in their own right, and the very condition for their existence is the collapse of previous systems. Moreover, since all linguistic systems are independent, there is no sense in which one system owes anything to another. Analyses valid for earlier systems are totally inapplicable to their successors: indeed, the most profound analytic mistake that can be made for Saussure is to continue to apply classifications and criteria that are derived from an earlier system, as if the later system were the same. The only reality of a system is the reality it has for its present users: to this reality the past contributes nothing. This implied rejection of the nineteenth century's insistence on always looking back to the past in order to explain the present is, as much as any other single feature, what established Saussure's credentials as a thoroughly 'modern' theorist.

The Saussurean identification of synchrony with the viewpoint of current language users ([117]ff.) is a further factor which requires *la langue* to be construed in terms of an equation between social institution and individual cognitive system. For the working of the social institution in its totality is something which the individual speaker is *in no position to observe*, unless the linguistic community is a very small one indeed. In larger communities, however, we cannot as individuals going about our daily linguistic business claim to be in contact with all our fellow speakers. In that sense, an individual can no more command a view of the totality of *parole* in the community than of the totality of the other social transactions being conducted. The guarantee that all speakers are speaking 'the same language' cannot come from anyone's acquaintance with the totality of the community's *parole*, since in many communities no individual can claim anything remotely approaching such an acquaintance. Hence the need to postulate that somehow all speakers have already acquired a standard representation of *la langue* inside their heads 'rather like a dictionary of which each individual has an identical copy' ([38]). How they manage to do this is something of a mystery, but it is simply assumed that somehow or other they do.

Without this assumption, clearly, the descriptive statements of linguistics could never be scientific statements in the sense in which Saussure was trying to establish linguistics as a science. The reasons why take us back again to the 'Saussurean paradox'. If access to *la langue* could not be obtained through the testimony of individuals, there would be strictly nothing scientific to be said about English, or about French; for since no linguist could possibly set about the Herculean task of observing – let alone analysing – the totality of English or French speech, descriptions would be simply provisional codifications of minute fragments of *parole*. No generalizations about *la langue* would be possible. These are the considerations which dictate Saussure's choice of a model of speech communication.

CHAPTER II
Saussure's Theory of Communication

Every linguistic theory presupposes a theory of communication; and Saussurean linguistics is no exception. However minimal or inexplicitly formulated such a theory of communication may be, it has an essential role to play because nothing else can provide the conceptual underpinnings necessary for a more detailed account of how an interactive social activity like language works. If Saussure had called his *circuit de la parole* instead a *circuit de la communication orale*, this might have avoided the unfortunate impression that the reader is expected to accept *la parole* on trust as a process, before the theorist can supply any clear articulation of the distinction between *la parole* and *la langue*. Calling it a *circuit de la parole* sounds suspiciously like taking one term of a theoretical dichotomy for granted, in order thereby to define the other. If, on the other hand, we read the speech circuit as a general theory of oral communication, it does not prejudge the dichotomy in advance. Furthermore, the place of importance which the circuit is given right at the beginning of the *Cours* would then be seen as the logical place to introduce general theoretical assumptions about a communicational whole which involves both *langue* and *parole*.

The theory of oral communication which Saussure's speech circuit summarizes was by no means new, and did not originate within the disciplinary confines of linguistics. The *Cours* makes no reference to these origins, but as a matter of intellectual history they can scarcely be open to doubt. When the speech-circuit model is scrutinized, it becomes clear enough that although Saussure explicitly divided the circuit into its physiological, psychological and physical sections, those divisions were not based upon contemporary findings in psychology, physiology or physics. At the time the *Cours* was published, the neurological, motor and acoustic processes involved in speech were not sufficiently well understood to offer the basis for such a model. Apart from one passing reference to the work of Broca (which, as noted earlier, is used to support a merely negative conclusion), nothing suggests that Saussure's analysis of oral communication was in any way founded on nineteenth-century advances in the sciences dealing with the actual mechanisms of speech. Its ancestry is more venerable.

Saussure's speech circuit is essentially a schematic summary, not of the directly observable facts of speech activity, nor even of unobservable micro-events hypothesized as taking place during speech, but of a psychological explanation of oral communication of the kind propounded in its classic form in the seventeenth century by John Locke, and sometimes called the 'translation theory' of understanding (Parkinson 1977). Saussure simply takes over two basic claims of this old psychological theory and incorporates them as premises in his model. These are: (i) that communication is a process of 'telementation' (that is, of the transference of thoughts from one human mind to another), and (ii) that a necessary and sufficient condition for successful telementation is that the process of communication, by whatever mechanisms it employs, should result in the hearer's thoughts being identical with the speaker's. Although this theory is perhaps most clearly expounded by Locke in its application to language, elements of it can be traced back much further in the philosophical tradition. Plato's theory of forms, for example, as Cornford (1935:9) points out, reveals an 'underlying assumption ... that every common name must have a fixed meaning, which we think of when we hear the name spoken: speaker and hearer thus have the same object before their minds. Only so can they understand one another at all and any discourse be possible.'

The term 'translation theory' refers to the fact that, according to the theory in question, when language is the vehicle of communication understanding requires a double process of 'translation': a speaker's thoughts are first translated into sounds, and then the sounds uttered are translated back again into thoughts by the hearer. This is clearly the basic idea behind Saussure's account of what happens when A and B engage in discourse. A and B are each responsible for the translation required in their respective sections of the circuit. A cannot translate on behalf of B, nor B on behalf of A: this is of the essence of *la parole*. It is conceived by Saussure as an individual enterprise, as distinct from the social or collective enterprise which constitutes *la langue*. If for any reason either A or B fails in this individual responsibility, or the process of double translation is otherwise prevented, the speech circuit is broken and the speech act abortive.

It is interesting to compare Saussure's model with accounts of speech communication which were still being offered fifty years later by authorities in linguistic theory, phonetics and speech pathology. The family resemblance is unmistakable.

In some modern versions, the metaphor of translation is replaced by that of 'encoding' and 'decoding': as for example, in the following generativist formulation:

Linguistic communication consists in the production of some external, publicly observable, acoustic phenomenon whose phonetic and syntactic structure encodes a speaker's inner, private thoughts or ideas and the decoding of the phonetic and syntactic structure exhibited in such a physical phenomenon by other speakers in the form of an inner, private experience of the same thoughts or ideas. (Katz 1966:98)

Similarly, Crystal describes three phases of the speech chain as 'neurological encoding', 'anatomical-physiological encoding', and 'brain decoding' (Crystal 1980:72ff., 93 ff., 119 ff.).

The code metaphor is not merely 'terminological': it is spelled out in quite elaborate detail. For instance:

We may ... think of the speech chain as a communication system in which ideas to be transmitted are represented by a code that undergoes transformations as speech events proceed from one level to another. We can draw an analogy here between speech and Morse code. In Morse code, certain patterns of dots and dashes stand for different letters of the alphabet; the dots and dashes are a code for the letters. This code can also be transformed from one form to another. For example, a series of dots and dashes on a piece of paper can be converted into an acoustic sequence, like 'beep-bip-bip-beep'. In the same way, the words of our language are a code for concepts and material objects ...

During speech transmission, the speaker's linguistic code of words and sentences is transformed into physiological and physical codes – in other words, into corresponding sets of muscle movements and air vibrations – being reconverted into linguistic code at the listener's end. This is analogous to translating the written 'dash-dash-dash' of Morse code into the sounds, 'beep-beep-beep'. (Denes and Pinson 1963: 7-8)

Some versions (e.g. Moulton 1970:23) restrict the terms 'encoding' and 'decoding' to those parts of the circuit which correspond to Saussure's 'psychological' sections. (Thus the transmission from A's brain to A's speech organs, for example, would not count as part of the 'encoding' process.) Others apply the metaphor to physiological processes as well.

It is evident that the substitution of the code metaphor for the translation metaphor alters nothing in the account of communication, except perhaps to make even more perspicuous the point that the objective is the recovery by B of exactly the same conceptual package (the 'message') as A originally formulated.

More emphatically than Saussure, his generativist successors half a century on stressed the inadequacy of restricting the study of language to the 'public' sections of the speech circuit:

Behaviouristically oriented investigations of linguistic communication focus exclusively on the publicly observable aspects of communication situations: speech sounds, nonverbal behavior of the participants in the situation, and physical properties of the available stimuli. Thus, such investigations neglect the essential aspect of successful linguistic communication, the congruence of speaker's and hearer's thought and ideas that results from verbal exchanges. (Katz 1966: 98)

With all this Saussure would doubtless have agreed.

In Katz's view, as in Saussure's, a linguistics restricted to the analysis of publicly observable features of linguistic activity would simply fail to come to terms with the principal function which a language is called upon to serve:

> To understand the ability of natural languages to serve as instruments for the communication of thoughts and ideas we must understand what it is that permits those who speak them consistently to connect the right sounds with the right meanings. (Katz 1966: 100)

Saussure could scarcely have hoped for a more whole-hearted endorsement from posterity of his assumption that the speech-circuit model provides not only a correct but an essential communication theory for linguistics. Most linguists of the nineteenth century had certainly failed entirely to appreciate the need for any such theoretical basis, having concentrated almost exclusively on the publicly observable features of linguistic activity, and even then in a second-hand form (via written records). By adopting and adapting the Lockean model to the purposes of twentieth-century structuralism, the *Cours* makes a decisive break with the crypto-positivism which had reigned in language studies from Bopp to the Neogrammarians.

The main features in which later versions of the speech circuit do not tally with Saussure's are two; and both are significant with respect to the distinction between *langue* and *parole*. First, later accounts tend to give a more elaborate account of the initial and final phase. For example:

> The first thing the speaker has to do is arrange his thoughts, decide what he wants to say and put what he wants to say into *linguistic form*. The message is put into linguistic form by selecting the right words and phrases to express its meaning, and by placing these words in the correct order required by the grammatical rules of the language. (Denes and Pinson 1963: 4)

According to Moulton (1970: 23) the initial phase of encoding is divisible into three consecutive steps, as follows:

Encoding the message $\left\{ \begin{array}{l} \text{1. Semantic encoding.} \\ \text{2. Grammatical encoding.} \\ \text{3. Phonological encoding.} \end{array} \right.$

These are matched by a parallel sequence in reverse order at the hearer's end of the chain:

$$\left. \begin{array}{l} \textit{Decoding} \\ \textit{the message} \end{array} \right\} \begin{array}{l} \text{9. Phonological decoding.} \\ \text{10. Grammatical decoding.} \\ \text{11. Semantic decoding.} \end{array}$$

All that Saussure has to say about the initial phase is the brief reference to concepts 'triggering' sound patterns in the brain ([28]); while the final phase is described as the 'psychological association' of the *image acoustique* with the 'corresponding concept' ([28]).

The second discrepancy concerns a 'loop' in the speech circuit which Saussure omits, but which later accounts supply. The point here is that A and B are both listeners: 'there are two listeners, not one, because the speaker not only speaks, he also listens to his own voice. In listening, he continuously compares the quality of the sounds he produces with the sound qualities he intended to produce and makes the adjustments necessary to match the results with his intentions' (Denes and Pinson 1963: 6). This 'double listening' is regarded as important in providing models of language disability. Furthermore, it is recognized as a complex process. 'Auditory feedback is perhaps the most noticeable way in which we monitor our own communications, but it is not the only way. There is also *kinesthetic* feedback – the feelings of internal movement and position of our muscles, joints, etc. which we have while we are speaking ... Knowing (at an unconscious level) where our tongues are in our mouths is an important factor in maintaining our clarity of speech' (Crystal 1980: 58-9).

It would be uncharitable to suppose that these two discrepancies highlight matters which scholars of Saussure's generation had simply never thought about. Why is there no inclusion of them in Saussure's speech circuit? The first omission sends us back to the question of the Lockean ancestry of Saussure's model, and raises a point on which Saussure was subsequently criticized by the generativists of the 1960s.

Locke and Saussure both seem to assume that the basic item on which the understanding of oral communication operates is a single, indivisible unit of some kind. For Locke this is the 'word', and for Saussure the *signe linguistique*. (In Locke's case, 'word' has to be put in scare quotes. One commentator claims: 'his definition is such that any sound at all will be a word' (Woozley 1964: 36). This rather sweeping charge seems to have been brought on the ground that since Locke is wrong about words anyway, he might as well be hung for a sheep as a lamb. A charge that would stick with more plausibility is that Locke treats words as identified by (what Saussure would have regarded as) their phonetic 'substance'. But then, so do many people for all practical purposes. To object to this is to object to a very usual way in which the term *word* is ordinarily used.)

But Locke has a reason for adopting this kind of unit, which Saussure ostensibly lacks. It is connected with Locke's account of perception and his taxonomy of ideas. According to Locke, when we hear a word such as *man*, or *horse*, or *sun*, or *water*, or *iron* 'everyone who understands the language frames in his mind a combination of those several simple ideas which he has usually observed, or fancied to exist together under that denomination' (Locke 1706: 2.23.6). No such doctrine of simple ideas is supplied by Saussure, who, unlike Locke, was not engaged in the larger theoretical endeavour of constructing a general, internally consistent account of the human mind. Locke's interest in what we understand by words such as *man, horse, sun, water* and *iron* is connected with his intellectual role as epistemologist to the founders of the Royal Society (Aarsleff 1982). Saussure played no comparable role: he was not committed to any particular alliance with contemporary philosophers of science, much less to taking sides in a debate with very considerable religious implications.

The second discrepancy between Saussure's speech circuit and later models also sends us back to Locke. For a theory of understanding, the feedback loop in the communicational mechanism is simply an irrelevance. B's hearing what A says is in no way on a par with A's hearing what A says. If it were, Saussure would have to claim that A does not grasp the meaning of his own utterance until he hears it. *Quod est absurdum*. This is what supplies the internal logic of Saussure's insistence ([27]) that at least two individuals are needed to complete the speech circuit. In strictly Saussurean terms, talking to oneself does not count as a speech act at all.

There are differences between Locke's version of the translation theory of oral communication and Saussure's. Locke evidently supposed that there could be thought without language, and that the mind could engage in it without the aid of any linguistic instrument. 'Language does not exist, then, because man is a rational being; it exists, according to Locke, because man is "a sociable creature", and language is "the great instrument and common tie of society" ' (Parkinson 1977: 2). Saussure emerges as a sceptic on this score. He does not explicitly discuss the question of whether or to what extent human beings could think without language, but he describes prelinguistic thought as amorphous. 'Psychologically, setting aside its expression in words, our thought is simply a vague, shapeless mass' ([155]). More specifically still, '... were it not for signs, we should be incapable of differentiating any two ideas in a clear and consistent way ... No ideas are established in advance, and nothing is distinct, before the introduction of *la langue*' ([155]). This marks a significant shift of emphasis away from Locke, and meshes with an important historical evolution in the philosophical status of linguistic inquiry, which is characteristic of the late nineteenth and twentieth centuries. The evolution in question tends towards seeing language not as a gratuitous social bonus for purposes of communication, but as a *sine qua non* for the articulation of any analytic structure of ideas whatsoever.

This, in one sense, is the essential message of Saussurean structuralism for the whole of the humanities: language is not peripheral to human understanding of reality. On the contrary, human understanding of reality in every sphere revolves about the social use of linguistic signs.

To this extent it could perhaps be argued that it is unfair to saddle Saussure with a crude, old-fashioned Lockean theory of communication. For Saussure would certainly have denied that the systems of concepts on which communication depends are given independently of the system of vocal signals. In Saussure's theory, therefore, there is strictly no question of 'translation' between two systems: on the contrary, both are constitutive of one and the same *langue*. Although a defence of Saussure along these lines is perfectly justified, and shows that in his case the translation metaphor cannot be pressed too far, it nevertheless remains true that Saussure, like Locke, is forced to concede that knowing the meaning of a word is quite different from knowing its pronunciation. Ultimately, the reason for this is that both Saussure and Locke claim that the linguistic sign is arbitrary. It follows that neither Saussure nor Locke can explain speech communication simply by reference to a shared set of vocal forms. For, as Locke points out, being able to utter a word is no guarantee of understanding it: 'he that uses the word *tarantula*, without having any imagination or idea of what it stands for, pronounces a good word; but so long means nothing at all by it' (Locke 1706: 3.10.32.). But it is only possible to pronounce the word *tarantula* without having any idea of 'what it stands for' because *tarantula* is an arbitrary vocal form, having no natural connexion with the creature of which it happens to be the name. If A and B both use the word *tarantula* but neither knows what it means, or only one of them, then on both Saussure's account and Locke's there is no communication. The speech circuit breaks down at the point where no conceptual 'translation' of the word *tarantula* is available.

Thus far Locke would have agreed with Saussure, inasmuch as both theorists postulate complete symmetry between the encoding and the decoding of the vocal signal. Decoding has to recover exactly what was originally encoded. B's understanding of A is simply a mirror image of A's expressing the thought in the first place. The only differences between expression and comprehension that the Saussurean speech circuit allows are (i) a difference in physiological processing (between phonation and audition), and (ii) a difference in the direction of flow, as it were (the flow between *concept* and *image acoustique* being reversed, as shown by the arrows in Saussure's diagram). A point to note is that whereas this symmetry of encoding and decoding is again for Locke grounded in a general account of how the mind works (of which understanding what other people say is only one part), Saussure gives the reader no general account of how the mind works which could provide a comparable anchorage. So what was originally a motivated feature of

Locke's account survives as an article of faith in Saussure's.

A related difference is that Saussure leaves himself room to dissent from Locke's claim that men talk 'only that they may be understood; which is then only done when, by use or consent, the sound I make by the organs of speech excites in another man's mind who hears it the idea I apply to it in mine when I speak it' (Locke 1706: 3.3.3.). For Saussure is apparently concerned only with giving an account of communication in so far as it is mediated by *la langue*: he has nothing to say about the more general problem of understanding between individuals. So, for example, the word *tarantula* might excite a somewhat different idea in B's mind from the idea excited in A's (because, for instance, B is pathologically afraid of spiders whereas A is not, or because one knows more about tarantulas than the other); but that would not matter for Saussure's purposes provided both A and B were in agreement about the linguistic meaning of the term *tarantula*. At first sight, this restriction might seem to give Saussure's theory of communication an advantage over Locke's. But arguably, on the contrary, it presents Saussure with a pivotal problem never satisfactorily resolved in the *Cours*. To phrase it in terms of Locke's example, the problem would be to determine which of the mental associations connected with tarantulas in the minds of A and B count as 'the linguistic concept "tarantula" ' (in other words, the *signifié* of the sign *tarantula*). This is left unclarified in the *Cours*, apart from vague remarks about signs receiving the collective ratification of the linguistic community. But what this ratification consists in, and how the linguist would discover whether it had been collectively given or collectively withheld, are questions passed over in silence. This silence is, to say the least, awkward for Saussurean linguistics; because if there is no answer *la langue* becomes in practice undescribable. Perhaps it is this silence which, in the end, explains why the *Cours* never appeared in print in Saussure's lifetime.

There is an analogous problem too concerning the vocal form of the speech signal. Phonetically sophisticated post-Saussurean versions of the speech circuit make this quite explicit. 'Although we can regard speech transmission as a chain of events in which a code for certain ideas is transformed from one level or medium to another, it would be a great mistake to think that corresponding events at different levels are the same. There is some relationship to be sure, but the events are far from being identical. For example, there is no guarantee that people will produce sound waves with identical characteristics when they pronounce the same word. In fact, they are more likely to produce sound waves of different characteristics when they pronounce the same word. By the same token, they may very well generate similar sound waves when producing different words' (Denes and Pinson 1963: 8). But there is no mention of this in Saussure.

Once the problem is recognized, it poses an embarrassing question for the whole of Saussure's theory of communication. For that theory is based on identities. Once we allow that oral communication between A and B is based not on identities but on disparities, the notion of *la langue* as a fixed code is immediately vulnerable to objections.

Locke here encounters parallel difficulties about identity of ideas and of words, to which his *Essay* similarly offers no solution. The difference is that Locke, unlike Saussure, is not trying to elaborate a theoretical foundation for linguistics. More importantly, the comparison points up a question which Saussurean commentators have been slow to answer. Why did Saussure apparently try to adapt to his own ends a theory of communication which ostensibly served a quite contrary purpose? To put the point more sharply, why did Saussure take over a (Lockean) theory of communication concerned obviously (in Saussurean terms) with *la parole*, and apply it instead to *la langue*? A facile answer might be that Saussure had read Durkheim – an advantage history denied Locke. But there is more to it than that. For Saussure – unless he were very naive – could hardly have failed to see that by so doing he simply inherited Locke's problems writ (collectively) larger.

Saussure's adoption of this Lockean psychological model consequently cannot be explained away on general epistemological grounds. Bloomfield apparently thought the reason was simply Saussure's ignorance of anything more sophisticated: '(he) seems to have had no psychology beyond the crudest popular notions' (Bloomfield 1923). Bloomfield goes on from this to make the point that Saussure 'exemplifies, in his own person and perhaps unintentionally' the irrelevance of psychology to the study of language. The conclusion Bloomfield should have drawn was almost the opposite: namely, that a theoretical framework for the study of language may be shaped in many important respects by the communicational assumptions underlying it.

Hjelmslev was probably nearer the mark when he observed that pre-Saussurean linguistics treated language as being reducible, in the final analysis, to a constitutive totality of individual linguistic acts (Hjelmslev 1942: 30). Such a view is completely antithetical to any form of structuralism, and Saussure could not accept it. In rejecting it, however, he inherited the obligation to offer at least a minimal account of the individual linguistic act, in order to avoid the charge that his theory was an abstraction which simply failed to come to terms with the realities of everyday speech. Looking at the problem from this angle, one can see why Saussure would have found a modified Lockean model of communication attractive. In effect, it offered two welcome guarantees. In the first place, it established the role of linguistics in the human sciences. By interposing *la langue* between the individual speaker and *la parole* within a Lockean framework, Saussure ensures that the study of language cannot be reduced either to the psychology of individual speech acts, or to social analyses of the communication events which such acts constitute. For the individual acts depend on the existence of a linguistic system, of which neither the psychology nor the sociology of the nineteenth century offered any detailed description. In the second place, reducing *la parole* to the individual implementation of resources provided by *la langue* ensured that within linguistics the study of the latter take priority over the former and be independent of it. Thus built into the speech-circuit model there is what amounts to a double guarantee of autonomy: (i) autonomy of linguistics among the disciplines dealing with human speech behaviour, and (ii) autonomy of the study of *la langue* within linguistics.

Where Saussure's speech circuit marks an advance over Locke is that Locke's account is still basically a form of nomenclaturism (Harris 1980: 67 ff.). For Locke, words 'stand for' ideas in the mind: but the mind forms its ideas independently of language. Saussure rejects this psychocentric surrogationalism in favour of giving theoretical priority to the linguistic sign itself (envisaged as an indissoluble combination of *signifiant* and *signifié*). A compromise with Locke is still visible in one feature, however. 'Concepts' remain, in Saussure's account, the prime movers in the activity which occupies the speech circuit: they 'trigger' a process which would have no other plausible starting point.

This still leaves unanswered the question of how a seventeenth-century theory of understanding could plausibly be resuscitated for the purposes of a 'new' twentieth-century science. For however strong Saussure's interest in seeking a basis for establishing linguistics as an autonomous branch of scientific inquiry, it was not an interest so widely shared by fellow academics that any model suitable for that purpose would automatically have commanded general approval (or, at least, general immunity from criticism). Therefore, to explain why Saussure adopted the speech-circuit model of the individual act does not explain why his choice of model met with such widespread acceptance. Part of the answer to this rarely-asked question lies in a nineteenth-century revolution in another field altogether: technology.

Modern technology is deeply committed to circuit models. Without them, it is no exaggeration to say, technology as the modern world knows it could scarcely exist. (The earliest scientific application of the term *circuit* recorded by the *Oxford English Dictionary* dates from 1800 and relates to electricity.) Bearing this in mind, it is not a naive question to ask why Saussure (unlike Locke) insisted that speech involved a *circuit*; and whether as a matter of fact *circuit* was an appropriate term to choose. For Saussure's predecessors, even those most committed to viewing language as a summation of individual acts of speech, had not described the basic process of communication in this way.

The first point to note is that the speech-circuit model is a transmission model. It represents communication as involving passage through a succession of phases arranged in linear progression along a track or pathway. In this succession there are no gaps. The process is envisaged as a continuous journey or transfer of information from one point in space to another point in space: that is, from a location in A's brain to a location in B's brain or, in the reverse direction, from B's brain to A's. Now a model of this kind undoubtedly receives much support from numerous expressions used in everyday speech to describe the processes of communication. For example, ideas are said to be *put into* words; words are *exchanged*; verbal messages are *put across* or *got over, sent* or *passed on*; and eventually *received* and *taken in*. This way of talking about communication as transmission has been described as 'the conduit metaphor' (Reddy 1979), and it is a metaphor with extensive ramifications in various European languages. The influence of this metaphor in predisposing us to accept any transmission model of speech as plain 'common sense' is not to be underestimated.

Saussure's model, however, purports to be one particular type of transmission model. The very term *circuit* implies a contrast with other geometrical configurations. In principle, circuit models of communication must be distinguished from at least two other configurational types: from rectilinear models on the one hand, and from helical models on the other. The difference between a circuit model and a rectilinear model is the difference between a circle and a straight line. The difference between a circuit model and a helical model is the difference between a circle and a helix or spiral. Of these three types, only helical models (Dance 1967) are formally appropriate to capture the dynamic or developmental aspects of speech communication. Circuit models can make no allowance for the progressive modification of the communication situation through time. For circles always lead back to an original point of departure. The only aspect of temporal progression a circuit model allows for is the time it takes for information to pass from one point in the circuit to another point, and the only aspect of modification allowed for is the alteration in the form of the signal as it passes from one section of the circuit to the next.

There is no doubt, then, that Saussure's model is not a helical model. But is it really even a circuit model? On closer inspection, it becomes obvious that the Saussurean 'circuit', in spite of its name, is made up simply of two rectilinear sections joined together. It envisages no feedback of any kind, except a verbal reply following exactly the same progression as the verbal message first transmitted, but with the direction of flow reversed. It incorporates no guarantee that B's utterance is in any way a direct linguistic 'continuation' of or response to A's. Nor is it a 'single-track' rectilinear model, however. For if it were, Saussurean linguistics would be in principle unable to cope with a situation of the type where A and B, meeting in the street, simultaneously utter the words 'Good morning'. In short, the so-called Saussurean 'circuit' would more accurately be described as a two-track rectilinear model of speech communication. Messages can be transmitted independently along either track. All that is precluded is the simultaneous use of one track for the transmission of two messages travelling in opposite directions.

From the foregoing discussion it should be quite clear that the so-called Saussurean speech circuit is in fact an amalgam of two quite independent concepts. One is the concept of what later theorists called the 'speech chain': that is to say, the biological interlinking of processes which are physically and physiologically distinct. (Saussure mentions a *chaîne acoustique* ([64]) and a *chaîne parlée* ([65],[77]): but only in the context of discussing sound sequences. In other words, Saussure's 'chain' is a phenomenon on the syntagmatic level, and not part of the mechanism which itself makes syntagmatic phenomena possible.) The other concept is that of reciprocal exchange: B's response to A is a processual mirror of A's original speech-contact with B. But it is in no way a necessary condition for the existence of speech chains. Neither speech-chaining nor reciprocality of exchange, separately or conjointly, guarantee the identities on which the Locke-Saussure model of communication relies. The missing link is also the missing loop in Saussure's circuit. The assumption, in other words, is that 'what B hears' is nothing other than 'what A hears'. Since A, as an individual, is in sole and undisputed control of the act of *parole* in question ([30]), it must follow that *if* B is to understand A then B and A must both independently hear the same thing.

Once the logical geometry of the Saussurean speech circuit is analysed in these terms, it becomes evident that the only symmetry between its two rectilinear halves is a symmetry of message conversion. Whether the message travels from A to B or from B to A makes no difference. Somehow or other, what starts off as an idea is converted into a physiological process, which is in turn converted into sound, which is in turn converted back into a different physiological process and back again into an idea. The origin of this type of model is not difficult to discover. It has been universally employed in all the natural sciences to account for observed and measurable correspondences in spatio-temporally connected processes involving continuity between different forms of energy. The prototype, in short, is the concept of energy-conversion; but with the caveat that nothing of communicational relevance is 'lost' on the way.

Why, it may be asked, should energy-conversion strike a linguist of Saussure's generation as a plausible exemplar for explaining speech communication? To answer this, we need look no further than the major technological innovations in communication which transformed everyday life in Western industrial society during the course of the nineteenth and early twentieth centuries. They were telegraphy, telephony and broadcasting: all forms of energy-conversion applied to the transmission of verbal messages. It can hardly be a coincidence that the illustration of A and B talking in the *Cours* shows them schematically linked by what look suspiciously like telephone wires. Nor is it a coincidence that the misapplied term *circuit* which Saussure borrowed for his own model of speech communication comes from the technical vocabulary of the electrical engineer. By representing speech as a closed, causally determined process in every way analogous to the energy-conversion processes of physics and chemistry, linguistics was provided in advance with a forged *carte d'entrée* to the prestigious palace of modern science.

It is also worth noting the socio-political implications of the way the speech circuit presents the role of the individual in speech. It is a model which relies on the existence of a fixed code which belongs to the community as a whole. (The *Cours* refers to *la langue* as a *code* on p.[31].) Membership of the linguistic community is implicitly defined by reference to this code. In speech, therefore, the individual merely makes use of a verbal communication system institutionalized collectively, in just the same way as any member of the community has access to public transport, the post office or any of the other organized communication services of modern society. Even as a sender of messages by way of this public code, the individual's initiative is curiously limited. The speech-circuit model simply postulates that a message comes into the mind of the sender already pre-programmed, as it were, for public transmission. How this is possible Saussure never explains. But that is an obscurity which lies outside the point of entry to the speech circuit itself. So even in this humble initiative as a sender of messages, the individual is already mysteriously indebted to the community. We are dealing with a model which assigns to the individual vis-à-vis *la langue* a role which matches exactly the socio-political role assigned to the individual vis-à-vis the institutions of the modern nation-state. As a member, the individual can do no more than what the community, through its institutions, makes it possible for an individual to do.

Predictably, the internal difficulties with such a model arise from the need to reconcile what is basically a mechanical transmission circuit with the notion that the individual retains at least some control over its operation. Clearly, one has to allow for the fact that an individual may formulate a verbal message mentally, but decide not to utter it. The decision to speak, therefore, together with the decision as to what to say, must both fall within the province of voluntary activity on the part of the speaker. This consideration would seem to dictate that both belong to *parole*: for Saussure says of *parole* that it is 'an individual act of the will and the intelligence' ([30]). He proceeds to distinguish in respect of *parole* '(1) the combinations through which the speaker uses the code provided by the language in order to express his own thought, and (2) the psycho-physical mechanism which enables him to externalize these combinations' ([31]). There are at least two problems here. One is that the key process of *parole* according to this account is the individual speaker's selection of a desired combination of signs. This corresponds to the activities going on at the 'linguistic level' in the Denes and Pinson model described above. Yet there is no part of Saussure's circuit which allows for the execution of this process. The description the reader is given of how the circuit operates ([28]) begins straight away with A's concepts 'triggering' the appropriate sound patterns in the brain. Now 'triggering', presumably, is an automatic process, and one over which the individual has no control. Yet it is precisely this section of the circuit which Saussure identifies ([30]) with *parole*. Likewise, it is presumably because the hearer has no control over how to hear the spoken message that Saussure explicitly allows the passive, 'receptive' section of the circuit linking sound-patterns with concepts to be instrumental in the formation of *la langue* in the individual. So we have the odd situation in which the process of associating concepts with sound patterns apparently belongs to *parole*, whereas its mirror-image, the association of sound patterns with concepts apparently does not. Yet the one is no more 'voluntary' than the other.

Similar conundrums arise in respect of the so-called 'psycho-physical mechanism' permitting the speaker to 'externalize' the selected combinations. This again, apparently, belongs to *parole*: but it is difficult to see in what sense the speaker has any voluntary control over this mechanism. What the speaker can do is decide whether or not to try to exercise the mechanism to achieve certain articulatory results: but it is operation of the mechanism itself which constitutes the flow of activity over that particular section of the speech circuit, and this is not a process subject to acts of will. (A speaker does not, for example, decide to send an articulatory 'message' via one neuromechanical pathway rather than another, or decide whether to pay attention to or ignore the feedback systems which guide the whole articulatory process.) But is the reader, it might be asked, intended to understand that physiological events themselves are part of the *acte de parole*? It would seem so. For the *Cours* here speaks of the impossibility of photographing such an act in all its details ([32]). Now this impossibility is not presented as the logical impossibility of photographing a decision: on the contrary, the difficulty is specifically said to reside in the 'infinite number of muscular movements' involved in phonation. This, as part of *parole*, is contrasted with the much simpler corresponding unit in *langue*, which is the *image acoustique*, comprising only a limited number of elements. What is certainly the case is that once the message has been 'externalized', the speaker no longer has any control at all over the further progression round the speech circuit: there is no question of exercising acts of will over the sound waves. Yet, one might argue, it is precisely when the message has at last emerged from 'inside' the speaker and taken on this spatio-temporally unique but fleeting acoustic form that we can most readily grasp its reality as a fact of *parole* and appreciate that facts of *parole* are separate from facts of *langue*. Along this section of the circuit, however, the transmission is under the control neither of A nor of B. It is at the mercy of all kinds of external factors in the communication situation (gusts of wind, extraneous noise, etc.)

These problems of the speech circuit are intrinsic to it, and are never satisfactorily resolved in the *Cours*. It is difficult on this issue to exculpate Saussure (or his successors) from the charge of commitment to a gross category mistake: a mistake perhaps induced, but certainly compounded, by the decision to adapt a mechanical transmission model in order to explicate concepts which, in the final analysis, are not explicable by reference to mechanical processes at all. What is remarkable is that the attempt should have been made in the first place. That it was, however, bears witness to the extent to which the plausibility of this general picture of speech-communication is indebted to the cultural paradigms of a particular phase in Western civilization. Whether it would appear at all convincing if seen against a totally different cultural background must be doubtful. Its persuasiveness derives essentially from the fact that, at a particular time and place in human history, all the relevant analogues and justifications – metalinguistic, philosophical, technological and political – came together to provide what could be seen in that context as a necessary and sufficient conceptual framework for the analysis of speech.

CHAPTER III

Individuals, Collectivities and Values

The extent to which a Saussurean model of communication relies on *la langue* being a fixed code will already be evident from the discussion in the immediately preceding pages. There the requirement is that the code be fixed in the sense of being invariant across individuals and occasions. But that in turn requires that the code be fixed in a further sense. The point commentators have missed is that Saussurean theory needs a fixed code in this other sense too in order to support Saussure's 'first principle of linguistics': that is, in order to explain why, although the connexion between *signifiant* and *signifié* is arbitrary, it nevertheless cannot in any one *état de langue* vary beyond certain limits. This emerges perhaps most clearly in the remarks on writing on p.[165]. Commenting on the variety of different ways in which the letter *t* may be written, Saussure explains this as due to the fact that in writing, as in speech, values are based on contrasts within a fixed system. 'Since the written sign is arbitrary, its form is of little importance: or rather, is of importance only within certain limits imposed by the system' ([165]). In other words, there is a general semiological connexion between the arbitrariness of signs and their membership of fixed systems. Only a fixed system makes it possible to have signs which, although arbitrary, are not free to vary arbitrarily and thus take on *any* form.

It is important not to confuse this latter question with how, given a fixed code, its stability is maintained – or not maintained, as the case may be – throughout a certain community, length of time or geographical area. To stability questions the *Cours* gives mainly straightforward social (i.e. 'external') answers ([104]ff., [281]ff.). This kind of account could in principle apply to types of social institution other than languages. But the question of what fixes the code belongs to a different order of questions altogether. Here we are dealing not with the *état de langue*, but with the idiosynchronic system itself. To give a 'social' answer in that case would be, from a Saussurean point of view, to plunge the whole of linguistic theory into a never-ending circularity; or, perhaps even worse, to bind linguistics hand and foot in dependence on social anthropology.

The way the problem is dealt with in the *Cours* simultaneously demonstrates the brilliance and the vulnerability of Saussure's theoretical acumen. It also brings us to the theoretical core of structuralism. The Saussurean explanation of what fixes the code is archetypally holistic, and it has to be. Nothing 'outside' *la langue* determines the connexion between a *signifiant* and a *signifié*: so whatever does so must be 'inside'. But 'inside' there is nothing apart from other signs. If *la langue* included at least a few fundamental signs which were fixed on the basis of external relations, it might be possible to explain all the other signs as being somehow fixed relatively to these few invariant ones. But for Saussure there are no such fundamental signs of a non-arbitrary character to be found. The only necessary and sufficient condition for establishing the identity of any individual sign is that it be distinct from other signs. However, this can presumably only be so if the system as a whole is structured in such a way as to allocate to each sign its own unique semiological 'space'. Therefore Saussure accepts that adopting the principle that the linguistic sign is arbitrary forces us to conclude that it can only be the total network of interrelations which establishes individual connexions between *signifiants* and *signifiés*. So the Saussurean answer to the question 'What fixes the code?' is that what fixes the individual signs is their reciprocal interdependence in a system, which in turn is fixed simply by the totality of internal relations between its constituent signs. That explains simultaneously why altering just one set of relations disturbs the whole system, and also why, in spite of the arbitrary connexion between any one *signifiant* and any one *signifié*, it is not easy to break that connexion. Altering just one sign encounters the passive resistance of the entire structure. Thus everything in *la langue* is fixed by its structural interdependence with the rest, in the same way that the rungs of a ladder are held in position by being inserted into the vertical struts, which in turn are held in position by the rungs.

In the *Cours*, Saussure offers both a psychological and a social version of how this holistic fixing of the signs is to be construed. The psychological version is represented by the interface metaphor, which likens the contact between thought and sound to the contact between air and water ([156]). According to this version, the two substances are themselves totally amorphous, and structured only as a result of the contact between them. Although this is, in one sense, the purest possible variety of structuralism, it does not explain very satisfactorily how mere contact between intrinsically amorphous substances can automatically produce a structured system. Saussure supplements it, however, by a social version. This is represented by the economic metaphor. The crucial difference between the two versions is that in the latter there is 'contact' between two already independently structured systems, one monetary and the other comprising goods or services. Striking a balance of correlations between units in two separate systems, according to this second metaphor, is what produces a third system of values, which did not exist before.

The advantage of the latter version is that it makes it much easier to understand why contact should result in a structured system and not in chaos: for contact was not between amorphous masses in the first place. That is also the reason, however, why Saussure might not be entirely happy with this second version. For it suggests that there may be other structures 'outside', which in the end determine the resultant pattern of the system of bi-planar correlations. On the other hand, his theory of 'sound types' needs precisely this foundation if it is to underpin the Saussurean account of the *signifiant*. That account would be incoherent if it were not supposed that the physiology of the vocal apparatus was given in advance by Nature. To that extent, speech sound is not amorphous, but already structured by the possibilities inherent in something external to the idiosynchronic system.

There is ultimately no compromise available between the two versions of how it is possible for a system to be fixed holistically by bi-planar correlations. Nor does the *Cours* attempt a compromise: it simply offers both. In one case systematicity somehow emerges magically *ex nihilo*, whereas in the other systematicity arises from the attempt to adjust units of one kind to units of another kind. On either version, however, it has to be a systematicity which for Saussure will underwrite the concept of a linguistic *state*.

In recent years, linguistic advocates of the so-called 'dynamic paradigm' have urged that no 'static paradigm', whether specifically Saussurean or not, can come to terms with the fact that languages are inherently unstable and continuously evolving. If this is so – and the *Cours* concedes the point that in languages we never find *l'immobilité absolue* ([193]) – the question must arise whether *la langue*, conceived as a fixed code, corresponds to any linguistic reality at all. How Saussure might have replied to 'dynamic paradigm' critics we can only speculate. But we can suppose that a Saussurean answer would maintain, come what may, that *la langue* is not a concept which has to be – or could be – maintained at the expense of sacrificing the dichotomy between synchrony and diachrony; and furthermore that *la langue* is indeed a linguistic reality and not a theoretical abstraction.

Defenders of Saussure have sometimes urged that a careful reading of the *Cours* shows a full awareness of the allegedly neglected dynamic aspect of *la langue*. De Mauro (1972: 454) cites in this connexion the explicit statement in the *Cours* that 'At no one time does a language possess an entirely fixed system of units' ([234]). One might counter this, however, with other explicit statements from the *Cours*. For example, that each language uses 'a fixed number of distinct speech sounds' ([58]), that 'every language has an inventory of sounds fixed in number' ([303]), that 'each language constitutes a closed system' ([139]), that in writing as in languages, values 'are solely based on contrasts within a fixed system' ([165]). Is it possible to read the *Cours* in a way which allows both static and dynamic linguistic paradigms to co-exist within a Saussurean framework? Can the fixed system be sufficiently elastic to accommodate the observed heterogeneity?

The problem revolves around the controversial Saussurean notion of 'value'. For to *fix* a value presupposes the invariance of certain elements and relations. This is as true in the linguistic case as in the economic case which Saussure offers for comparison ([159-60]). The value of a five-franc coin does not remain the same over a period of years simply because it remains equivalent to five one-franc coins. We cannot suppose Saussure thought that: for that would be to reduce a system of values to a mere mathematics. The whole point of his economic analogy is that coins have to be exchanged for something *other than* coins (bread, clothes, services, etc.).

But nor does the value of a five-franc coin remain constant simply because, for instance, the price of bread remains constant. For there are many other factors affecting its value than the price of just one commodity. On the contrary, a fixed price is *eo ipso* no guarantee of anything without considering whether or not it costs more or less to produce the commodity than it used to. Analogously in the linguistic case, it proves nothing to show that the word *unfashionable* has at all times in its history been divisible into the same three morphemic units, nor even that it has always been defined as meaning 'not fashionable', if what is at issue is whether there have been changes in the system of lexical values to which it belongs. Saussure's economic analogy, therefore, seems at first sight only to render the problem more acute: for economic values seem to vary continuously. On the other hand, purchases are made, deals are struck, business is done. How is this possible?

Two attempts to dissolve or at least to minimize the problem on Saussure's behalf will be considered here. One is the explanation given by Ullmann, and evidently approved by de Mauro (1972: 454-5). This presents Saussure as recognizing that *in fact* linguistic phenomena exhibit continuous variation; but deciding to ignore the variation for certain purposes. Thus 'it is not the language which is synchronistic or diachronistic, but the approach to it, the method of investigation, the science of language' (Ullmann 1959: 36). The duality, in Ullmann's view, 'is not entwined in the linguistic material itself.' Thus, apparently, it is a mistake to see Saussure as caught here in any kind of dilemma. There are simply two points of view, and Saussure recognizes the validity of both. One point of view sees *la langue* as a static system, while the other recognizes change. Therefore, presumably, Saussure's reply to 'dynamic paradigm' critics would be that it is *they* who are confused: for they naively reason from the fact that in real time different synchronic systems co-exist to the conclusion that there are no *états de langue* at all. In other words, theirs is yet another failure to distinguish between *faits de langue* and *faits de parole*.

This apologia, however, dodges the real issue. Although it is perfectly true that for Saussure it would be essential not to mix up in the same analysis synchronic and diachronic facts, there is no justification in the *Cours* for supposing the distinction between synchronic and diachronic to be merely in the eye of the analyst. The separation of synchrony from diachrony is neither just a descriptive convenience nor an artifact of linguistic theorizing. To think otherwise would be to make nonsense of Saussure's objection that the viewpoint of the historical linguist does not correspond to any reality in the experience of the speaker. 'The first thing which strikes one on studying linguistic facts is that the language user is unaware of their succession in time: he is dealing with a state. Hence the linguist who wishes to understand this state must rule out of consideration everything which brought that state about, and pay no attention to diachrony. Only by suppressing the past can he enter into the state of mind of the language user' ([117]). Here is as clear a statement as one could wish. It shows that if the linguist adopts the distinction between synchronic and diachronic, that is not simply for descriptive convenience, nor because there is any analytic obligation to do so, but because that distinction is imposed by the nature of linguistic realities for the linguistic community.

Furthermore, the Ullmann-de Mauro defence of Saussure supplies no genuinely Saussurean answer to the question of what 'fixes' the code. It simply papers over the cracks to suggest *if* one adopts the diachronic point of view *then* the code is not fixed at all. This is no more than a bland attempt to please everybody by turning a blind eye to the fact that Saussurean theory subordinates the distinction between synchronic and diachronic to the prior distinction between *langue* and *parole*. After all, everyone presumably agrees that what was the case yesterday or yesteryear may no longer be the case today. That is *not* the same as having grasped the Saussurean distinction between synchrony and diachrony. It is not a question of saying to oneself: 'Today the situation is as it is; but yesterday it was different. Therefore, one must conclude that change has occurred. However, today I cannot foresee anything about tomorrow. Therefore, at the moment, I cannot say that change is occurring. So today, I describe the situation as "static".' On that reasoning, 'today' (however long it may last) is always static. Some Saussurean commentators give the impression of having to defend – or attack – ratiocination of this order. This merely shows that they have failed to grasp the implications of such classic Saussurean dicta as 'it is *la parole* which causes *la langue* to evolve' ([37]) and 'everything which is diachronic in *la langue* is only so through *la parole* ([138]).

Some advocates of the dynamic paradigm argue that the Saussurean position is in any case based upon a *non sequitur*. For from the fact that speakers are ignorant of the past development of the language they speak, it does not follow that from their point of view the language is static, unless the term 'static' is interpreted broadly enough to include the varied patterns of observable change in progress. But if it *is* thus interpreted, then the Saussurean dichotomy between synchronic and diachronic is immediately threatened, and the notion of *la langue* as a homogeneous system cannot be maintained.

Washabaugh identifies three characteristics of the systematic patterning of language variations which advocates of the dynamic paradigm regard as inexplicable within a Saussurean framework. One is the way in which these patterns show up numerically. 'Only by taking a statistical average of a large number of people do systematic relations appear' (Washabaugh 1974: 29). Investigation of the speech behaviour of individuals, on the other hand, shows that the individual is prone to unsystematic fluctuations. The second characteristic is the diachronic nature of the patterning, which is difficult to account for if one assumes with Saussure that linguistic change depends on the acceptance or rejection by the community of innovations initiated by individuals. The third characteristic is the heterogeneity of the patterning. That is to say, whereas Saussurean linguistics assumes a homogeneous language, uniformly employed by all members of the community, observation suggests that speakers are constantly choosing between alternative sets of forms, but dealing with this non-uniformity in a systematic manner.

Washabaugh argues that the first of these three alleged inadequacies of Saussurean linguistics involves a basic conflict between different views about social facts. One is a Durkheimian view, which treats social facts as discoverable only by statistical methods, since there is no guarantee that any individual is perfectly typical of the community. But Saussure's mature theory of language, Washabaugh holds, is non-Durkheimian or even anti-Durkheimian, since 'for Durkheim there is no such thing as psychological reality of a social fact; there is no analogue to Saussure's *la langue individuelle* or *la faculté du langage*' (Washabaugh 1974: 28). Washabaugh rejects the view that Saussure was influenced by Durkheim as based upon 'hearsay', and claims that the resemblances between Saussure and Durkheim are 'only terminological'.

Washabaugh goes on to argue that the other two alleged inadequacies of the Saussurean paradigm in principle have Saussurean solutions, although Saussure himself did not develop them in detail. The key to these solutions lies in Saussure's recognition of *langage* as a human faculty, common to all individuals but independent of particular languages. This faculty, Washabaugh claims, can be construed as a source of universal constraints accounting for the diachronic and heterogeneous patterns detectable in a community's linguistic behaviour. So, paradoxically, far from denying the validity of a dynamic paradigm, Saussurean linguistics actually provides the dynamic paradigm with a sound theoretical basis, and makes it unnecessary to have recourse to any Durkheimian approach to linguistic facts.

An observant reader cannot fail to notice that at various points in the *Cours* there is an uneasy tension between the role attributed to the individual and the role attributed to the collectivity. Saussure speaks, for example, of individual innovations but of collective ratifications, and this is intimately bound up with the basic dichotomy between what belongs to *parole* and what belongs to *langue*. Nowhere, however, does it emerge very clearly what exactly collective ratification amounts to. For theorists who, like Durkheim, deny that social facts are reducible to sets of facts about individuals, a collectivity has to be something more than a mere aggregate of people. Saussure, on the other hand, often seems to assume that the essential process by which linguistic innovations become generalized is simply the imitation by one individual of another individual. But this would reduce collective ratification to a matter of counting heads, and raise in a rather acute form the descriptive problem of deciding at what percentage level a linguistic practice should be judged to have gained general acceptance by the community. Durkheim's frank commitment to a statistical methodology (Durkheim 1895: 9-10) has no obvious echo in the *Cours*.

Washabaugh's defence of Saussure is certainly a more interesting one than any attempt merely to juggle with the application of the terms 'synchronic' and 'diachronic'. The contrast drawn between Saussurean and Durkheimian approaches to social facts invites a number of comments. A long line of commentators, from Doroszewski (1931) down to Dinneen (1967), have claimed or assumed that Saussure was influenced by Durkheim. But this has also been denied, notably by Koerner (1973: 45-71), who points out that 'there is not a single text from either Saussure himself or from lecture notes taken by his students which mentions the names of Durkheim, Tarde or Walras'. More important for a reading of the *Cours* than debating the evidence for 'influences' at this level is how the concept of social facts which we find in the *Cours* compares with Durkheim's. Via what historical route the two are related, if at all, need not concern us.

Catlin (1938: xv) points out that Durkheim's principal criterion of a social fact, that of 'being general throughout the extent of a given society' at a given stage in the evolution of that society, by implication distinguishes a social fact from a psychological fact which is universal to human nature. So at least on this score there is no basic difference between the Durkheim of *Les règles de la méthode sociologique* and the Saussure of the *Cours*, granted the interpretation of Saussurean *langage* as something 'universal to human nature' and of *langue* as a social product in the sense that every language presupposes a particular culture or community whose purposes it serves. Moreover, the implication is that for Durkheim such facts as are 'universal to human nature', even though they will clearly affect people's social behaviour, lie outside the scope of sociology.

Now if for 'the scope of sociology' we substitute 'the scope of linguistics', Saussure's position is in essence no different. It does not fall within the scope of Saussurean linguistics to investigate universal constraints which derive from factors outside the human language faculty, or, more exactly, which are independent of that semiological faculty which is *la faculté linguistique par excellence* ([27]). The reason why is made quite clear in Saussure's remarks about the 'panchronic' point of view ([134-5]). For Saussure 'there is no panchronic point of view' ([135]). This is *not* a denial of the possibility of formulating generalizations of various kinds about linguistic phenomena; but it is both a denial that *faits de langue* can be identifed on any basis 'outside' *la langue*, and an affirmation that the only generalizations which concern linguistics are those concerning *faits de langue*. Clearly, if there are no *faits de langue* which are panchronic facts, then *a fortiori* there are no psychological facts 'universal to human nature' which can be the concern of linguistics, other than those deriving from the *faculté linguistique*.

Durkheim, like Saussure, sees both languages and currencies as obvious examples of social systems which cannot be explained in terms of a fortunate conformity between individual practices. 'The system of signs I use to express my thought, the system of currency I use to pay my debts, the instruments of credit I utilize in my commercial relations, the practices followed in my profession, etc., function independently of my own use of them. And these statements can be repeated for each member of society. Here, then, are ways of acting, thinking and feeling that present the noteworthy property of existing outside the individual consciousness' (Durkheim 1895:4).

What solves for Durkheim the problem of identifying a distinctive subject-matter for the science of sociology is, as Catlin points out, positing the existence of a collective consciousness. Now the phrase *conscience collective* is by no means unfamiliar to a reader of the *Cours*. But in the *Cours* the role played by this notion is not *overtly* that of making it possible to identify a distinctive subject-matter for the science of linguistics. It does, however, serve a no less crucial function: that of distinguishing synchronic from diachronic linguistics ([140]). And since for Saussure synchronic linguistics takes priority, in that diachrony is defined negatively with respect to synchrony, it becomes clear that *indirectly* the notion of a collective consciousness plays for Saussurean linguistics a theoretical role which is exactly parallel to that which it plays in Durkheimian sociology. Positing *la langue* as a supra-individual system solves for Saussure simultaneously the problems of defining and organizing linguistics internally 'as a science'. Unless there is a collective consciousness, the notion of a supra-individual *system* does not make sense in Saussurean terms, systems being defined holistically. Moreover, without a collective consciousness, diachrony would be reduced to relations of chronological succession. For Saussure, clearly, a collective consciousness has to extend across generations to unite individuals whose linguistic lives may be widely separated in 'real time', and however ignorant such individuals may be of the linguistic practices of their forebears.

Catlin says of Durkheim that he demarcated sociology from psychology by limiting psychology 'by definition to the level of individual consciousness' (Catlin 1938: xxvii). What Saussure did was rather different, although the strategy employed was the same. For even if *la langue* was for Saussure in some sense psychological in nature (at least to the extent that *la langue* exists as a cognitive system in the individual), academic psychology in Saussure's days had no established techniques for studying it, other than those which a 'scientific' linguistics was to provide. A psychology which attempted to study speech in the individual *qua* individual would merely be studying aspects of *parole*. Durkheim, says Catlin, believes 'that he is studying a supermind, immanent in society' (Catlin 1938: xxx), and the description is remarkably apposite to Saussure. Although *la langue* is manifest only in the speech behaviour of individuals, *elle n'existe parfaitement que dans la masse* ([30]).

But Saussure runs into both practical and theoretical difficulties in trying to have his collective linguistic bun and eat it, where Durkheim wisely refrains; and this brings us back once again to the 'Saussurean paradox'. There is no corresponding 'Durkheimian paradox' because Durkheim does not attempt to treat the individual as an idealized representative of the community. The practical consequences of the 'Saussurean paradox' were to have a quite marked effect on the subsequent development of linguistics, which can still be seen today. Although the distinction between *langue* and *parole*, as Giglioli points out, 'seemed at first to draw linguistics and sociology together, actually, unwittingly or not, it produced the contrary result. For if *langue* is defined as a set of grammatical rules existing in the mind of everyone, it becomes unnecessary to bother with the study of actual speech in social interactions' (Giglioli 1972: 7). The reason Durkheim gives for rejecting introspection as a way of discovering the collectivity's conception of a social institution is that it 'does not exist in its entirety in any one individual' (Durkheim 1938: xlvi-xlvii). Now although Saussure's *elle n'existe parfaitement que dans la masse* pays lip-service to this too, it can only be lip-service. Otherwise, Saussure's model of communication would not work. There is no way of resolving a conflict between an account of *la langue* as an instrument of communication which assumes that by definition communication resides in the telementation of messages which are identical for any speaker and any hearer, and a general account of social institutions (including *la langue*) which allows that by definition different individuals may have different – and *in any case* will have only imperfect – degrees of mastery of the institution which unites them. The Durkheimian approach cannot – and makes no attempt to – evade the question of *how* it is possible in practice to study social institutions which are complete only *dans la masse*. Saussure, unfortunately, pretends that the problem does not exist. Or, if it does, it is merely a practical and not a theoretical problem. The trouble is that it automatically does become a theoretical problem in the context of any attempt to lay the foundation of linguistics as a science. To set out the theoretical basis for a science which cannot be done is *eo ipso* to reduce the notion of a science to absurdity.

According to Washabaugh, Saussure borrowed the notion of a language as a social institution from Whitney, not from Durkheim, and he quotes Mounin to the effect that the term *institution* does not appear in Durkheim (Washabaugh 1974: 28). This is simply wrong. On the contrary, Durkheim claimed that it is permissible to 'designate as "institutions" all the beliefs and all the modes of conduct instituted by the collectivity' (Durkheim 1895: xxii). Here we seem to have clear evidence that a language for Durkheim does count as a social institution, since it is difficult to see what a language is if not a 'mode of conduct instituted by the collectivity'. For Saussure, *la langue* is precisely that. It is not instituted by the individual. (Saussure goes out of his way to assert that the individual is powerless to affect *la langue* in any way, apart from producing innovations which may – or may not – be subsequently incorporated into *la langue*.) Nor is it instituted by Nature. Those linguistic theorists who subscribed to what was later called 'the innateness hypothesis' do not find themselves in conflict with Durkheim on this score, since Durkheim's 'modes of conduct' manifestly include conduct based in various ways on human natural abilities. There may be a sense in which speaking English and speaking Chinese are based on the same natural abilities. But no one seriously supposes that the differences between the 'mode of conduct' which comprises speaking English and the 'mode of conduct' which comprises speaking Chinese are to be accounted for in terms of genetic differences.

Durkheim continues in the same passage: 'Sociology can then be defined as the science of institutions, of their genesis and of their functioning' (Durkheim 1895: xxii). It is a definition which could easily be adapted to fit Saussurean linguistics. If for 'institutions' we substitute 'linguistic institutions', we can derive a definition which is eminently Saussurean in spirit: 'Linguistics can then be defined as the science of linguistic institutions, of their genesis and of their functioning.' For just previously Durkheim has spelled out an account of the relationship between the freedoms of the individual and collective constraints which is tailor-made for the *Cours*. He says that the idea of a social constraint 'merely implies that collective ways of acting or thinking have a reality outside the individuals who, at every moment of time, conform to it. These ways of thinking and acting exist in their own right. The individual finds them completely formed, and he cannot evade or change them' (Durkheim 1895: lvi). Similarly, the *Cours* tells us that *la langue* 'is not a function of the speaker' ([30]) and that the individual 'is powerless either to create it or to modify it' ([31]). Where Saussure goes further – as he must in order to fulfil the requirements of his model of communication – is to claim that *la langue* also exists in the brain as 'the product passively registered by the individual' ([30]). There is no talk here of a 'collective brain': brains, for Saussure, are things only individuals have. This important difference between Durkheim and Saussure means that Saussure supplies himself in advance with a purely mechanistic psychological explanation of social conformity. The *mécanisme de la langue* is just that. It operates not at the collective but at the individual level, ensuring that the processes of telementational transference required by the *circuit de la parole* can actually take place.

Durkheim comments on the relationship between the social institution and the individual in terms which make an interesting comparison with the remarks on this topic in the *Cours*. He says 'Because beliefs and social practices thus come to us from without, it does not follow that we receive them passively or without modification. In reflecting on collective institutions and assimilating them for ourselves, we individualize them and impart to them more or less personal characteristics. Similarly, in reflecting on the physical world, each of us colours it after his own fashion, and different individuals adapt themselves differently to the same physical environment. It is for this reason that each one of us creates, in a measure, his own morality, religion and mode of life' (Durkheim 1895: lvi-lvii, n.7). This passage could almost stand without modification as an explication of the Saussurean claim that 'all the individuals linguistically linked in this manner will establish among themselves a kind of mean: all of them will reproduce – doubtless not exactly, but approximately – the same signs linked to the same concepts' ([29]). The difference is that whereas Durkheim recognizes the consequences for sociological investigation, Saussure does not. Saussure uses the appeal to a 'collective consciousness' as a way of circumventing the methodological problems consequential on the fact that the larger the linguistic community the less chance there is that any two individuals will have been 'linguistically linked' in the manner required to reproduce 'approximately' the same system of signs.

The only concession Saussure makes to the problem is to admit that in large communities languages tend to fragment dialectally. But his theoretical move here is then to treat each of the resultant dialects as a separate linguistic system in its own right. This is the thrust of his decision to replace the notion of synchrony by that of idiosynchrony. To identify idiosynchronic systems, it may be necessary to pursue 'a division into dialects and sub-dialects' ([128]). The move is clumsy on at least two counts. First, it is quite unclear how the investigator in the field will be able to identify these sub-dialects which constitute separate idiosynchronic systems: for Saussure does not deny that communication may be possible *across* dialects and sub-dialects of the same language, while at the same time conceding that in some cases it may not be ([275]). But if this is so, communication is no criterion for identifying differences between idiosynchronic systems. Second, how can this be reconciled with Saussure's circuit model of communication? That model was based on the assumption that the interlocutors A and B shared the same idiosynchronic system. But if linguistic communication is possible without that common factor, clearly the model proposed is inadequate as a basis for linguistic theory. We would need at the very least a model which showed how it was possible to translate from A's idiosynchronic system into B's idiosynchronic system: whereas in the Saussurean model it is the single idiosynchronic system itself which takes care of the transmission problem of equivalences.

Here the tension between the collective 'social institution' component of *la langue* and the individual 'cognitive system' component of *la langue* stretches the link to its theoretical breaking point. For there is not much sense to be made of the notion that *la langue* is a social institution if the institution cannot provide the most basic of social requirements, which are those of communication between the members of society. Analogously, it would make little sense to treat a monetary system as a social institution if it failed to provide the members of society with a means of buying and selling things. Once language and communication become theoretically divorced, the key Saussurean concept of *valeur* is itself rendered vacuous; and for just the same reason as in the economic analogy, where a five-franc coin simply has no value if *nothing* can be bought with it. (Obviously, that would not prevent it from having a value in some other sense – aesthetic value, historical value, sentimental value: but these other possible dimensions of value are irrelevant to the case.)

The root of the problem with Saussurean linguistics is that it has not worked out the connexion between language and communication in any theoretically satisfactory way. Although it couples language with communication in an intimate partnership, the two partners are condemned to dancing in perpetuity to the tune of what one linguist has called Saussure's 'hesitation waltz' (Gagnepain 1981: 149). This odd composition is the result of starting linguistic theory from the wrong end. Saussurean linguistics begins by focussing upon the properties of the individual linguistic sign in the abstract, and hoping that somehow at the social end, where signs are put to everyday use, everything will work out satisfactorily in terms of communicational corollaries. Unfortunately, it does not work out at all. But it could have worked out if only

Saussure had grasped the full implications of the economic analogy and seen that values are subordinate to transactions, and not the other way round. He might then have seen the wisdom of starting linguistic theory 'from the opposite end'.

The ultimate historical irony is that Saussure's error had been lucidly exposed in advance by Durkheim. (Perhaps that is one reason for supposing that the linguistic theorist who delivered the Geneva lectures had not read *Les règles de la méthode sociologique*; or, if he had read it, had failed to assimilate it.) Durkheim writes sceptically of the academic economics of his day:

> If value had been studied as any fact of reality ought to be studied, the economist would indicate, first of all, by what characteristics one might recognize the thing so designated, then classify its varieties, investigate by methodological inductions what the causes of its variations are, and finally compare these results in order to obtain a general formula. Theory would be introduced only when science had reached a sufficient stage of advancement. On the contrary, it is introduced at the very outset. In order to construct economic theory, the economist is content to meditate and to focus attention upon his own idea of value, that is, an object capable of being exchanged; he finds therein the idea of utility, scarcity, etc., and with these products of his analysis he constructs his definition. (Durkheim 1895: 25)

Transposed into linguistic terms, that advice would provide a charter for general linguistics of a quite different theoretical stamp from the Magna Carta which the *Cours* was subsequently taken to provide.

Saussurean linguistics stands or falls by the Saussurean concept of linguistic values. This is made eminently clear in the *Cours*, where that concept is presented – rightly – as Saussure's most original contribution to modern thinking about language, and indeed to linguistic thought of any era. For no thinker in the entire Western tradition before Saussure ever proposed a view which could be encapsulated in what is perhaps the most famous and contentious of all the Saussurean dicta: *la langue est un système de pures valeurs* ([116]). Whether we accept that view or not, it is one which extends the scope of Western thinking on the subject in unprecedented and challenging ways.

The greatest challenge of all, doubtless, is to pinpoint exactly where Saussure's concept of linguistic value is radically defective. Like the economists' concept of value, Saussure's does not yield constants *unless* we take the further step of assuming that the system of exchange is closed. Only then is there any assurance of that holism which will guarantee determinate identities to the individual items which are or may be exchanged. Without the logical necessity of closure, there just are no constants of the kind Saussurean synchronic theory postulates: no determinate forms, no determinate meanings, no determinate linguistic structure of any kind. It is hardly coincidental that most of Saussure's academic career had been spent in studying dead languages: for nothing imposes the appearance of closure on a system more convincingly than its recession into the irrecoverable past, where it remains perpetually 'frozen' in the form of writing.

By failing to see that values are subordinate to transactions, not transactions to values, Saussure forced his own thinking about language into a theoretical *impasse*. In the linguistic case no less than in the economic case, values are never 'fixed' except by and for the purpose of particular transactions. To recognize this would have necessitated a radical revision of Saussure's evaluation of *parole*. (It is by no means out of the question that a re-evaluation of this order might have ensued from the projected course of lectures on *linguistique de la parole*.) In any case, reversing out of that theoretical *impasse* is inevitable if the Saussurean concept of *valeur* is to be rescued at all. The fact that last week at Sotheby's I bought a vase by Hamada for £500 does not in any way guarantee *either* that the vase has the same value this week *or* that £500 sterling will this week buy me something equivalent to my Hamada vase. Nor can this dilemma be resolved by invoking such explanations as that, perhaps, 'I paid too much for the vase last week,' or alternatively, that 'I got a bargain'. These are simply historical – i.e. diachronic – comments. There is no sense in which they entail that there was a 'correct' value for the vase which I either paid or failed to pay when I bought it. *Mutatis mutandis*, the same applies to linguistic values: and anyone who fails to understand that fails to understand what kind of activity language is.

What happened when I bought the vase was that *by* paying £500 for it I established its value (in that particular commercial context). That I bought it at auction does not affect the example: the same would apply had I bought it in a shop at the price the dealer asked. (Asking prices are not values, even though they may both reflect and be reflected by values.) The price paid for the vase on that occasion automatically becomes an item in its commercial history. It may affect to some extent the price it fetches when next sold. And irrespective of its commercial history, it may affect the prices paid for other Hamada vases in London auction rooms. None of this validates a theory of economics which posits that buying and selling demands a fixed system of values. Furthermore, all the considerations mentioned carry over to the linguistic analogue: for example, the word *vase*. Was this pottery artifact sold for £500 'really' a vase? Might it not have been a bowl, dish, or even a traditional Japanese form for which there is no exact English term? It was, in any case, a unique piece of pottery, fashioned in a certain manner, and sold on this occasion 'as a vase'. The fact that it was catalogued as a 'vase', like the fact that it was sold for £500, becomes part of its history, and may or may not affect how similar pieces of pottery by Hamada are described in English. The meaning of the English word *vase* is no more fixed than the purchasing power of the pound sterling.

It is disappointing that Saussure managed to get so far with the concept of *valeur*, and yet in the end did not quite get far enough. Saussure, as de Mauro (1972: v) points out, saw a major problem of synchronic linguistics as being the problem of sameness: i.e. identity of linguistic signs. The pronunciation of a word may vary as between different instances, and its exact interpretation may also vary according to context. (Exactly the same variations apply to the cases of buying and selling.) From this Saussure draws the unobjectionable conclusion that, in the linguistic case, neither pronunciation nor interpretation *per se* provide adequate criteria for identifying the same item on all occasions. But Saussure, unfortunately, is committed to a model of speech communication which depends essentially on being able to produce and recognize 'the same' linguistic items irrespective of the occasion. How can such a symmetry between production and recognition be established irrespective of any occasional differences? The notion of *la langue* as a value system is intended to provide the answer. But to do this, it has to be a *fixed* value system; that is, it must be invariant across particular occasions. The sameness of a word resides not in having an identical pronunciation or an identical interpretation on all occasions, but in occupying a determinate and unique place in a total system which is supra-individual. This is the Saussurean solution to a problem which a long line of French writers had discussed, going back to Destutt de Tracy and beyond him to Condillac. The topic in question is sometimes referred to as the 'subjectivity of language' (Aarsleff 1982: 343 ff.), and the problem arises for anyone who accepts a Lockean model of speech communication: it is what Taylor calls 'Locke's puzzle' (Taylor 1984).

The Saussurean solution encounters two potential difficulties, one difficulty hidden behind the other. The more obvious difficulty is that unless the system itself is the same for *all* its users, it can hardly yield for them a uniform identification of linguistic signs. That is why change and variation *across users* must be excluded from the system as such. However, since the investigator has access only to the users, and not directly to the system, a plausible programme of linguistic investigation must explain how to circumvent that difficulty.

The less obvious but more serious difficulty is that one cannot get rid of change and variation merely by banishing them by fiat to the diachronic realm. For there is no sense to be made of the notion that an *état de langue* is simply a changing and variable linguistic continuum, but minus the changes and variations. That would be like trying to explain standing still as being the same as running, but without movement. Not only is the proposal incoherent, but in linguistics it automatically defeats its own purpose.

It leaves the synchronic theorist with no principled way of deciding what belongs to the system and what counts as a change or variation to be ignored. ('But since languages are always changing, however minimally, studying a linguistic state amounts in practice to ignoring unimportant changes' ([142]).) In other words, the invariant signs on which speech communication is deemed to depend remain *descriptively* unidentifiable amid the flux of actual discourse with all its individual idiosyncrasies. It follows that in order to have any explanatory utility, the system has to be envisaged as a *whole*, complete in itself, standing apart from the speech acts which it sponsors and the individuals who use it. Hence, as Calvet points out (Calvet 1975: 61) the theorist, although proclaiming *la langue* to be a social institution, ends up by postulating an abstract linguistic system which stands 'outside' society altogether.

Otherwise, in the constant flux of social interaction, there is no stable totality to provide the linguistic framework within which particular linguistic signs can be located and identified. If it were in principle possible that a given speech act by a given individual could (like buying a Hamada vase) itself introduce a modification into the system of values, that would be tantamount to seeing *la langue* as intrinsically open-ended and indeterminate. But then speech communication would be at the mercy of unpredictable innovation, and the basis for a systematic identification of linguistic signs would be lost. Just as in the economic case, it is only if we postulate that *the economy is a closed system* that it makes sense to speak of fixed currency values and equivalences. Once it is conceded that the supply of goods is constantly changing and that particular economic transactions may affect the availability of goods or the demand for them, then a theory of fixed values is no longer viable.

It would be a mistake to think that Saussure was unaware of the problem. The awareness is most obviously apparent in Chapter V of Part II, where there is an attempt to back away from the awkward question of how it is possible for the linguist to delimit the *état de langue* in its entirety. Saussure's holistic theory of linguistic structure requires such a delimitation. On the other hand, he cannot see any plausible *a priori* basis on which to restrict the range of either associative or syntagmatic relations. So he has to concede that 'an associative group has no particular number of items in it: nor do they occur in any particular order' ([174]) and that 'where syntagmas are concerned ... one must recognize the fact that there is no clear boundary separating *la langue*, as confirmed by communal usage, from *la parole*, marked by freedom of the individual' ([173]).

These are damaging admissions. To concede that 'any given term acts as the centre of a constellation, from which connected terms radiate *ad infinitum*' ([174]) is to concede that associative series are in principle open-ended, while to concede that the items occur in no particular order is to concede that the series themselves are internally unstructured. But series which have *no limit* and *no order* can hardly be the basis of any system of fixed communal values, or supply that *tout solidaire* ([157]) from which, by a process of analysis, the constituent elements are eventually reached. If the series are both open-ended and unstructured, there can be no guarantee that different individuals will not subdivide them in different ways, and thus recognize different associative groups; which amounts to saying that different speakers may be operating with different systems of *valeurs*. Thus in Saussurean terms they will be speaking different *langues*, even though the differences may not be obvious from the data of *parole*.

Similarly, in the case of syntagmatic relations, to concede the impossibility of drawing a boundary between individual initiative and collective usage is to concede that in descriptive syntagmatics the linguist will be unable to tell in many cases whether the facts described are *faits de langue* or *faits de parole*. If the status of linguistics as a science depends precisely on not conflating *langue* and *parole*, this concession is in any case a disaster for Saussure; but it is a double disaster inasmuch as the indeterminacy of syntagmatic relations also entails the impossibility of a fixed system of *valeurs*.

This time the paradox is one well worthy of Zeno. For if linguistic units have a value only in virtue of being determinately placed in relation to one another in the context of larger networks of units, each of which in turn functions interdependently with others in still larger networks, then determining the value of even the smallest unit in the system presupposes the completion of an apparently unlimited process of incremental re-contextualization, involving networks of larger and larger size, with structuring of ever-increasing complexity. *C'est du tout solidaire qu'il faut partir pour obtenir par analyse les éléments qu'il renferme* begins to sound less like an invitation to linguistic analysis and more like a warning against the futility of attempting it.

Thus in the end we see Saussurean holism running up against the apparently insuperable difficulty arising from the absence of any clear analytic criteria for identifying the limits of the system, either in the associative or in the syntagmatic dimension. Along neither road does the linguist come to a Checkpoint Charlie, where visas are demanded for crossing the border from Individual Freedom into Collective Coercion, or vice versa. Given that in Saussurean linguistics parts depend on wholes, and analysis proceeds from the latter to the former, this leads straight to the problem that it becomes impossible for the linguist to identify with any assurance the postulated *entités concrètes de la langue*. Saussure is thus ensnared in a theoretical trap of his own making. Proclaiming on the one hand that in linguistics it is the viewpoint chosen which creates the linguistic object, he fails on the other hand to be able to demonstrate that his recommended viewpoint creates any scientifically identifiable object at all.

* * *

It is intrinsic to any theoretical endeavour that failure has the potential to teach as many valuable lessons as success. Saussure's ultimate failure to resolve the contradiction between a fixed-code model of languages and the linguistic freedom of the individual teaches a difficult lesson of the highest value; perhaps still the most valuable lesson in linguistics that could possibly be learned. If linguists subsequently ignored or forgot or evaded it, that is nothing for which the blame can retrospectively be laid at Saussure's door.

The same lesson is a lesson for other social sciences, and for epistemology in general. One has only to substitute for *la langue* the designation of any other social institution to see that a conceptual framework of the kind proposed in the *Cours* will encounter parallel problems in other disciplines. In one sense, it would have made no difference if Saussure had been writing about sartorial systems, kinship systems, or transport systems. His prophetic subordination of linguistics to semiology already presages this extension. The basic questions the *Cours* deals with are questions which will arise wherever a discipline is concerned with elucidating the mechanisms by which the individual and the collectivity are mysteriously united in social interaction. Consequently, the *Cours* can be read as a kind of pioneering enterprise in theorization, relevant for all disciplines which must, sooner or later, face Durkheim's challenge to recognize social facts as constituting an independent order of reality. It is Saussure's *Cours* which, if anything does, validates Lévi-Strauss's claim that linguistics occupies a 'special place' among the social sciences (Lévi-Strauss 1945).

The explanatory conflict dramatized in the *Cours* is between holism and individualism: and that is a conflict which demands a larger academic stage than any that linguistics alone can offer (d'Agostino 1979, Sampson 1979, Pateman 1980). 'Holism versus individualism in history and sociology' appeared forty years later as the title of a well-known paper by Gellner (which makes no mention of Saussure at all, although its themes are essentially Saussurean). What is even more interesting from a Saussurean point of view is that the original published title of Gellner's paper was 'Explanations in History'. It is interesting to speculate which of these two formulations Bally and Sechehaye would have preferred if choosing a subtitle for the *Cours*. In either case, they might have been glad of the kind of epigraph which Gellner provides when he writes of this very conflict that 'when reductions fail, the fact that they do so and the reasons why they do so, give us some understanding of the nature of the unreduced concepts' (Gellner 1959: 490 n.1.): or even 'The problem of explanation in history is also the problem of the nature of sociology' (Gellner 1959: 489).

Therefore, to recommend reading the *Cours* as a record of failure is not a nonsense. The apt comparison is with certain types of experiment in engineering, where a structure is submitted to progressively increasing stress until finally it collapses. The *Cours* is a text of this order. It takes a very simple structure of explanation, based on just two principles, and proceeds to pile more and more upon this framework, in order to demonstrate just how much it will bear. One should not be surprised by the eventual collapse, but amazed by its unsuspected strength, and intrigued to see just where it will fracture. That is why there is no substitute for reading the *Cours* as it stands; and why, as it stands, it remains one of the most impressive intellectual landmarks of modern thought.

Bibliography

H. Aarsleff, *The Study of Language in England, 1780-1860,* Princeton, 1967.
From Locke to Saussure, London, 1982.
F.B. d'Agostino, 'Individualism and collectivism: the case of language,' *Philosophy of the Social Sciences,* vol. 9, 1979.
G.P. Baker and P.M.S. Hacker, *Wittgenstein: Meaning and Understanding ,* Oxford, 1980.
Ch. Bally, 'L'arbitraire du signe: valeur et signification,' *Le français moderne,* vol. 8, 1940.
R. Barthes, *Eléments de sémiologie,* Paris 1964. Tr. A. Lavers and C. Smith, London, 1967.
L. Bloomfield, *An Introduction to the Study of Language,* New York, 1914.
Review of Ferdinand de Saussure, *Cours de linguistique générale, Modern Language Journal,* vol. 8. 1923.
Language, London, 1935.
L.G.A. de Bonald, *Législation primitive,* Paris, 1802.
G. Broadbent, R. Bunt and C. Jencks (eds.), *Signs, Symbols and Architecture,* Chichester, 1980.
E. Buyssens, *Les langages et le discours,* Bruxelles, 1943.
L.-J. Calvet, *Pour et contre Saussure,* Paris, 1975.
G.E.G. Catlin, Introduction to E. Durkheim, *The Rules of Sociological Method,* tr. S.A. Solovay and J.H. Mueller, New York, 1938.
CFS: *Cahiers Ferdinand de Saussure,* Genève, 1941-.
A.N. Chomsky, *Syntactic Structures,* The Hague, 1957.
'Current issues in linguistic theory'. In J.A. Fodor & J.J. Katz, *The Structure of Language,* Englewood Cliffs, 1964.
Aspects of the Theory of Syntax, Cambridge, Mass., 1965.
R.G. Collingwood, *The Idea of History,* Oxford, 1946.
F.M. Cornford, *Plato's Theory of Knowledge,* London, 1935.
D. Crystal, *Introduction to Language Pathology,* London, 1980.
J. Culler, *Saussure,* London, 1976.
F.E.X. Dance, 'A helical model of communication'. In F.E.X. Dance (ed.), *Human Communication Theory,* New York, 1967.

P.B. Denes and E.N. Pinson, *The Speech Chain*, Garden City, N.Y., 1963.

F.P. Dinneen, *An Introduction to General Linguistics*, New York, 1967.

W. Doroszewski, 'Sociologie et linguistique (Durkheim et de Saussure),' *Actes du 2e congrès international de linguistes*, Paris, 1933.

E. Durkheim, *Les règles de la méthode sociologique*, Paris, 1895. [(Page references are to the standard modern reprint of the second edition, Paris, 1937. English versions of the passages quoted are from the translation by S.A. Solovay and J.H. Mueller, *The Rules of Sociological Method*, New York, 1938.)

U. Eco, *A Theory of Semiotics*, Bloomington, 1976.

R. Engler, 'Théorie et critique d'un principe saussurien: l'arbitraire du signe,' *Cahiers Ferdinand de Saussure*, vol. 19, 1962.

'Compléments à l'arbitraire,' *Cahiers Ferdinand de Saussure*, vol.21, 1964.

Edition critique du 'Cours de linguistique générale' de F. de Saussure, Wiesbaden, 1967.

'La linéarité du signifiant'. In R. Amacker, T. de Mauro and L.J. Prieto (eds.), *Studi saussuriani per Robert Godel*, Bologna, 1974.

J.R. Firth, 'The technique of semantics,' *Transactions of the Philological Society*, 1935.

'Personality and language in society,' *The Sociological Review*, vol. 42, 1950.

'Modes of meaning,' *Essays and Studies*, 1951.

(Page references are to the reprints in: J.R. Firth, *Papers in Linguistics 1934-1951*, London, 1957.)

G. Frege, 'Über Sinn und Bedeutung,' *Zeitschrift für Philosophie und philosophische Kritik*, vol.100, 1892.

H. Frei, 'Saussure contre Saussure?', *Cahiers Ferdinand de Saussure*, vol.9, 1950.

E.C. Fudge, 'Phonology'. In J. Lyons (ed.), *New Horizons in Linguistics*, Harmondsworth, 1970.

J. Gagnepain, 'On language and communication,' *Language & Communication*, vol.1, 1981.

A.H. Gardiner, *The Theory of Speech and Language*, Oxford, 1932.

E. Gellner, 'Holism versus individualism in history and sociology'. In P. Gardiner (ed.), *Theories of History*, Glencoe, 1959. (Page reference to this edition.) Originally published as 'Explanations in history,' *Proceedings of the Aristotelian Society*, 1956.

P.P. Giglioli (ed.), *Langue and Social Context*, Harmondsworth, 1972.

R. Godel, *Les sources manuscrites du Cours de linguistique générale de F. de Saussure*, Genève/Paris, 1957.

'De la théorie du signe aux termes du système,' *Cahiers Ferdinand de Saussure*, vol.22, 1966.

R. Harris, *The Language-Makers*, London, 1980.

A. Henry, 'La linéarité du signifiant'. In J. Dierckx and Y. Lebrun (eds.), *Linguistique contemporaine: hommage à Eric Buyssens*, Bruxelles, 1970.

L. Hjelmslev, 'Langue et parole,' *Cahiers Ferdinand de Saussure*, vol.2, 1942.

Omkring sprogteoriens grundlæggelse, Copenhagen, 1943. Tr. F.J. Whitfield, *Prolegomena to a Theory of Language*, Baltimore, 1953.

C.F. Hockett, 'Two models of grammatical description,' *Word*, vol.10, 1954.

A. Hovelacque, *La linguistique*, 2nd ed., Paris, 1877.

C.M. Hutton, *The type-token relation: abstraction and instantiation in linguistic theory*, Oxford, 1986 (unpublished D.Phil. thesis).

R. Jakobson, *Selected Writings. I: Phonological Studies*, The Hague, 1962.

O. Jespersen, *Language; its Nature, Development and Origin*, London, 1922.

Mankind, Nation and Individual from a Linguistic Point of View, Oslo, 1925.

M. Joos (ed.), *Readings in Linguistics I. The Development of Descriptive Linguistics in America 1925-56*, Chicago, 1957.

J.J. Katz, *The Philosophy of Language*, New York, 1966.

J.J. Katz and P.M. Postal, *An Integrated Theory of Linguistic Descriptions*, Cambridge, Mass., 1964.

E.F.K. Koerner, *F. de Saussure: Origin and Development of his Linguistic Thought*, Vieweg, 1973.

A. Lange-Seidl, *Approaches to Theories for Nonverbal Signs*, Lisse, 1977.

G.C. Lepschy, *A Survey of Structural Linguistics*, London, 1970.

C. Lévi-Strauss, 'L'analyse structurale en linguistique et en anthropologie,' *Word*, vol.1, 1945.

J. Locke, *An Essay Concerning Human Understanding*, 5th ed., London, 1706.

N. Love, 'Psychologistic structuralism and the polylect,' *Language & Communication*, vol. 4, 1984.

J. Lyons, 'Human language'. In R.A. Hinde (ed.), *Non-Verbal Communication*, Cambridge, 1972.

Semantics, vol.1, Cambridge, 1977.

B. Malmberg, 'Le circuit de la parole'. In A. Martinet (ed.), *Le langage*, Paris, 1968.

A. Martinet, 'De quelques unités significatives'. In R. Amacker, T. de Mauro and L.J. Prieto (eds.), *Studi saussuriani per Robert Godel*, Bologna, 1974.

T. de Mauro, *Edition critique du 'Cours de linguistique générale' de F. de Saussure*, Paris, 1972.

C. Metz, *Langage et cinema*, Paris, 1971.

C. Morris, *Signification and Significance*, Cambridge, Mass., 1964.

W.G. Moulton, *A Linguistic Guide to Language Learning*, 2nd ed., Menasha, 1970.

F.M. Müller, *Lectures on the Science of Language*, vol. II, London, 1864.

J.A.H. Murray, *Oxford English Dictionary*, vol.1, Oxford, 1888.

C.K. Ogden and I.A. Richards, *The Meaning of Meaning*, London, 1923.

G.H.R. Parkinson, 'The translation theory of understanding'. In G. Vesey (ed.), *Communication and Understanding*, Hassocks, 1977.

T. Pateman, 'Nature and culture in language and speech: another comment on d'Agostino,' *Philosophy of the Social Sciences*, vol. 10, 1980.

'What is a language?', *Language & Communication*, vol.3, 1983.

H. Paul, *Principien der Sprachgeschichte*, Halle, 1880. 2nd ed. (1886) tr. by H.A. Strong, *Principles of the History of Language*, London, 1890. (Page references are to and quotations from the translation.)

C.S. Peirce, *Collected Papers*, 8 vols., ed. C. Hartshorne and P. Weiss, Cambridge, Mass., 1931-58.

L.J. Prieto, *Messages et signaux*, Paris, 1966.

'La sémiologie'. In A. Martinet (ed.), *Le langage*, Paris, 1968.

M.J. Reddy, 'The conduit metaphor – a case of frame conflict in our language about language'. In A. Ortony (ed.), *Metaphor and Thought*, Cambridge, 1979.

N. Ruwet, 'Linguistique et science de l'homme,' *Esprit*, November 1963.

G. Sampson, 'Comment on d'Agostino,' *Philosophy of the Social Sciences*, vol.9, 1979.

A. Schleicher, *Die deutsche Sprache*, Stuttgart, 1860.

A. Sechehaye, 'Les trois linguistiques saussuriennes,' *Vox Romanica*, vol. 5, 1940.

M. Silverstein (ed.), *Whitney on Language*, Cambridge, Mass., 1971.

H. Spang-Hanssen, *Recent Theories on the Nature of the Language Sign*, Copenhagen, 1954.

N.C.W. Spence, 'A hardy perennial: the problem of *langue* and *parole*,' *Archivum Linguisticum*, vol.9, 1957.

'*Langue* and *parole* yet again,' *Neophilologus*, vol.44, 1962.

(Page references are to the reprints in: N.C.W. Spence, *Essays in Linguistics*, München, 1976.)

T.J. Taylor, 'Linguistic origins: Bruner and Condillac on learning how to talk,' *Language & Communication*, vol.4, 1984.

B. Toussaint, *Qu'est-ce que la sémiologie ?*, Toulouse, 1978.

M. Toussaint, *Contre l'arbitraire du signe*, Paris, 1983.

S. Ullmann, *The Principles of Semantics*, 2nd ed., Glasgow, 1959. *Semantics*, Oxford, 1962.

J. Vendryes, 'Sur la dénomination,' *Bulletin de la Société de Linguistique de Paris*, vol.48, 1952.

W. Washabaugh, 'Saussure, Durkheim and sociolinguistic theory,' *Archivum Linguisticum*, vol.5, 1974.

W.D. Whitney, *Language and the Study of Language*, London, 1867.

L. Wittgenstein, *Philosophische Untersuchungen*, tr. G.E.M. Anscombe, 2nd ed., Oxford, 1958.

A.D. Woozley (ed.), *John Locke, An Essay Concerning Human Understanding*, Glasgow, 1964.

Index

Aarsleff, H., 6, 9, 28, 121f., 209, 233
abstract entities, 97ff., 136ff.
agglutination, 158ff.
d'Agostino, F.B., 236
alphabet, 44f., 47ff., 52, 78; 'physiological', 49
alphabetical order, 117
alternation, 144
analogy, 148ff., 153f., 155f., 158, 160f.
anthropology, 11f., 188, 195, 220
anti-historicism, 202
arbitrariness, 5, 16, 26, 28, 30, 53, 55ff.,
80ff., 88f., 111, 122, 131ff., 143,
154f., 161, 188, 190, 219f.; absolute
and relative, 131ff., 150
Aristotle, 57f., 119, 169
associative relations, 124ff., 128ff., 134,
146, 234f.
astronomy, 7
auditory feedback, 208
axes of simultaneity and succession,
88ff., 104, 200

Baker, G.P. and Hacker, P.M.S., 56
Bally, Ch., vii, x, 66, 191, 196, 236
Barthes, R., 15, 26f., 29
behaviourism, xiii, 9, 206
Bible, 56
bilingualism, 173
bi-planar correlations, 21, 45, 50, 62,
221
Bloomfield, L., x, xiif., 8f., 17, 52, 89f.,
126f., 212
Böhtlingk, O., 9
Bonald, L.G.A. de, 122
Boole, G., xiv
Bopp, F., 4, 7, 42, 175f., 183, 207
borrowings, 38, 146f., 179
botany, 7f.

Bréal, M., 9, 121
Broadbent, G., Bunt, R. and Jencks,
C., 26
broadcasting, 215
Broca, P., 16, 19, 20, 204
Bühler, K., x
Buyssens, E., 27, 30

Calvet, L.-J., xif., xvi, 23, 197, 201, 234
Catlin, G.E.G., 225-7
chemistry, 216
Chomsky, A.N., xivf.
classification: grammatical, 136ff.; of
languages, 150; of linguistic facts,
16, 21, 35, 39, 202; of sounds, 47,
52f.; of words, 117; semantic, 127
codes, 205ff., 219ff.; see also Morse
code
cognition, 29, 76
collective consciousness, 87, 139, 226f.,
229
collective ratification, 211, 225
Collingwood, R.G., 200
collocation, 124f.
communication, 26f., 107, 131, 227,
230, 234; and linguistic change, 106,
153; animal, 28; face-to-face, 25,
106; channel of, 31; model of, 22,
204-18, 230; theory of, 25, 27, 204-18
communicative functions, 18
communicative intentions, 28
comparative grammar, see comparative philology
comparative philology, xii, 3f., 7ff., 30,
62, 145, 175, 183f.
comparativists, see comparative
philology
comparison, 172
competence, linguistic, xiv, 33

concepts, 22f., 58ff., 208, 210, 213, 217
concrete entities, 98, 108ff., 235
Condillac, E.B. de, 233
conduit metaphor, 214
consonant, 49, 74, 142
conventionalism, 66ff.
Cornford, F.M., 205
Cours de linguistique générale: editors,
    viiff., 23f., 37, 39, 41, 44, 52, 59, 65,
    74, 76, 84f., 138, 160, 163, 181, 191f.,
    195f.; expository technique, xvi;
    hidden premises, xvi, 5, 17, 31, 43,
    78, 106, 109ff., 169; influence of,
    xiff.; publication, vii; reviews of,
    xif.; sources, viiiff.
creativity, 149f.
Culler, J., 10, 23, 165

Dance, F.E.X., 214
Denes, P.B. and Pinson, E.N., 206ff.,
    211, 217
Derrida, J., x
Destutt de Tracy, A.L.C., 233
diachronic identities, 162ff.
diachronic illusions, 148, 161ff., 201
diachronic realities, 162ff., 182
diachronic units, 162ff., 168
dialects, 37, 147, 165, 171, 173, 177,
    179, 229f.; d.boundaries, 171, 177
Diez, F., 4
Dinneen, F.P., 225
Dionysius Thrax, 4
discovery procedures, 49, 110
distinctive features, 70, 130
Doroszewski, W., 225
duality of linguistic phenomena, 15,
    25, 47, 55f.
Durkheim, E., x, 157, 212, 224ff.
dynamic paradigm, 221ff.

Eco, U., 26f.
écriture, see writing
energy conversion, 215f.
Engler, R., ix, xvii, 56
état de langue, see linguistic state
ethnicity, 188
ethnography, 188
etymology, 14f., 57f., 166, 170; popular,
    155ff.
exclamations, 65

Finck, F.N., 9

Firth, J.R., xiii, xv, 30, 124
form and substance, 11f., 31, 118ff.,
    201
Frege, G., xiv, 58
Frei, H., ix
Fudge, E.C., 49

Gabelentz, G. von der, x
Gagnepain, J., 230
Gardiner, A.H., xiii
Gellner, E., 236
geology, 7, 182
Giglioli, P.P., 227
Gilliéron, J., 85, 176
Godel, R., 69
grammar, 3, 5, 9, 38, 90, 134f., 136ff.,
    149; and sound change, 144ff.;
    comparative, *see* comparative
    philology; descriptive, 87; general,
    8, 103; geographical, 179; historical,
    xiii, 87ff., 98, 134f., 142, 162, 179,
    201; subdivisions of, 134f.; tradi-
    tional, 4f., 8, 91, 134f., 137; trans-
    formational-generative, xiv
grammarians, 4f., 49, 168; modistic, 6,
    57
grammatical categories, 136
grammatical change, 96ff., 140, 146
grammatical classifications, 136ff.,
grammatical relations, 126, 146
Grimm, J., 42

Harris, R., 57, 213
Henry, A., 72ff., 77
historiography, ixf., xvii
history, 90, 169, 184, 200f.; of linguis-
    tics, xv, xvii, 3ff., 8f.; reality of, 169,
    184f., 200f.
Hjelmslev, L., 23, 30, 212
holism, 220ff., 236; *see also* struc-
    turalism
homonymy, 115f.
horticulture, 8
Hovelacque, A., 6ff.
Humboldt, W. von, x
Hutton, C.M., 115

idiosynchronic systems, 94ff., 103,
    108ff., 147, 165, 177, 200, 219, 221,
    229f.
image acoustique, see sound pattern
imitation, 153, 178f., 225

immediate constituent analysis, 126f.
individualism, 236
innateness hypothesis, 228
intercourse, 172, 178
intonation, 73
introspection, 110
irregularity, 148, 156

Jakobson, R., xiv, 70
Jespersen, O., xif., 52
Jones, D., 49
Jones, W., 7
Joos, M., xiv

Katz, J.J., 207
kinesthetic feedback, 208
Koerner, E.F.K., 225

Labov, W., 198
langage, 16, 21, 34, 37, 55, 150, 156, 160, 225
Lange-Seidl, A., 26, 29
language: definition of, 5, 21f., 26, 32, 118, 197; faculty, 16, 19, 50, 55, 150, 154, 224, 226; heterogeneity of, 16, 224; organ, 20; written, *see* writing
language acquisition, 18, 36
language boundaries, 171, 177
language families, 190
languages: as codes, 205ff.; as cognitive systems, 198ff., 227, 230; as idiosynchronic systems, 94ff.; as instruments of communication, 227; as mathematical systems, xiv; as organisms, 3, 7, 9f.; as sign systems, 16f., 20, 34, 109, 202; as social conventions, 16; as social institutions, 67ff., 80ff., 89, 101, 150, 188, 198ff., 205, 226, 228, 230; as synchronic systems, 30, 92ff.; as systems of differences, 118, 128; as systems of values, 88, 123, 134, 231, 233, 235; dead, 48, 232; earliest, 183; grammatical, 150; lexicological, 150; literary, 173; relations between, 172; typology of, 150, 190f.
langue, xii, xivf., 10, 13, 15f., 19ff., 28ff., 33ff., 37ff., 41ff., 46ff., 55ff., 107, 118, 198f.; and writing, 41ff.; as an aggregate, 198f.; as an average, 198f.; as the social part of *langage*, 23f., 34, 149ff.; compared to a

dictionary, 35; compared to a sheet of paper, 120; compared to a symphony, 33; compared to a system of currency, 120ff., 221; compared to air in contact with water, 119f., 220; compared to chess, 38, 40, 92ff., 100f., 104f.; compared to the crosscut of a plant stem, 92, 104;
laws, 12, 95ff., 113, 178; diachronic, 95ff., 100f., 191; of linguistic diffusion, 178; of sound change, 44, 53, 165, 201; panchronic, 101f.; phonetic, 97; semiological, 30, 172; synchronic, 95ff., 100f.
Lepschy, G.C., 70f.
Lévi-Strauss, C., x, 236
lexicography, 4, 14f, 117
lexicology, 134
linear cohesion, 111ff.
linearity, 53, 55ff., 69ff., 124ff., 129, 170, 187, 213
linguistic atlases, 171, 176
linguistic awareness, 111, 136, 146, 149ff., 156f., 159f., 167, 190, 223
linguistic change, 80ff., 106f., 139f., 148ff., 153ff., 188f., 190f.; compared to changes in the solar system, 91
linguistic community, 79, 81, 83ff., 95, 99, 107, 163, 211
linguistic comparison, 172, 183f.; *see also* comparative philology
linguistic diffusion, 178ff.
linguistic geography, 171-80
linguistic intuitions, 110f.
linguistic invariants, 131, 222ff.
linguistic paleontology, 188
linguistic procedures, 159ff.
linguistic processes, 159ff.
linguistic reconstruction, 184ff., 188
linguistics: aims of, 11ff.; and other sciences, 11ff., 188f.; and phonetics, 46ff., 51f.; and semiology, 28ff., 33; autonomy of, 30, 38, 77, 199, 213; data of, 11ff, 40; definition of, 5ff., 11, 26, 32; diachronic, 30, 34, 39, 79f., 87ff., 113, 139f., 141ff., 144ff., 148ff., 153f., 155ff., 158ff., 162ff., 167ff., 178ff., 181f.; evolutionary, *see* linguistics, diachronic; external, 18, 37ff., 153f., 171ff., 179, 201; general, xiif., 3, 6, 195ff.; geographical, 37, 105f., 171-80; historical, 4, 9, 30, 62,

80, 87ff., 153f., 163f., 201; history of, xv, xvii, 3ff., 8f.; internal, 37ff.; methods of, 15; object of, 11, 14ff., 32, 42, 76, 181f., 184, 191f., 235; of *la langue*, 33ff., 37ff., 197; of *la parole*, 33ff., 37ff.; prospective diachronic, 181f.; retrospective diachronic, 181f., 184; static, 87ff., 103ff.; synchronic, 4, 10, 30, 39, 79f., 87ff., 103ff., 114ff., 118ff., 124ff., 128ff., 167ff.

linguistic sign, 11, 16, 31, 55ff.; arbitrary nature of, 5, 16, 26, 28, 30, 53; identity of, 110ff.; invariability of, 79ff.; theory of, 21; variability of, 79ff.; zero s., 61

linguistic state, 89ff., 103ff., 146, 165, 179, 185, 200f., 233f.

linguistic structure, 30, 33ff., 113, 132, 143, 156, 180, 188f., 190f.

linguistic units, 15, 108ff., 114ff., 128ff., 131; compared to chess pieces, 117; syntagmatic, 128ff.

linguistic universals, 12, 47f., 53, 74, 78, 101, 110, 113, 172

Littré, E., 7

localization of language, 16, 19, 23f.

Locke, J., 28, 205ff.

logic, xiv, 4, 8

Love, N.L., 111, 165

Lyons, J., 17, 115

Martinet, A., xvii, 129

mathematics, xiv

matière, see linguistics, data of

Mauro, T. de., xi, xiv, xvi, 6f., 10, 28, 37, 41, 46f., 56, 59, 63, 65f., 70, 79f. 153, 163, 191, 221ff., 233

mechanism: language m., 128ff., 137, 156, 158, 229; psycho-physical m., 216f.

medical science, 14f.

Meillet, A., vii, xi

Mémoire sur le système primitif des voyelles dans les langues indo-européennes, xii, 6, 50

mentality, group, 188f.

mental lexicon, 60

mental representation, 74ff., 146, 202

Merleau-Ponty, M., x

methodological postulates, 113

methodological principles, 199

Metz, C., 26

mistakes, 156f., 158, 164

morphological function, 142

morphology, 134

Morris, C., 28

Morse code, 31, 33, 206

Moulton, W.G., 18, 206ff.

Mounin, G., 228

Müller, F.M., 7, 9f., 49

Murray, J.A.H., 18f.

naturalism, 66ff.,

Neogrammarians, 3, 6, 8f., 43f., 142f., 167ff., 207

nomenclaturism, 56ff., 176, 213

nominalism, 185

objet, see linguistics, object of

Ogden, C.K. and Richards, I.A., xiii, 62f.

onomatopoeia, 65

Oxford English Dictionary, 18, 213

panchronicity, 85, 101f., 145, 165, 226

Parkinson, G.H.R., 205, 209

parochialism, 172, 178

parole, xii, xiv, 10, 22ff., 27, 33ff., 37ff., 41ff., 46ff., 55ff.; and analogy, 148ff., 160; and diachrony, 106, 149, 223; and linguistic structure, 143; as the 'individual' part of *langage*, 23, 34, 198f., 213, 216, 227, 234; *circuit de la, see* speech circuit

parts of speech, 117, 136

Pateman, T., 198, 236

Paul, H., x, 8f., 43f., 87ff.

Peirce, C.S., 26f., 115

performance, linguistic, xiv, 33

Piaget, J., x

philology, ixf., 3f., 6ff., 12, 30f., 89, 191

phonation, 34, 48, 72, 217

phoneme, 48ff.

phonetic doublets, 146f.

phonetic identity, 131, 186f., 211f.

phonetics, 14, 30f., 33f., 46ff., 52f., 90, 119f., 186f., 205; articulatory, 52; auditory, 52; combinatory, 53; historical, 142

phonology, 50, 70

physics, 204, 216

physiology, 30, 46ff., 195, 204

Plato, viiff., xvi, 66, 119, 169, 205
polysemy, 115f.
Port Royal, 4, 8, 77
prehistory, 188
prescriptivism, 3f., 5, 9
Prieto, L.J., 26f.
primary theoretical problems, 195ff.
Priscian, 4
productive forms, 150f.
pronunciation, 18f., 43ff., 143
prototypes, 183
psychological reality, 136
psychologism, xiii, 9, 90
psychology, 11, 28, 120, 179, 195, 204, 212, 227

Quintilian, 121

race, 188
'radical historicity', 10, 80
Reddy, M.J., 214
regularity, 148ff., 156f., 160
representational discreteness, 112f.
Robins, R.H., 150
romanticism, 4f.
Royal Society, 209
rules, 3, 24, 93f., 100, 148f., 153, 207, 227
Ruwet, N., 70

Sampson, G., 236
'Saussurean paradox', 198ff., 227
schéma, 23
Schleicher, A., 6ff.
science, 3ff., 11ff., 107, 228; historical, 7; natural, 7, 20, 215; of human speech, xiii; of language, xiii, 3ff., 15, 19ff., 23, 38, 51, 55, 57, 62, 88, 95, 135, 175f., 184, 195ff., 226f., 228; of signs, *see* semiology; philosophy of, 12, 209
scriptism, 78
Sechehaye, A., viif., xf., 39, 191, 196, 236
secondary theoretical problems, 199f
segmentation, 108ff., 169
semantic change, 96, 99f., 140, 145, 159ff.
semantics, 100
semeiōtikē, 28
semiological space, 220
sémiologie, see semiology
semiology, ix, xv, 11, 17ff., 21, 25ff., 33,

41, 43, 51, 219, 236; laws of, 30, 172; principles of, 18, 93, 113
semiotic, 26
sentences, xiv
signe, 58ff.
signifiant, 21, 53, 58ff., 81, 99, 108ff.; auditory nature of, 72
signifié, 21, 53, 58ff., 81ff., 99, 108ff.
signs: definition of, 27; science of, *see* semiology; social, 29, 31; systems of, 26, 108ff.; types of, 26; visual, 72; zero, 61; *see also* linguistic sign
Silverstein, M., 85
sociolinguistics, 142, 176
sociology, 11, 195, 226f.
Socrates, viif., xi, 67
sound, 25, 46ff., 119; amorphous nature of, 47, 52; s. laws, 44, 53, 165, 201; s. systems, 186; s. types, 44, 47f., 53, 78, 100, 186; s. waves, 34
sound change, 30, 34, 53, 93, 99f., 140, 141ff., 144ff., 148f., 163, 165, 178f., 188f.; absolute, 141; combinative, 141; conditioned, 141; laws of, 44, 53, 165; spontaneous, 141f.
sound pattern, 22ff., 41, 44f., 52, 57ff., 208, 217
Spang-Hanssen, H., 29f.
spectrogram, 74, 142
speech; as 'execution', 23f., 34; definition of, 22f.; physiology of, 16, 19; primacy of, 17f., 21; science of, xiii; s.act, 22, 35f.; s.circuit, 22ff., 34, 73, 198, 204-18, 230; s.communication, 25; s.comprehension, 25; s.pathology, 205; s.production, 25; s.sounds, 31; units of, 25
spelling, 43ff., 142
Spence, N.C.W., xiii, 23, 35
sterile forms, 150
stress, 72f.
structuralism, xiii, xv, 11, 50, 86, 122, 142f., 179, 201f., 207, 210, 212, 219ff.
subjective and objective analysis, 167ff.
substance, vs. form, 11, 31
substantialism, 200f.
substitution, 139f., 162ff., 172
surrogationalism, 213
syllable, 48, 72f., 142; syllabic stress, 72f.

symbol, 29
synchronic identities, 114ff., 131, 212
synchronic realities, 114ff., 182, 186, 202, 221, 223
syntagmas, 124ff.
syntagmatic interdependences, 131
syntagmatic relations, 124ff., 128ff., 134, 234f.
syntax 134, 137
systematicity, 92ff., 102, 132f., 148, 200, 221
systematization, 196

tâche, see linguistics, aims of
Taylor, T.J., 233
technology, 213ff.
telegraphy, 215
telementation, 205ff., 227, 229
telephony, 215f.
terminology, 168
time, 71, 76f., 83f., 88ff., 103ff., 175f., 178, 200, 227
Toussaint, B., 26
Toussaint, M., 55
transcription, 46ff., 52f.
translation theory of understanding, 205ff.
type-token relations, 35, 115ff., 125

Ullmann, S., 63f., 115, 155, 222f.
usage, 23

valeur, see values
values, 11, 60f., 86, 88f., 98, 114ff., 118ff., 124ff., 136, 145f., 219ff., 231ff.; two orders of, 124ff.
Vendryes, J., 155
vocal apparatus, 16, 19f., 46, 48f., 186f., 221
vowel, 49, 74, 142

Washabaugh, W., 224f., 228
Watson, J.B., xiii
Whitney, W.D., x, 16, 66f., 81f., 85, 228
Wittgenstein, L., 56, 58
Wolf, F.A., 4
Woozley, A.D., 208
word, 102, 109, 114ff., 142, 208f.; and sound change, 97, 142, 144ff.; w. composition, 144f.; w.identity, 114ff., 144f., 165, 197; w. order, 74
writing, vii, 3, 12, 16ff., 25, 30f., 35, 41ff., 46ff., 52, 55, 77f., 106, 109, 219, 232; ideographic, 42, 45, phonetic, 42ff., syllabic, 48
Wundt, W., xiii

zero: z. change, 141; z. elements, 111; z. signs, 61